Helen Chen's

Chinese

Home

Cooking

Helen Chen's

Chinese

Home

Cooking

Illustrated by Earl C. Davis

Hearst Books / New York

Copyright © 1994 by Helen Chen
Illustrations copyright © 1994 by Earl C. Davis

It is the policy of William Morrow and Company, Inc., and its imprints
and affiliates, recognizing the importance of preserving what has been
written, to print the books we publish on acid-free paper, and we exert
our best efforts to that end.

Library of Congress Cataloging-in-Publication Data

Chen, Helen.
    [Chinese home cooking]
    Helen Chen's Chinese home cooking.
        p.   cm.
    Includes index.
    ISBN 0-688-14609-0
    1. Cookery, Chinese. I. Title. II. Title: Chinese home
    cooking.
TX724.5.C5C5374   1994
641.5951—dc20   93-49726
                                                          CIP

Printed in the United States of America

First Hearst Paperback Edition

3   4   5   6   7   8   9   10

Book design by Richard Oriolo

This book is lovingly dedicated to my mother,
Joyce Chen

My mother was diagnosed with multi-infarct dementia over ten years ago. All her symptoms and the progression of her illness lead her doctors to believe that she is also a victim of Alzheimer's disease. Today at seventy-six, my mother lives in a nursing home and cannot speak or care for herself.

Many years ago, before the illness manifested itself, my mother used to talk to me about her wish that one day we would write a mother-daughter cookbook. As the weeks became months and the months became years, our busy lives never brought us together in the kitchen to accomplish this collaboration. With the advance of my mother's illness and dementia I thought that dream was gone forever.

I was wrong. One morning I awoke with the realization that my book *was* the collaborative effort my mother wished for after all. Instead of having my mother beside me, I had her thoughts, her philosophy, her recipes, and her stories as my guide.

My mother's cookbook, which has been out of print for many years, contains many recipes from our family meals — those "hot and noisy" dinners with our Chinese friends, the simple family meals and get-together meals celebrating birthdays, festivals, and special events in our lives. I am happy to be able to bring some of those recipes, together with my own, for you to enjoy.

We can't recapture our past or change our destiny, but with my mother's recipes I truly feel that she has actually been with me, leading me through the maze of her recollections, stories, traditions, experiences, and food that she once prepared. Once in a while I'd be working on a recipe and think of her so much I would have to drive over to the nursing home to be with her.

In my mind I see her now as she used to be — smiling, talking, spatula in hand, apron on, warm fragrant aromas wafting from our little kitchen in Cambridge. That's how I remember my mother, Joyce Chen, who passed away on August 23, 1994.

Acknowledgments

My mother used to say that we are all born the same. Everything we know comes from someone else. Although I cannot possibly thank all whose lives have influenced me, I wish to express my gratitude to those whose contributions made this book a reality:

First and foremost I wish to thank my mother, Joyce Chen, for teaching me everything I know about cooking. To my late father, Thomas Chen, for instilling in me the values of honesty, hard work, and perseverance.

I am grateful to my two brothers, Henry and Stephen, for answering questions, suggesting recipes, and helping me recall childhood stories and memories, of which there would be far fewer without them.

To my publicists, Lisa and Lou Ekus, for their friendship and guidance that led me to William Morrow and Company.

To Judith Weber, my agent, for her wise professional judgment and advice.

To Harriet Bell, my editor, for her encouragement, wisdom, and gentle guidance through the intricacies of writing a book.

To Skip Dye of William Morrow, who enthusiastically believed in me and my book from the start.

A special note of gratitude to Nancy Verde Barr for her insightful critique and editorial assistance.

And to the following people whose collective design and production talents made this book possible:

Bill Truslow, photographer; Jane Sutton, stylist; Susan Derecskey, copy editor; Richard Oriolo, designer; and Earl Davis, illustrator.

To my friends and neighbors who cheerfully tasted and honestly critiqued the recipes. In particular, a special thanks to close friend and fellow food enthusiast, Barry Lockard, who so generously offered his assistance in testing and tasting recipes.

To Mel Novatt, mentor, trusted adviser, and friend in business and in life.

To our family friend, Bob Bradford, who shared his expertise on wines.

To Wilson and Warren Wong of Sun Sun Company, Inc., who helped me with the glossary of ingredients.

To Shirley Fong-Torres and her husband, Bernie Carver, for their warm friendship and for introducing me to San Francisco's Chinatown.

To my cousins, Chen Zu-ying and Zhao Lung-hai, for their help with the *pinyin* spelling and Chinese characters. To my number one aunt, Wu Chen, and my sixth aunt, Chen Zai-chen, for being the link to my parents' China.

To Alice Chang and Lenny Li, for translation help; and to chefs Lee Yuen-gong and Li Xiao-xu, for their recipe ideas and suggestions.

To Betty Woodmansee for her computer expertise and Dorise Boujoulian for her ever-ready smile and administrative support.

To my sister-in-law, Barbara Chen, for information and advice on Chinese ingredients.

To my mother-in-law, Dorothy Ohmart, for her willing assistance with proofreading, and for being the best mother-in-law anyone could ask for.

To Gus Dallas, for his friendship, encouragement, and determination to have me taste every Chinese chicken salad in Los Angeles.

To longtime friends Deli Bloembergen and Anna Ku Lau, for recipe ideas, and to Valarie Hart Ross for inspiring me to create the only cookie recipe in the book.

To Gregory Lee for his assistance with the Chinese calligraphy.

To Nana, my loving cat, for her faithful companionship during the writing of this book.

And last but not least, to my devoted husband and partner-in-life, Keith, for his love, understanding, unwavering trust, and steadfast support in everything I do.

Contents

Preface
前言
How It
All Began

My mother, Joyce Chen (Liao Jia-ai) 廖家艾, was born in Peking (Beijing), China, to the family of a prominent public official. She was the youngest in a family of nine, the seventh daughter. Being the youngest and only child of my grandfather's second marriage after the death of his first wife, she was the apple of her father's eye and often accompanied him on business trips. She was encouraged by both parents to be self-reliant and independent. Undoubtedly this early exposure and encouragement influenced her later interest and success in business. As a young girl, she also enjoyed spending time in the kitchen watching the family chef prepare meals. She would stir and mix and make miniature dumplings alongside the head chef's wife. Her parents frequently entertained friends at home, so her childhood memories were of parties, guests, and food.

My father, Thomas Chen (Chen Da-chong) 陳大中, was born in Hangchow (Hangzhou), China, to the principal of a high school. He was the youngest in a family of eleven (one died as a child) and was named Big Middle. It was his family's tradition that all the boys be named after the points on a compass and the girls after the seasons. By the time my father was born, all the compass points were taken, so he became Big Middle. My father's sixth sister was named Again Spring because she was the fifth daughter.

My older brother, Henry, and I were born in Shanghai, China — at home because in those days women were afraid their babies might be switched at the hospital. My brother Stephen, the youngest in the family, was born in Cambridge, Massachusetts. In the Chen tradition, all the children in the male line were given the same middle name. Only the last character of our name is our own. Thus all the Chen cousins have very similar names. Even if we never knew each other, we would realize our relationship because of our names. Henry's Chinese name is Chen Zu-ming 陳祖明, I am Chen Zu-hua 陳祖華 and Stephen is Chen Zu-chang 陳祖昌.

The foresight my mother's parents had in encouraging her interest in cooking so that she "wouldn't have to eat raw rice" was prophetic. In 1949, when my parents immigrated to the United States on the last boat to leave Shanghai before the closing of China, a new life was to start for them. In those early years in Cambridge, there were very few northern Chinese from Shanghai. Although many of us ate regularly in Chinatown where the food was southern — mainly Cantonese — there was nowhere to get our hometown specialties. My parents had become acquainted with a handful of northern Chinese students at nearby Harvard, M.I.T., and Boston University; they were also homesick for their regional foods. My parents often played hosts to these students and my mother's reputation as a cook became established. She would cook wonderful meals for everyone, and they would talk and reminisce about China and sometimes play mah-jong into the night. I remember having houseguests every weekend, and it is interesting that my childhood memories are of parties, guests, and food — just like my mother's.

My mother's reputation as an excellent cook grew and led to the opening in 1958 of the first of three Joyce Chen restaurants in Cambridge. She began teaching Chinese cooking at local schools and adult centers and in 1962 she published the *Joyce Chen Cook Book,* from which some recipes have been taken for this book. A year after her cookbook was published, she starred in her own public television series, "Joyce Chen Cooks." She was the first Asian to have her own television show. In 1972, also for public television, we made "Joyce Chen's China," a documentary recounting our trip to China and our reunion with our family. At that time my mother also founded Joyce Chen Products, a company that my husband, Keith, and I now operate. Joyce Chen Products designs, develops, and markets a line of quality Asian cooking utensils especially for the Western kitchen.

Although I have lived in America since childhood, I have a strong bond to China and to being Chinese. As a child I never knew any relatives outside of our immediate family. For a long time, I thought I had none. Since the opening of China in 1972, I have come to know some of my numerous relatives, who still reside all over China in such places as Hunan, Szechuan (Sichuan), Shanghai, Hangchow (Hangzhou), Peking (Beijing), and Nanking (Nanjing). I have assembled a family tree of Liaos (my mother's side) and Chens and discovered to my delight that we have over forty first cousins alone!

By writing this book, I hope to share with you, as my mother did, the rich cultural heritage of China, through my personal memories, traditions, and family recipes.

Introduction

For many people, Chinese cooking remains a mysterious and esoteric cuisine that requires exact and difficult cooking techniques with specialized cooking utensils and exotic ingredients. For others, it is a style of cooking that they occasionally do at home but find the taste is never on a par with the food at their favorite Chinese restaurant. Still others have unsuccessfully attempted Chinese cooking at home and given up in utter frustration. Do any of these sound like you?

What is it about Chinese cooking that people love — and why is it so elusive to most? In addition to the fact that it just tastes good, all of today's nutritional information points to Chinese food as "just what the doctor ordered." For the most part it is low in saturated fat and cholesterol, uses small amounts of meat, and incorporates an abundance of fresh vegetables cooked in a short amount of time to retain texture and nutrition. Unfortunately, there is so much misinformation as to cooking techniques and necessary ingredients that many people are confused as to what is actually right. High heat: What about the food burning in the pan? Small amounts of oil: What about the food sticking? When to cook vegetables and when to cook meat? Together? Separately? Pushed up the sides of the pan? Marinate the meat? Don't marinate meat? What's the answer?

As with most things, there is no one answer that will take care of everything. Cooking is a variable science and art. It all depends upon the kind of stove you have, the type and quality of the cookware you are using, the temperature, the size and type of ingredients, and so on. Understanding some simple techniques and controlling these variables will help you master the Chinese cooking experience.

Before you begin exploring on your own, you need to learn the basics in order to build a firm foundation for experiences yet to come. I will also try to tell you the "why" as well as the "how" of Chinese cooking. Once you understand why, rules become meaningful. Eventually you don't even have to try and remember them. They are yours.

Home-style Cooking

禄　Chinese cuisine holds a vast, largely untapped richness of family tradition, recipes that are passed down from generation to generation but are rarely written down. This is home-style or family-style cooking. It is a personal culinary expression. In spite of improved transportation and the institution of a national dialect, the Chinese still cling tenaciously to the provincial dishes of their home. People from Shanghai love Shanghai food and those from Peking (Beijing) prefer Peking food.

In preparation for this book, I spent a long time thinking about what I really wanted to do for you. I realized after a few false starts that what my mother said to me over thirty years ago, when she was writing her own cookbook, was still true today. Westerners love Chinese food for its quick cooking, economy, taste, nutrition, and variety. Isn't this exactly what the Chinese also love about their own cuisine?

Instead of concentrating on classic Chinese cuisine, this book focuses on the simpler, home-style cooking that I learned from my mother, and she from hers. It's a style of cooking that is simple to prepare. We stir-fry more than deep-fry; steam more than roast; use fresh, seasonal ingredients instead of exotic delicacies; and use less meat in favor of more fresh vegetables.

Besides a simpler approach to ingredients and cooking techniques, home-style cooking is also quick and economical. Although highly processed foods, frozen dinners, and fast-food restaurants are practically unknown in China, the Chinese have their own prepared foods. Understanding and learning to use some of these convenience foods provide a fast way to expand your Chinese cooking repertoire the way the Chinese do.

Although most of us love to get right down to the recipes in a cookbook, I encourage you to read each chapter to help build that foundation I talked about earlier. Once you have established a base of knowledge, you will be ready to put that knowledge to work in the kitchen.

A *Word on* Pinyin
Romanization

禧   After the founding of the People's Republic of China in 1949, the Mandarin dialect became the national language, thereby uniting all the provinces in a common tongue. This language is known in China as *putong hua,* or common speech. At the same time, China adopted a new system for romanizing Chinese words called *pinyin* or piece-together-sound. *Pinyin* is currently used by the Western world to replace the older Wade-Giles and Yale systems.

    In most instances in this book, I have used the new *pinyin* words. However, some place names are more recognizable by their older romanized form and I have retained them for their familiarity to the reader.

Shopping in Chinatown

採購

Shopping at an Asian market can be daunting. The sights, sounds, and smells are all at once exotic, exciting, and intimidating. Although Chinese home cooking can be done without a single visit to a Chinese market, it adds to the culinary experience to browse through an Asian grocery store. And with the burgeoning Asian population in the United States, Asian markets are sprouting up in suburbs and shopping centers all over the country.

They are vibrant and active places, filled with live, fresh and frozen, canned and bottled, dried and pickled food. The shelves are usually stacked from the floor to the ceiling with every imaginable ingredient. Many will be new and unknown to even the veteran Chinatown shopper, for there are always new foods being imported from the Far East to tempt even the most jaded palate.

When I was a child, going to Chinatown was a family affair. Every Sunday we would all pile into the car and my father would drive from Cambridge to Boston's Chinatown. The first order of the day was to find a restaurant and eat. My mother was never one to just sit and wait, so while we waited for our food, she often ventured out to a nearby Chinese pastry shop to see what was fresh. She sometimes came back with some sweet dim sum for dessert. After our meal, the shopping would start in earnest at our favorite store on Hudson Street. It was a dusty dark place with wooden shelves that reached to the ceiling, wooden stools, and a hardwood table where the shopkeepers tallied and wrapped the purchases — and ate their meals. The store seemed to be an endless string of rooms since they had broken through the walls on either side to expand over the years. At the time, it was one of the largest markets in town and we used to spend hours there — or so it seemed to a five-year-old. Every week the owner would treat me to a piece of crystal-clear rock candy on a string that kept me occupied and quiet as my mother shopped. After the grocery store, there were stops at the noodle shop, pastry shop, roast-meat shop, and bean sprout factory.

Things have changed since those Sundays in the dark recesses of an old-fashioned Chinese market, but shopping and eating in Chinatown is a tradition that is carried on to this day. Just one look at the crowds and the bustle on weekends will confirm this. The grocery store we now frequent is a small but busy place. It is brightly lit, well stocked, and clean, with checkout counters just like Western supermarkets. It's only thirty-five hundred square feet, but it carries over three thousand different items!

Understanding and Using Chinese Ingredients

*T*housands of different ingredients, from the common to the exotic, are used in Chinese cuisine. New food products from the Far East appear constantly, just as in American supermarkets. Since the opening of China in the 1970s and with the large influx of peoples from Vietnam, Laos, Thailand, and Cambodia, Chinese ingredients are imported from all over Asia and the Pacific Rim, making grocery stores truly pan-Asian. Although a Chinese grocery store may carry a huge variety of foods, not even the Chinese use all of them.

In this chapter, I will introduce you to the important special ingredients that are used in my recipes as well as to some standard ingredients that need some care in their use. I do not believe it's necessary to stock your pantry with many esoteric and expensive ingredients that you may use only once. Instead, I will show you how a few good-quality, well-chosen specialty ingredients will expand your Chinese cooking repertoire.

You will also be pleased to learn that most Chinese ingredients keep practically forever. Sauces, spices, preserved, dried, and pickled condiments seem to keep indefinitely. When I was young, I used to help my mother clean out the refrigerator and cupboards every once in a while. There would be jars and plastic bags containing, to my eye, indistinguishable matter in them. I would be ready to throw them out, having seen them there the last time we cleaned the cupboard. My mother would come rushing over to retrieve them from my hand saying, "Don't throw those away! They're still good." Now, I too have such jars and bags in my refrigerator and cupboard.

Ingredients are listed below in alphabetical order according to their English names. Below the English I have given the name in Mandarin romanization or *pinyin* (page 5). I have also given the Chinese calligraphy (all Chinese read the same characters) and for those ingredients that are sold most often by their Cantonese name, I have given that pronunciation. To be sure you are getting the right item, I suggest you bring your book with you or make a copy of the pages. If you are completely at a loss, you can show the shopkeeper the book and point to the ingredient you want. The shopkeeper, although perhaps reticent with English, often is happy to answer your questions.

Azuki Beans. See Dried Red Beans.

Bamboo Shoots

Mandarin: sŭn

Recommended brands: Ma Ling (China) Winter Bamboo Shoots, Narcissus (China)

Bamboo is a grass, and it grows extremely fast. When the Chinese talk about things that grow quickly, they refer to them as "bamboo after a spring rain." My mother used to tell me that some people claimed they could hear the bamboo shoots pushing up through the ground in the spring!

Bamboo shoots are difficult to obtain fresh in the United States, so canned bamboo shoots are commonly used. As far as canned vegetables go, bamboo shoots and water chestnuts retain much of their original flavor and texture even when canned. Any slight metallic taste can be removed by blanching the shoots in boiling water, then immediately draining and refreshing them under cold water.

Canned bamboo shoots come in different sizes and cuts; sliced bamboo shoots are most common in American supermarkets. Chinese markets carry canned bamboo shoots that are whole, sliced, or in strips (shredded). They usually sell both the long, slender spring bamboo shoots and the thick, stubby winter bamboo shoots, which are favored by the Chinese. The winter shoots (*dong sun*) are more tender and flavorful. In general, higher quality bamboo shoots are canned whole.

Once opened, canned bamboo shoots may be stored for about one week, covered with cold water in a lidded container. Change the water daily. If the bamboo shoots smell sour or the water in which they are stored becomes viscous, the bamboo shoots are spoiling and should be discarded.

Bean Curd

豆腐 *Mandarin:* doù fú

Japanese: tofu

Bean curd, or tofu, is made from soy beans that are soaked, ground, and mixed with water to make a soy milk. The milk is heated, and when the curds separate, they are pressed into soft cakes. Bean curd is rather bland in flavor and takes on the taste of the sauce in which it is cooked. It is a healthy alternative to meat since it contains a high amount of protein and calcium without fat.

Chinese grocery stores sell individual three-inch square cakes of bean curd from water-filled tubs or pails. Fresh bean curd from a Chinese bean curd shop has a marvelous fragrance and an almost sweet taste, but it is very perishable and should be used as soon as possible for the best flavor.

Fresh bean curd is now readily available in supermarkets; it comes packed in sealed plastic containers. There are different kinds, but for the recipes in this book I use either the firm Chinese-style or the soft Japanese-style bean curd.

Store bean curd submerged in water in a covered container in the refrigerator. Change the water daily. Fresh bean curd will keep for five to six days, but if it smells sour, discard it. If I am unable to use the bean curd right away, or if I purchase extra cakes on sale, I put some in the freezer for longer storage. The water inside the bean curd freezes, and when it is thawed, the water flows away, leaving a spongy network behind. My mother used to cut frozen bean curd into bite-size cubes to add to a savory soup. They would soak up the tasty liquid in which they were cooked. Frozen bean curd is a traditional ingredient for the popular Peking (Beijing) winter dish called Fire Pot, in which raw ingredients are cooked in hot broth right at the table.

Besides the familiar fresh type, bean curd comes in many other forms — dried bean curd sticks and sheets made from the skin formed on the soy bean milk; little dark cakes of pressed and seasoned bean curd; light, airy puffs of fried bean curd; deep-fried bean curd; and bean curd noodles.

Fermented bean curd that is cured in salt and wine is known in Mandarin as *fú rǔ* 腐乳 ; it is also called wet bean curd. It is sold in small cakes packed in glass jars. The cakes are mashed and used for stir-frying vegetables such as watercress (page 272) and Chinese water spinach (page 274). It is also eaten right out of the jar as a breakfast condiment with rice gruel known as congee. Fu ru is available in a white (not spicy) or red (spicy) version. It keeps indefinitely in the refrigerator.

Bean Paste or Bean Sauce

豆瓣醬

Mandarin: dòu bàn jiàng

Japanese: miso

Recommended brands: Koon Chun (HK) Ground Bean Sauce (pureed or whole bean), Sze Chuan Food Products Co., Ltd. (Taiwan) Spicy Szechuan Sauce

Thick, salty, fermented soy bean paste is used as a base for sauces. It is available in whole-bean or pureed form; in this book I use only the puree. Both are sold canned and in thirteen-ounce glass jars. Choose the glass jars whenever possible.

Spicy Szechuan-style hot bean sauce is made with yellow soy beans, salt, flour, chili, sesame oil, sugar, and pepper and comes packed in cans or small jars. It is the base for such dishes as Szechuan Spicy Bean Curd (page 246).

The Japanese make a very good quality bean paste called miso (pronounced mee-so) that is packed in sealed plastic bags or plastic tubs. There are many types of miso available, mainly white (*shiro*) and red (*aka*). My mother used to buy white and red miso and mixed them together half and half. I like to use the white miso for its lighter and slightly sweeter taste.

Store bean paste in the refrigerator after opening. If it came in a can, transfer it to a tightly lidded glass or plastic container. It will keep indefinitely.

綠豆芽 Bean Sprouts

Mandarin: lù dòu ya

Although at one time they could only be purchased in Asian markets, fresh mung bean sprouts are now popular and easily obtainable in most Western supermarkets. Be sure the sprouts that you buy are fresh and plump with no sign of wilting, browning, or sogginess.

I do not recommend canned bean sprouts. If bean sprouts are needed for flavoring such dishes as fried rice and are not available, substitute shredded pieces of the thick white part of iceberg lettuce. This does not work well in dishes where bean sprouts are the main ingredient.

The Chinese do not like to eat raw vegetables. Even for salads, they blanch the bean sprouts first to remove the raw taste. For special banquets they break off the hair root and head of each sprout by hand so the finished dish will look more beautiful.

Store bean sprouts in a plastic bag in the crisper in the refrigerator; they will keep fresh for about one week.

粉絲 Bean Thread
Mandarin: fěn sī

Bean thread is also known as cellophane noodles, glass noodles, Chinese vermicelli, and green bean thread. The first two names are a reference to the clear appearance the noodles have once they are cooked. Made from mung bean flour, the noodles are most often packed in tight two-ounce bundles and come eight bundles to a net bag. They are used in soups, stir-fried, or added to vegetarian fillings.

Bean thread will keep indefinitely in a cool, dark, dry place.

Black Mushrooms. See Dried Black Mushrooms.

白菜 Cabbage
Mandarin: bái cài
Cantonese: bok choy

Many different varieties of Chinese cabbage or bok choy (literally, white vegetable) are available. Chinese cabbage has a milder flavor and softer texture than the common green cabbage. The first three varieties of Chinese cabbage listed below are the most versatile and widely available; they are the ones used most often in this book. The fourth, Shanghai bai cai, is currently available only in Chinese markets. The taste, texture, and appearance are so special, you should try to find it when you can.

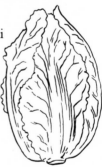

山東白菜 *Napa cabbage.* Also known as Shandong Bai Cai, this is a barrel-shaped cabbage with tightly packed large crinkly leaves. The leaves are light yellow-green in color with white stems. Napa cabbage is a favorite of mine because it is extremely versatile, cooks up tender without a strong cabbage aroma, and stores well.

天津白菜 *Chinese celery cabbage.* Also known as Tianjin bai cai, this cabbage has long, slender leaves that form a compact, cylindrical head, hence the name celery. The pale green leaves are proportionally smaller than the more significant white stalk.

白菜 *Bok choy*. Called Bai Cai in Mandarin, this is a loose-leaf cabbage with thick white stems and dark green leaves. It is used most often in stir-fry dishes.

上海白菜 *Shanghai bai cai or bok choy*. Also called Shanghai bok choy, this diminutive (about six inches long) loose-leaf cabbage has a loose, green leaf structure similar to bok choy, but the leaf stems are green instead of white. The cabbage is usually split or quartered, if large, and stir-fried or parboiled.

Tight-leaf cabbages, like napa or Chinese celery cabbage, will keep a month or more, wrapped in plastic and stored in the vegetable drawer of the refrigerator. Loose-leaf cabbages, like bok choy or Shanghai bai cai, are more perishable and should be used within a week.

Cellophane Noodles. See Bean Thread.

Chili Oil

辣油 *Mandarin: là yŏu*

Recommended brand: Joyce Chen (USA) Szechuan Stir Fry Oil

This bright red-orange chili oil is also known as hot oil. It may be purchased in Chinese grocery stores, or you can infuse your own (page 329). Chili oil is not meant for cooking but to be used as a garnish or seasoning for dips and stir-fry dishes.

The oil may be kept at room temperature in a cool, dark place for about six months or refrigerated for longer storage. If it begins to smell rancid, discard.

Chili Pepper

辣椒 *Mandarin: là jiāo*

Small (about 2 inches long) dried red chili peppers are useful to have on hand; they are a must-have if you like spicy-hot food. Most dried chili peppers come from Thailand and are packed in three- to four-ounce plastic bags.

To keep a finished dish looking attractive, I remove the pepper seeds before cooking. It's easy to do. Simply take a small pair of scissors, snip off the stem, and cut the chili open on one side. With one blade of the scissors scrape up and down the chili and the dry seeds will all fall out. Discard the seeds and use the pod only. Always add the dried peppers to cold oil and heat them up slowly to avoid burning.

You may substitute crushed red pepper for the whole chili. In general, if one teaspoon of flakes is added to a dish that serves four, it will be mild-hot; two teaspoons, hot; and three to four teaspoons, fiery!

Store dried chili peppers in a tightly lidded clean jar in your cupboard. They can get buggy over time.

芥藍 ## Chinese Broccoli or Chinese Kale
Mandarin: gài lán
Cantonese: gai lan

This vegetable is part of the cabbage family and resembles Chinese cabbage rather than broccoli. The flat leaves, which are the predominant part of the vegetable, grow from the stem, they are dark green with a blue haze. The narrow stalks often have small yellow or white flowers at the tips. Chinese broccoli is appreciated for its slightly bitter taste and the crunchy stems. As with regular broccoli, I peel the outer skin off the stalks if it is tough. Chinese broccoli may be substituted for regular broccoli.

韭菜 ## Chinese Chives or Garlic Chives
Mandarin: jiǔ cài
Cantonese: gow choy

The long, grasslike leaves of Chinese chives are flat rather than round and have a stronger flavor and texture than regular chives. Chinese chives are green or if grown away from the light, yellow. If the white ends are tough, they should be snipped and the discolored or wilted leaves pulled off and discarded before use.

Chinese chives are easy to grow as a perennial herb. Seedlings or seeds are sold in garden shops as garlic chives (*Allium tuberosum*). You can use the greens in Chinese dishes and to garnish and flavor Western dishes much as you would use regular chives. The lovely swirl of white flowers that bloom in August are edible and make a nice garnish.

Store Chinese chives in a plastic bag in the vegetable drawer of the refrigerator. To prevent rotting from too much moisture, I like to lightly wrap the chives in a layer of paper towels before sealing in a plastic bag. They will keep fresh for about one week.

Chinese Mustard Greens

芥菜 *Mandarin: jīe cài*

Cantonese: gai choy

The kind of mustard greens commonly used by the Chinese looks like a distorted head of green cabbage with loose, swirling leaves. Often the leaves are trimmed, contributing to an even more ragged appearance. Fresh Chinese mustard greens have a pleasant, slightly bitter taste. They are used in soups, stir-fries, and for making pickles.

Mustard greens will keep about one week in a plastic bag stored in the vegetable drawer of the refrigerator.

Chinese Sausage

香腸 *Mandarin: xiāng cháng*

Cantonese: lop chong

Storebought Chinese sausages are very tasty, keep well, and are readily available in Chinese markets. The ones I use most often are the thin links about six to eight inches long, made with pork or with duck liver. The sausages are dried and shrink wrapped in plastic or, in some stores, hung from hooks in bunches. As with most sausages, they tend to be fatty, but they are versatile as a flavoring condiment or side dish. Since the taste is slightly sweet, they are sometimes referred to as sweet sausages. As a quick side dish, my mother used to fashion a tray out of aluminum foil, place the sausages, sliced into bite-size pieces, on it, and steam the sausage with the rice for the last ten to fifteen minutes of cooking.

Chinese sausage will keep for months in the refrigerator and indefinitely in the freezer.

香菜 Cilantro, Coriander, or Chinese Parsley

Mandarin: xiāng cài

The Chinese call cilantro "fragrant vegetable," and so it is. It resembles flat-leaf parsley but has a strong, distinctive aroma. Some people find the taste a bit too strong. I recently read that to many children, cilantro tastes like soap. I remembered that was the exact reaction I had when I first tasted it as a child. But now I love it and like to garnish cold meats, soups, and steamed seafood with sprigs of this herb.

Store cilantro in a plastic bag lined with a paper towel. Without the paper towel, the cilantro rots faster, especially if it was moist from the market. Be sure to rinse cilantro thoroughly before using as it can be gritty.

菱粉 玉米粉 Cornstarch

Mandarin: líng fěn (water chestnut starch)
Mandarin: yù mǐ fěn (cornstarch)

Cornstarch is used in Chinese cooking as a thickener, binder, and coating to hold in natural juices so that the food does not dry out. As a thickener, cornstarch is ideal. It mixes easily with water, cooks quickly, and makes a clear sauce. When used as a thickening agent, the cornstarch is always mixed first with water and stirred in quickly while the food is still cooking. It should never be added dry or it will form a lumpy, powdery mess. In Chinese restaurants a container of cornstarch mixed with water — a slurry — is always on hand, ready to use. The amount of slurry needed to thicken a dish depends upon how much liquid there is to thicken. If you like your sauces thicker, add a little more cornstarch slurry, judging the consistency as you stir. If the sauce is too thick, add some water or unsalted broth to thin it out.

As a binder, cornstarch is added to ground meat, as in Lion's Head (page 205). cornstarch locks in the juices and binds the soft meat together.

As a coating, cornstarch keeps the juices of meat and seafood sealed in during stir-frying and deep-frying. The drawback is that the cornstarch has a tendency to stick to the pan. If this happens, add some water — not oil — to the pan. The water will dissolve and lift the cornstarch, forming a gravy in the process.

When cornstarch is mixed with water to form a slurry or is used to coat meat or seafood, it has a tendency to separate and sink to the bottom of the bowl before it is added to the pan. Stir up anything that has cornstarch in it just before adding it to the pan. That way you'll be sure you haven't left most of the cornstarch behind.

If you are allergic to cornstarch, substitute Chinese water chestnut starch, available in Chinese grocery stores, or arrowroot.

You can store cornstarch indefinitely in a dark cupboard.

咖喱粉 Curry Powder or Paste

Mandarin: gā lí fěn

Curry is not a single spice but a combination of different spices; each curry has its own distinctive taste. I recommend purchasing Madras Indian curry in powder or, preferably, paste form in specialty ethnic markets since it has a

Chinese

Ingredients

good, strong flavor. Curry pastes with oil and chili have a more complex taste than curry powder.

I store curry paste or powder in the refrigerator. The paste will keep practically indefinitely. Curry powder should be replaced when it no longer has a rich aroma.

Daikon
蘿蔔
Mandarin: *luo bŏ*

Japanese: *daikon*

Known most commonly by its Japanese name, which means big root, this radish is also called icicle radish or Chinese white radish. It is long and white, inside and out. Good daikon is heavy, juicy, solid, and crisp, not fibrous and dry. It is used for soups, red-cooked foods, or for pickling (page 320). Mother and I also used to eat daikon raw if it was not too sharp. We would peel the radish, cut it into sticks, and dip them into peanut butter.

Store daikon in the refrigerator as you would carrots. It will keep for about one month.

Dried Black Mushrooms
冬菇
Mandarin: *dōng gū*

Japanese: *shiitake*

The Chinese call these winter mushrooms. The Japanese sometimes use these mushrooms fresh, but the Chinese always use them dried, in which case the smoky flavor is more concentrated. Black mushrooms come in a wide variety of size and thickness, which determine the quality and price. The most expensive ones have thick caps with white cracks. For everyday use, where the caps may be sliced for stir-frying, use the less expensive thinner ones. Reserve the more expensive, thick-capped ones for special occasions when the mushrooms will be served whole.

Dried mushrooms must be reconstituted before using. Soak them in hot water for fifteen minutes, squeeze out the water, and cut off the stems with scissors. Use whole or cut into pieces.

Dried black mushrooms should be stored in a tightly lidded container in a cool, dark place. They will keep almost indefinitely.

Dried Golden Needles
金針 *Mandarin: jīn zhēn*

These dried unopened blossoms of a certain kind of day lily are used in vegetarian and northern-style dishes such as Peking Hot and Sour Soup (page 72) and Moo Shi Pork (page 192). The dried flowers must be softened in hot water, the hard stem knob cut off, and excess water squeezed out. If the flowers are long, line them up, and cut them in half before using. Golden needles come packaged in cellophane or plastic bags.

Store in a tightly lidded container in a cool, dry, dark place. They keep almost indefinitely.

Dried Orange or Tangerine Peel
陳皮 *Mandarin: chén pí*

Dried orange peel is used to flavor braised and stir-fried dishes as well as desserts. The Cantonese favor their use more than the northern Chinese. I purchase a small box of dried orange peels in Hong Kong each year. They come in clear plastic boxes and look quite prehistoric! I also dry orange peels as my mother did. She preferred to use Honey Tangerines (Murcotts) because the skin is highly fragrant and the pith is very thin so you don't even have to scrape it off. Score the skin before peeling so you get nice, even quarters of skin. Air-dry for several days, and then store in a cool, dry, dark place. They will keep indefinitely.

Dried Red Beans
紅豆 *Mandarin: hóng dòu*
Japanese: azuki

Red beans may be purchased in Chinese grocery stores or in some health food stores. Unlike Western-style beans, these are generally used to make sweets. They are cooked whole as in Sweet Red Bean Soup (page 342) or sometimes pureed. The beans are also popular as the main ingredient in cold drinks during the summer. Store as you would any dried bean in a sealed plastic bag or lidded jar.

Already prepared sweet red bean paste (*hong dou sha*) is available in eighteen-ounce cans in Asian markets. Look for Companion brand. The paste is made from boiled and pureed red beans, sugar, and water and used as a filling for steamed buns and such desserts as Eight Treasure Pudding (page 344). My mother used to make her own the traditional way by pureeing the cooked beans and mixing the puree with sugar and lard into a rich paste. After opening, store the paste in a tightly lidded jar in the refrigerator. It will keep for several months.

蝦米 Dried Shrimp
Mandarin: xiā mī

These tiny shrimps are salted and dried. They have a strong fishy flavor and may not appeal to everyone. Chinese enjoy snacking on dried shrimp, and when we were children, my mother always kept a good supply on hand, enough for cooking and snacking! When they are used as a condiment in salads, soups, and stir-fried dishes, I soften and rinse them in water to rid them of excess salt. They are not a substitute for fresh shrimp.

Store dried shrimp in a covered jar in the refrigerator. They will keep for months. The color should be orange. Brown means that they are old.

木耳 Dried Wood Ears
Mandarin: mù ěr

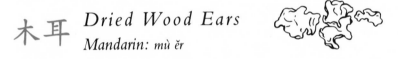

Also known as Black Fungus, Cloud Ears, or Tree Ears, wood ears are a kind of black, gelatinous fungus that grows on trees. They are appreciated for their crisp texture and not for their flavor, of which there is little. Look for small, black flakes, about half an inch or smaller in size, not the large pieces with grayish color on one side.

Wood ears are always sold dried and must be reconstituted in hot water for fifteen to twenty minutes. When softened, they expand to five or six times the dried size. After soaking, trim off the sometimes hard stem end and rinse thoroughly to get rid of any grit. Cut or break the caps into smaller pieces for cooking. Do not cook them too long or they will lose their texture.

Store dried wood ears in a tightly sealed container or sealed plastic bag in a cool, dry, dark place. They will keep indefinitely.

Duck Sauce
Mandarin: none

Recommended brand: Joyce Chen (USA) Sweet and Tangy Duck Sauce

Duck sauce is a sweet and pungent sauce that resembles a fine chutney of apples, plums, and/or apricots, sugar, and vinegar. It has no duck in it, although it is delicious served with duck. I sometimes add duck sauce to fried rice at the table. Our sales director for Joyce Chen Products, John Eaton, adds a little bit to his stir-fry at the end of cooking for a tangy-sweet taste. Duck sauce is very popular with Americans and is often served with egg rolls, fried wontons, and barbecued spareribs. On the East Coast of the United States it is known as duck sauce, but on the West Coast they call it plum sauce. It is probably not authentically Chinese. Unfortunately, the duck sauce served at most Chinese restaurants is thin and runny. This is because many restaurants thin out the prepared duck sauce with applesauce and pineapple juice to extend it.

Egg-roll Skins or Wrappers

Egg-roll skins are sold in Chinese grocery stores and in almost any full-size supermarket. They are a standard six and a half inches square and are sold in one-pound packages. Wonton skins or wrappers are basically egg-roll skins, but cut into fours. I find that egg-roll or wonton skins from Chinese grocery stores or noodle shops tend to be thinner and more tender than the ones in Western supermarkets. The thinner skin gives better results. When you work with egg-roll skins, cover them with a lightly dampened towel to keep the edges from drying out and getting brittle.

If not using before the expiration date on the package, freeze the skins for later use.

Fermented Black Beans or Salted Black Beans

豆鼓 *Mandarin: dòu chi*

Recommended brand: Pearl River Bridge Co. (China) Yang Jiang Preserved Beans with Ginger

Not to be confused with dried black beans, these are soy beans that have been salted and aged with spices. They have a rich, salty taste and a tender texture. Some cooks like to rinse them before using, but I find that good-quality black beans are not loaded with salt and do not have to be rinsed. In general, however, if you add black beans to a dish that does not call for them, reduce the amount of salt. Black beans should be coarsely chopped before using to release the flavor. The quality of black beans varies from brand to brand. I highly recommend Pearl River Bridge beans, which are actually less salty than most. They are packed in a seventeen-ounce yellow, blue, and brown paper drum. Most fermented black beans are packed in eight- to sixteen-ounce plastic bags.

Black beans keep indefinitely in a tightly sealed container in a cool, dry, dark place.

五香珍 *Five-spice Powder*
Mandarin: wŭ xiāng fĕn

This prepared spice powder is made with about five (sometimes more) different ground spices, including cinnamon, star anise, licorice, fennel, cloves, ginger, anise seed, and pepper. In Chinese it is called five-fragrance powder. Five-spice powder is used by the southern Chinese to marinate meat and poultry as well as a seasoning for Oven-roasted Spiced Peanuts (page 321).

Store tightly covered in a cool, dry, dark place as you would other powdered spices.

Fu ru. See Bean Curd.

薑 *Gingerroot*
Mandarin: jiāng

Fresh gingerroot is an ubiquitous flavoring in Chinese cuisine. It is an irregular shaped fibrous rhizome with a strong, spicy taste and wonderful aroma. Ground ginger is not a substitute for fresh gingerroot.

Recipes call for gingerroot to be sliced, crushed, minced, shredded, or grated. Generally speaking, if the gingerroot will not be eaten, it does not need to be peeled. Minced and grated gingerroot that will be blended into a dish and consumed should be peeled first. Chinese chefs peel gingerroot with small, deft strokes of the Chinese knife. You may find it easier to scrape or peel the skin off with a small paring knife. Peel only as much as you will use at a time.

Slices of gingerroot called for in this book are one inch in diameter and an eighth of an inch thick, about the size of a fifty-cent piece. For grated ginger, the ginger should be peeled and the exposed end scraped over the raised teeth of a ginger grater. Use the grated ginger that accumulates at the end of the dish; the fiber caught in the porcelain teeth can be rinsed off and discarded. Crush gingerroot with the side of a Chinese knife.

Choose a piece of fresh gingerroot that feels hard with a skin that is light tan. If the skin is shriveled and darkened or the rhizome feels spongy, don't buy it.

I have short- and long-term storage methods for gingerroot that work very well.

Short storage: about three months. Wrap the fresh gingerroot in a plain white paper towel and place it in a plastic bag. Place in the vegetable drawer of your refrigerator. When the paper gets too wet, replace with a fresh paper towel. If any mold begins to grow on the gingerroot or a portion turns brown and becomes spongy, trim it off and use the portion that is still hard.

Long storage: one year or more. Rinse the gingerroot and slice one eighth of an inch thick. Place the slices in a clean glass jar with a good lid. Cover the gingerroot slices with pale dry sherry, seal the jar, and store in the refrigerator. When you need some gingerroot, remove the slices with a pair of chopsticks or a toothpick. Although sherry-packed gingerroot is easy to use, I prefer to use fresh gingerroot whenever possible.

Golden Needles. See Dried Golden Needles.

海鮮醬 ### Hoisin Sauce
Mandarin: hǎi xiān jiàng
Recommended brands: Koon Chun (HK) and Joyce Chen (USA)

This versatile soy bean sauce, which is flavored with spices and garlic and sweetened, is used in cooking and as a dipping sauce for dishes served with Mandarin Pancakes, such as Moo Shi Pork (page 192) and Peking Duck. Hoisin sauce is one of those commercial sauces that no one makes at home, like ketchup. It can be served as it comes from the bottle or garnished with a little sesame seed oil.

Refrigerate after opening. It will keep indefinitely.

辣豆瓣醬 ## Hot Bean Paste. See Bean Paste.

麵 ## Noodles

Many types of noodles are used in Chinese cooking. The most popular are made from wheat or rice flour.

Wheat Noodles
雞蛋麵 *Mandarin: jī daǹ miàn (egg noodles)*
miàn (water-and-flour noodles)

Wheat noodles may be egg or eggless, thin or thick. The thin kind is comparable to Italian thin spaghetti and the thick variety to fettuccine. Both varieties are available fresh or dried. Interestingly, it is easier to find fresh Chinese-style noodles in Western supermarkets than dried. This may be due to the fact that with the great popularity of Italian-style dried noodles, there's no room on the shelf for dried Chinese noodles.

Dried noodles are available in boxes or bags. I like to buy five-pound boxes of Chinese-style plain dried flat noodles about an eighth of an inch wide for general use. In the early years when Chinese-style noodles were only available in Chinese noodle shops, my mother often used Italian dried spaghetti from the supermarket as a substitute. I still use it and have never had a problem with the success of a dish. I use thin spaghetti, spaghettini, vermicelli, or when I want a wider noodle, linguine.

Dried wheat noodles keep almost indefinitely.

Fresh noodles are usually in the produce department of the supermarket and are packed in plastic bags. I have found that Azumaya brand noodles, thick or thin, are very good. You'll find many dried and fresh noodles in Chinese grocery stores. Fresh noodles, egg or plain, are packed in plastic bags.

Fresh noodles cook up very quickly, so be careful you don't overcook them.

Fresh noodles should be stored in the refrigerator until ready to use or frozen for longer storage.

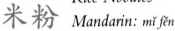

Rice Noodles

米粉 *Mandarin:* mǐ fěn

Recommended brand: Double Swallow Brand (China) Rice Stick

Rice noodles are made from rice and water and come thick or thin, dried or fresh. The most common rice noodle used at home is the thin, dried variety called rice sticks.

Before using, soak the noodles in warm water for ten to fifteen minutes until soft. Do not boil. Drain and use in soup noodle recipes or with other ingredients in a stir-fry.

The thin rice noodles can also be deep-fried in hot (375°F.) oil while they are still dry. Break them into three-inch pieces and fry small portions at a time. Remove with a wire skimmer as soon as they puff up and drain on paper towels. Use them as a garnish for stir-fry dishes or in salads.

Dried rice noodles keep for a long time.

Fresh rice noodles, which are popular with the southern Chinese, are available in Chinatown. They are very perishable and must be stored in the refrigerator.

油 *Oil*
Mandarin: y̌ou

There seems to be much confusion as to the *right* oil to use for Chinese cooking. There is no single right oil. Some are more right than others, however. Peanut oil has been touted by many, but my mother always used soybean oil because of its lighter flavor. Other oils that are fine to use are corn oil and so-called vegetable oil, such as Wesson or Crisco. I prefer canola oil, which is derived from the rapeseed, a plant of the brassica family. It is neutral in flavor and light in texture and does not interfere with the natural flavors of fresh or delicate ingredients. It is an excellent oil to use at high temperatures for stir-frying. Canola oil was used exclusively in the testing of all the recipes in this book.

If you would like to use a flavored cooking oil, the Joyce Chen cooking oils are all made with a base of canola oil.

Do not stir-fry with olive oil or sesame seed oil. These oils are not suitable for Chinese food because of their strong flavor and low smoking temperature.

蠔油 *Oyster Sauce*
Mandarin: ȟao yóu

Recommended brand: Lee Kum Kee Premium (HK) Oyster Flavored Sauce

This versatile and tasty Cantonese cooking sauce, also called oyster-flavored sauce, is made from oyster extract, salt, and spices. Contrary to its name, this thick brown sauce does not taste like oysters. Oyster sauce comes in glass bottles and is made by many manufacturers. If you are unsure of which brand to purchase, and the recommended brand is not available, choose a more expensive brand for better quality and taste. Refrigerate after opening. It will keep indefinitely.

Red Beans. See Dried Red Beans.

米 *Rice*
Mandarin: m̌i *(raw rice)*

飯
fàn (cooked rice)

Rice is the staple grain of Asia. There is long and short grain, brown and polished white rice, fragrant rices, like Basmati and Jasmine, popular in India and Thailand, respectively. The Chinese prefer long-grain white rice. This rice cooks up light and fluffy. The Japanese, on the other hand, prefer a short-grain white rice which is softer and stickier when cooked. For making congee, or rice gruel, we use short-grain rice for a smoother texture.

Originally, the northern Chinese ate many more wheat dishes like steamed breads and noodles because of the difficulty of growing rice in their cooler and drier climate. With better transportation rice is now served at every meal, although wheat remains a popular starch.

Rice is relatively inexpensive in the United States and easy to obtain in the supermarket or an Asian market. For convenience and savings, I buy a premium long-grain white rice by the twenty-five-pound bag. Precooked and instant rice are not recommended. They do not have the fresh flavor or soft texture of freshly cooked raw rice.

Glutinous rice, also known as sweet rice, is used in certain dishes as a filling or in desserts like the famous Eight Treasure Pudding (page 344).

Store raw rice covered in a cool, dry, dark place. It keeps indefinitely.

Glutinous rice is also ground into flour and used to make steamed sticky cakes, sweet rice balls like those in The Emperor's Nectar (page 340) and sweet soups like Almond tea (page 339). Sweet rice powder comes in one-pound boxes or bags from Japan, China, and Thailand.

Sweet rice wine is glutinous rice that has been yeast fermented. The rice is steamed, then mixed with a starter, covered and left in a cool, dark place until the rice is soft with a sweet, alcoholic liquid. Both the rice and its liquid are used in cooking such desserts as Emperor's Nectar. Although my mother always made her own sweet rice wine, I buy mine from the refrigerator section of an Asian market. It is sometimes called Sweet Rice Pudding.

Sesame Seed Oil
Mandarin: mā ýou

Recommended brand: *Kadoya (Japan) or Joyce Chen (USA)*

Oriental sesame seed oil is pressed from roasted sesame seeds. It is golden brown in color and highly fragrant. Since this oil has a low smoking temperature and is strongly flavored, it is not suitable for stir-frying. It is used as a garnishing oil or for making dressings and dips or added to fillings for flavor.

Store at room temperature in a dark, cool place. For longer storage keep in the refrigerator. Sesame seed oil tends to turn rancid in a few months. If it is used infrequently, buy a small bottle.

火腿 ## Smithfield Ham
Mandarin: hūo tŭi

Recommended brand: Smithfield Packing Co. (USA)

The Chinese call ham "fire thigh," and the most famous in China is from Jinhua in Zhejiang Province south of Shanghai. The closest in flavor to the famous *Jinhua* ham is Smithfield ham from Virginia. My mother used to keep a Smithfield ham hanging in the basement; now I do the same! When we needed to use it my father would bring it up and with a hacksaw, saw off a piece. The ham would then be rewrapped and taken back down to the cellar. If you do not want to deal with a whole ham, you'll find many Chinese markets with a meat department that have pieces of Smithfield ham already cut and packed for sale. The ham is used to flavor soups (Ham and Winter Melon Soup), or it is minced for a garnish.

Whole Smithfield ham keeps well in a cool basement. If there is any mold, just scrape or slice it off. For longer storage you may freeze the ham. Slices of ham should be stored in the refrigerator.

雪菜
雪裏紅 ## Snow Cabbage or Red-in-Snow
Mandarin: xùe caì or xùe lǐ hóng

Recommended brand: Ma Ling (China) Pickled Cabbage

What a beautiful name for a pickled vegetable! The imagery comes from the fact that the roots are red and that this leafy vegetable, a member of the mustard family, often sprouts in early spring through the snow. The leaves are pickled in brine and have a distinctive salty, pungent taste and crisp texture. Pickled snow cabbage is used as a condiment and flavoring, in soups, in stir-fries with pork, and as a filling for dumplings. Snow cabbage is usually available in cans.

After opening, transfer to a clean, tightly lidded glass jar and store in the refrigerator. It will keep indefinitely.

雪豆 ## Snow Peas
Mandarin: xùe dòu

Unlike regular peas, the whole pod of the snow pea is edible. In fact, the important part is not the pea, but the pod. Only use fresh snow peas; frozen snow peas will ruin a fine dish. Also called pea pods, snow peas have bright green, unblemished pods; they should snap when bent in two. To use, snap the ends of the snow peas and pull down the strings. Other edible pods, such as sugar snap peas, may be substituted for snow peas.

Store snow peas in a plastic bag in the vegetable drawer of the refrigerator where they will keep about one week.

Soy Sauce

醬油 Mandarin: *jiàng yóu*

Recommended brands: *Dark — Pearl River Bridge (China) Soy Superior and Joyce Chen (USA), Light — Pearl River Bridge (China) Superior Soy, Thick — Koon Chun (HK)*

A good Chinese soy sauce is critical to successful Chinese cooking. It is probably the most often used — and most misunderstood — Chinese ingredient. There are several different soy sauces, each with its own characteristic.

Supermarket soys are usually made from hydrolyzed vegetable protein, salt, caramel color, and preservatives. They lack both taste and texture. The popular Japanese soys are fine for Japanese food or for dressings and dips that call for their lighter, sweet flavor, but they are not suitable for Chinese stir-frying, which requires a more robust taste with a heavier, thicker texture.

The two most useful types of soy sauce to have on hand are dark and light. Dark soy sauce contains molasses and has a thicker texture (light refers to the thinner texture, not to the color or sodium content). You can tell the difference by shaking the bottle. Dark soy sauce will cling longer to the neck of the bottle. Light soy sauce, which is a little saltier than the dark, should be used for table dips and dressings or when a thinner coating is desired. Dark soy sauce should be used for cooking, where a richer taste and thicker coverage is desired.

The saltiness of different soy sauces varies a great deal. I suggest you omit or reduce the amount of salt called for when soy sauce is used. At the end of cooking, taste the dish and add salt as desired. This way, if the sauce you use is saltier than mine, you can adjust at the end of the cooking. This is especially true when using any Chinese prepared sauce, such as oyster sauce or bean sauce.

Many people ask me what restaurants use to give fried rice its dark color. It is not regular soy sauce, which would be too watery, but a thick, syrupy soy sauce called *thick soy sauce,* not to be confused with dark soy sauce. This has the consistency of honey and is made with molasses, salt, and soy bean extract. It is used primarily to give a deep, rich color to foods.

Store soy sauce in a cool, dark place. It is not necessary to refrigerate it. I like to buy large sizes of light and dark soy sauces and decant them into separate bottles with convenient pouring spouts.

八角 *Star Anise*
Mandarin: bā jiǎo

This lovely spice has five to eight cloves that form a star. The Chinese call them "Eight Corners" in reference to their star shape. They are most often used in Shanghai-style red-cooked dishes. Use star anise whole or break off cloves. Store in a tightly lidded glass jar in a cool, dark, dry place. Star anise keeps indefinitely.

Sweet Red Bean Paste. See Dried Red Beans.

花椒 *Szechuan (Sichuan) Peppercorns*
Mandarin: hūa jiāo

A dried spice, known as "flower pepper" in Chinese, Szechuan peppercorns are small reddish-brown husks that have partially opened to reveal tiny black seeds inside. They grow on bushes and are often packed with bits of twig that should be picked out before use. They are widely used in Szechuan cuisine for cooking, as well as for pickling and curing meats. They can be found in Chinese grocery stores, usually packed in four-ounce cellophane bags. Used in large quantities, they give a numbing sensation to the mouth. Transfer whole peppercorns to a covered glass jar and keep in a cool, dark, dry place. Use as long as they are fragrant.

Szechuan peppercorns are generally toasted and ground before use. Heat the peppercorns in an ungreased skillet over medium heat until the peppercorns are smoking and fragrant. Do not let them burn. How long it takes depends on the amount of peppercorns you are roasting. Let the peppercorns cool, then grind them in a mortar with a pestle or roll with a rolling pin between two pieces of paper. Sift through a strainer and discard the larger pieces that do not pass through. Store the powder in a clean, tightly lidded glass jar in a dark, dry place.

Szechuan peppercorns are also used to make a seasoned salt (page 332) that is used as a dip for fried foods. Stored in a tightly lidded container in a cool, dark, and dry place, the seasoned salt will keep indefinitely.

Chinese

Ingredients

27

Szechuan Vegetable

榨菜

Mandarin: zhā cài

Recommended brand: Ma Ling (China) Zhejiang Preserved Vegetable

The knobby, fleshy stems of a particular kind of mustard green are preserved in salt and chili powder for this Szechuan specialty. Its salty, sour, spicy taste and crisp texture enrich soups and stir-fry dishes. Szechuan vegetable comes in cans and is available whole or shredded. I like to buy the shredded one because it is easier to use. I always keep a can or two on hand for that quick soup or soup noodle dish. I usually rinse off the coating of red chili powder before using to tone down the spiciness and salinity. After opening the can, transfer the vegetable to a clean tightly lidded jar. It will keep indefinitely in the refrigerator.

Tofu. See Bean Curd.

醋

Vinegar

Mandarin: cù

Recommended brand: Cider — Heinz (USA), Rice — Marukan (Japan and USA) Genuine Brewed Rice Vinegar (green label), Chinese black — Gold Plum (China) Chinkiang Vinegar

There are three types of vinegars used in this book — cider, rice, and Chinkiang or Chinese black vinegar.

Cider vinegar My mother always used Heinz vinegars. I also find the taste of Heinz to be preferable to other brands.

Rice vinegar Less acidic than cider, this clear or yellowish vinegar is made from rice.

Chinkiang or Chinese black vinegar This rich, flavorful vinegar is comparable in taste to balsamic vinegar. It is made from water, glutinous rice, and salt. It is known as Chinkiang vinegar, for the city in which it is brewed. Store in a cool place away from direct sunlight.

馬蹄 *Water Chestnuts*
Mandarin: mǎ tí

Recommended brands: Ma Ling (China) or Companion (Taiwan)

Water chestnuts are available canned or fresh. Fresh water chestnuts are crunchy and sweet like apples, but it is difficult to find good-quality fresh ones. If the water chestnuts are spongy when pressed or are shriveled, don't buy them. Look for a hard fruit with a shiny mahogany-colored skin when rubbed. All fresh water chestnuts tend to be muddy. Wash, peel, and rinse thoroughly before eating. You may eat fresh water chestnuts raw or sliced and cook them in your favorite recipe. If the flesh is yellow or discolored, discard. Canned water chestnuts, available whole or sliced, are a fine substitute for the fresh. If your canned water chestnuts have a tinny taste or aroma, plunge them in boiling water for a few seconds, then immediately drain and rinse in cold water.

Store drained canned water chestnuts in a lidded container, covered with cold water. Change the water daily. If they begin to smell sour or the water becomes viscous, they are spoiled and should be discarded.

空心菜 *Water Spinach*
Mandarin: kōng xīn cài

Cantonese: ong choy

Water spinach is not related to spinach, but to the sweet potato. This trailing vegetable is available at Chinese markets. Stir-fried with fermented bean curd (page 9), it is a popular Cantonese country dish. The leaves become slightly slippery when cooked.

My introduction to the cultivation of water spinach was years ago when I lived in a two-family house in Somerville, Massachusetts, which I owned. My Chinese tenants downstairs asked permission one day to dig up a rather small and scraggly looking lawn for planting vegetables. I thought that neat rows of vegetables would look better than weeds, so I agreed. Little did I realize that they wanted to grow water spinach! True to its name it needs a very wet soil so instead of neat rows of tomatoes and peppers as I had imagined, the yard was transformed into wet, sunken beds filled with water spinach. When they moved out a few years later, it took quite a while to return the yard to lawn.

Water spinach will keep for about a week refrigerated in a plastic bag in the crisper.

酒 *Wine*
Mandarin: jĭu

In Chinese cooking, rice wine is usually used as a seasoning to cover up certain unwanted flavors, like fishiness from seafood. In some recipes such as Drunken Chicken (page 180), it is the main seasoning. Shaoxing wine, from Zhejiang Province, is a famous high-quality rice wine used both for cooking and drinking. Chinese rice wines are available in Chinese grocery stores, but in order to sell them as cooking wines and not table wines, for which they would need a special license, the wines are salted. Do not confuse Chinese rice wines with the Japanese rice wine called sake or mirin. It is not necessary to use Chinese rice wine. My mother always used pale dry sherry both at home and at our restaurants. I also prefer dry sherry. It is easy to get, inexpensive, and provides an excellent taste.

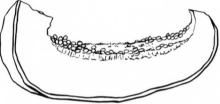

冬瓜 *Winter Melon*
Mandarin: dōng gūa

A member of the gourd family, this melon is prized for its thick, white rind. It grows very large (like a pumpkin) and is cut into wedges and sold by the pound. The skin is green with a white fuzz that makes it look as if it's frosted with snow. Winter melon rind is used in soups. At fancy banquets, a whole winter melon may be carved with an intricate design and used as the container to hold the soup. The rind is also candied and served during the lunar New Year along with candied water chestnuts and coconut slivers to ensure a sweet year ahead. Slices of fresh winter melon should be wrapped in plastic film and stored in the refrigerator. The melon will keep for about one week.

Wood Ears. See Dried Wood Ears.

福

Note　If you have difficulty obtaining any of the Chinese specialty ingredients or equipment used in this book, contact:

The Oriental Pantry
Mail Order Department
423 Great Road
Acton, Massachusetts 01720
Telephone: 1-800-828-0368
Fax: 617-275-4506

Tools in a Chinese Kitchen

he traditional Chinese kitchen is a rather spartan place and it's hard to believe that a few simple hand tools and a single pan could produce such incredible delicacies. These tools seem to remain confusing and awkward to most Western cooks. I hope the following guide will dispel the mystery. Some items may not be available in local stores. See the mail-order listing on page 30.

A Note on Quality

The cookware and cutlery of China are generally crudely made from inexpensive materials, such as cold rolled carbon steel and earthenware. This is not because the Chinese prefer them this way, but because China cannot afford better-made kitchenware. Just because a cooking tool comes from China or Taiwan doesn't necessarily mean that it is the best choice. The Western market is flooded with cheap Chinese equipment manufactured especially for export to be sold at low prices. It is ironic to me that so many home cooks insist on the "real" thing only to be disappointed with awkward-to-use, rusting cookware that ultimately ends up in the garage or trash can.

It was my mother's frustration with the lack of good or appropriate kitchenware that prompted her to create her own line of cookware, which continues to be distributed and marketed today under her name, Joyce Chen Products. Her original designs were the result of her knowledge of what a Chinese cook needs at home and what the Western kitchen can accommodate. I can recommend our products to you without reservation.

The Chinese Knife

福   The first piece of Chinese equipment people often think of is a wok, overlooking the most important tool — a good, sharp knife. Since the Chinese eat with chopsticks and not with knives and forks, almost all ingredients are cut up in the kitchen before cooking or serving. The most important cooking technique, stir-frying, is a fast sauté over high heat, and it is imperative that the ingredients be uniform in size so they cook quickly and evenly.

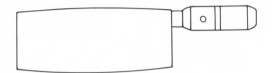

The traditional Chinese knife is a wide, rectangular carbon-steel blade with a wooden handle. It is sometimes referred to as a cleaver but I prefer to call it a knife, because the medium-weight style that is used most often is designed for cutting, slicing, and dicing, and not for chopping bones. Cleavers for chopping are heavier and made of a softer steel to avoid damage that may occur to a harder, more brittle blade.

A good knife should feel comfortable in your hand — well-balanced and solid. The blade and handle should be clean and properly packaged to prevent damage to the blade in transit. A poorly made knife will have a blade that is too thick and a handle that is awkward and fatiguing to hold.

The steel may be carbon or stainless. Some people feel that stainless blades are too difficult to sharpen because of their hardness, but I prefer a good stainless blade. It is much easier to maintain and won't rust, stain, or give a metallic taste to foods. The handle of a Chinese knife is traditionally made of wood, although there are some knives with metal, plastic, or rubber handles.

The top-of-the-line Chinese knife that we have designed for Joyce Chen Products is called the All-In-One Knife. It has a chrome molybdenum stainless steel blade and comes in two sizes, 85 mm (below left) and 63 mm wide (below right), with a full tang hardwood handle secured with three stainless steel rivets. The 85-mm knife is a full-size standard Chinese knife; the 63-mm is a slimmed-down version, made a little smaller and lighter for the smaller hand

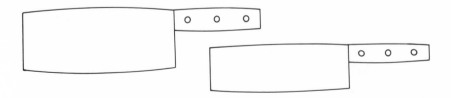

or for cutting vegetables. Our midline basic kitchen model is called The Chinese Kitchen Knife. It has a high carbon stainless steel blade with a traditional round wooden handle. Which knife to use depends upon your personal preference.

A Chinese knife should be cared for like any other good knife. It should never be placed in the dishwasher. Store it carefully so the blade does not rub up against hard objects that will chip or dull its edge. Keep the edge honed by running it over a sharpening or honing steel each time it is used. If the edge needs sharpening use a whetstone or a good quality sharpening tool.

See pages 41–48 for instructions on holding and using a Chinese knife.

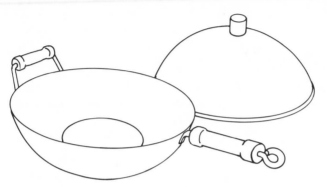

The Wok or Stir-fry Pan

禄 The next most important piece of Chinese equipment is the pan. Northerners who speak Mandarin call this pan a *guo,* or more familiarly *wok* in Cantonese. Manufacturers and distributors of Oriental-style cookware use the names stir-fry pan and wok interchangeably.

The original Chinese wok has a round bottom and metal ring handles on either side. It was designed to sit in an opening over a wood- or coal-burning brazier. This worked well for the Chinese for thousands of years, but on flat ranges in America, these round-bottom woks became inconvenient and even dangerous to use. To stabilize the wok, manufacturers devised a metal ring to be placed around a burner so the wok could sit on top. In the 1950s and 1960s this setup was all that was available to Western cooks wishing to stir-fry.

My mother never owned a round-bottom wok. She found it too difficult to use successfully on a Western stove. Before our cookware company was established, she used a pressure cooker or a deep heavy skillet from a professional kitchen supply house for stir-frying. It was the need for a proper pan that prompted her to develop the flat-bottom wok and stir-fry pan that became the hallmark of Joyce Chen Products.

When we introduced our first stir-fry pan, it was a revelation. My mother designed this new pan to be smaller and more compact than the fourteen-inch woks then available. The twelve-inch diameter fit better on a home stove top. She then eliminated the need for a ring stand by making the bottom of the pan flat. And instead of metal handles, she made one handle like a skillet handle. The body of the pan was made of heavy-weight carbon steel; in later years we added a nonstick surface for lowfat cooking.

Which pan is right for you? Some people are traditionalists and swear by the round-bottom carbon-steel wok. If it works for you and you are happy, that's fine. But, I would not recommend it for anyone with an electric or porcelain top stove. There, a flat-bottom wok is essential. Flat-bottom woks are also much better for gas stoves.

Uncoated carbon steel or nonstick? Some people prefer the traditional carbon steel that is seasoned on a regular basis to prevent rusting and to create a black patina on the inside of the pan. I find, however, that most people do not use their woks enough to keep the seasoned patina in perfect shape. Chinese people use the wok many times every day, it is constantly being cooked in, cleaned, and reseasoned. The complaint about sticky, tacky, dusty and eventually rusting woks is often a result of underuse. With a carbon-steel wok, the more you use it the better it gets.

Nonstick woks and stir-fry pans, on the other hand, do not require seasoning. All nonstick pans, however, are not equal. In general, many nonstick coatings applied on carbon steel do not tolerate well the high heat demands of stir-frying and, interestingly, even less the abuse from boiling water when the wok is used for steaming. Nonstick aluminum is stronger and more tolerant of temperature changes because aluminum, unlike carbon steel, spreads heat across the whole pan rather than concentrating it in one place.

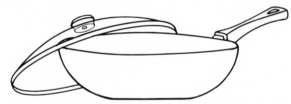

My personal preference is our top-of-the-line twelve-inch stir-fry pan called the Joyce Chen Peking Pan® Pro. It is made of heavy-gauge aluminum with a multicoat nonstick surface that helps you cut back on the amount of oil you use for cooking. Because the material is heavy-gauge aluminum you'll find that this pan takes a little longer to heat up than a carbon-steel pan. This is the pan I used to test all the recipes in this book.

If you choose a carbon-steel pan, make sure it is heavy for even heat conduction, but not so heavy as to be difficult to lift and move around. Handles should be securely attached to the pan with rivets or strong spot welds. Test the wok by holding the handles and pressing the sides together. A wok that is made of very thin gauge steel will be flexible, some can even be bent in half! Stay away from those. In addition to our Peking Pan Joyce Chen Products also offer a complete range of heavy gauge carbon-steel and nonstick woks.

Be wary of choosing wok sets by price alone. The difference between these sets may be more in the number of accessories than the quality of the pan.

I do not recommend electric woks. They generally do not provide enough heat for proper stir-frying, and they are difficult to control since the heating element is part of the pan itself.

How to Season a Carbon-Steel Wok

Carbon-steel woks are coated with a protective lacquer or oil to prevent rusting in transit. They must be cleaned and seasoned before use. Seasoning seals the carbon-steel cooking surface to prevent rusting. Successive uses of the wok will, over time, build up a black patina that will maintain the protective seasoning and provide a smooth, stick-resistant surface, much like a well-seasoned cast-iron skillet.

Thoroughly scrub the wok with hot soapy water to remove the factory-applied protective oil coating. Some woks come with a lacquer coating, this must be burned off before washing by placing the pan over medium-high heat until it smokes. Remove from the heat and cool. Wash and dry the pan thoroughly.

Pour about 2 tablespoons cooking oil into the wok and smear over the inside with a paper towel until the entire inside surface is coated with a film of oil. Place the pan over medium heat and allow it to heat up slowly for 10 to 15 minutes. With a paper towel, evenly distribute the oil over the entire cooking surface, tilting the wok over the burner so that the sides of the wok heat up as well as the bottom. The pan will be hot, so handle with care. The paper towel will blacken slightly as you do this. Repeat this oiling and heating process 3 or 4 times, letting the pan cool in between. Your wok is now seasoned and ready to use.

How to Maintain a Carbon-Steel Wok

After each use, rinse the wok with hot water and scrub away food particles with a dishwashing brush or nonmetallic scrubber. Use a dishwashing liquid only if necessary, as it may strip away the seasoning. Rinse the pan and dry thoroughly. To be sure all surface moisture is gone, place the wok over medium-high heat to finish drying. Allow the pan to cool. Before storing, wipe a thin film of cooking oil over the inside surface of the wok to prevent rusting and help maintain a seasoned surface. This last oiling may not be necessary every time if the pan is well seasoned and used often. If rust appears, simply scrub it away, rinse and dry the pan and season it again.

How to Maintain a Nonstick Wok

Wash a new nonstick wok with a mild dishwashing detergent and hot water. Dry thoroughly with a dish towel. After each use, clean with hot water and a mild detergent and dry by hand immediately. Never use scouring powder, abrasives, or metal scouring pads, which can damage the nonstick coating.

Never preheat nonstick woks without first adding cooking oil as called for in the recipe. The intense heat without something in the pan to help distribute it may damage the nonstick coating. Always use bamboo, wood, or plastic tools in your nonstick pan. Never use a metal spatula or sharp knives; these may scratch the nonstick coating.

To remove burned food, mix 3 tablespoons chlorine bleach with 1 tablespoon liquid dish detergent in 1 cup of water. Pour into the pan and soak for 20 minutes. Scrub gently with a soft nylon brush or sponge.

If you have a nonstick carbon-steel pan, apply a thin film of cooking oil to the entire surface of the pan after cleaning. This is to prevent rusting should the nonstick coating become scratched with use. It is not necessary to oil an aluminum nonstick pan.

Neither the carbon-steel or nonstick pans should ever be put into the dishwasher. Always wash by hand as soon as possible after cooking.

The Steamer

壽 After stir-frying, steaming is probably the most popular Chinese cooking method. Manufacturers now offer new electric steamers, but I prefer the Chinese stove-top steamers. They provide much more flexibility and control; flexibility in that larger steamers can hold whole fish or bowls of different sizes, control in that you can adjust the amount of heat as you wish.

The Chinese steamer is designed with numerous flat tiers — most commonly two tiers — and a lid. In the Far East, steamers can range in size from diminutive four-inch ones for dim sum to gargantuan tabletop steamers for commercial and restaurant use. For home use, the most common sizes are ten to twelve inches in diameter, these are available in bamboo, aluminum, and stainless steel.

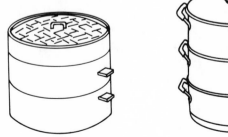

Bamboo steamers are handmade in Asia. Because bamboo can grow to over a hundred feet in height, very large as well as very small steamers can be made from this natural material. Some bamboo steamers in the American market are actually made of wood, with only the slats in bamboo. Some of the best bamboo steamers come from Sichuan (Szechuan) Province, where bamboo grows in profusion. The bamboo steamer is designed to sit over another pot, usually a wok, containing boiling water.

The benefit of a steamer made of bamboo is that as a natural material it absorbs condensation, keeping it from dripping back onto the food. When heated, it forms a hot container and can keep food warm for half an hour. A good bamboo steamer is also attractive enough to bring to the table and is generally reasonably priced.

Steamers made of aluminum and stainless steel come outfitted with a large base pot and tiers that fit snugly on top; there is no need to use a wok as the base. Metal steamers are the easiest to use if you plan do a lot of steaming. Most metal steamers have tiers that are high enough to accommodate a medium-size bowl for steaming soups. Ten-, twelve-, and fourteen-inch metal steamers are the most popular sizes for home use.

A drawback with metal steamers is that condensation forms inside the lid and drips onto the food, sometimes in a big stream when the lid is lifted. This is most troublesome when steaming breads and dumplings. To keep this from happening, the Chinese wrap the lid and the upper tier with a large piece of cotton cloth.

I use both metal and bamboo steamers at home. I prefer the bamboo steamers for steamed breads and dumplings because they don't allow condensation to form. I like the metal steamers because they accommodate bigger bowls and plates and can hold more water, so I don't have to replenish the boiling water as often. The larger steamers may be found in some Chinese markets or hardware stores in Chinatown.

The Rice Cooker

禄 Several kinds of rice cookers are available in the American market. Electric rice cookers are the most convenient to use. Once the rice and water are measured, all you have to do is to push a button and the rice cooker does the rest — cooks, turns itself off, and keeps the rice warm. Although an electric rice cooker can be expensive, it is a worthwhile investment if you like to eat rice.

Microwave rice cookers cook rice in twenty to thirty minutes. They are easy to use, although you need to cook the rice at two power levels and then let it sit to absorb moisture. Microwave rice cookers are inexpensive.

For saucepan-cooked rice a regular heavy-bottomed pot with a lid is fine. See page 88 for directions for cooking rice.

The Steam Pot

禧   The traditional Yunnan steam pot can also be used to cook rice. The steam pot is a special, hard-fired, unglazed clay pot that is handmade in China. It is designed with an interior chimney that rises from the floor of the casserole. It is through this tube that steam enters the casserole, condenses against the lid, and cooks the food in a moist, gentle heat. This pot comes from Yunnan Province. It is traditionally used to cook Yunnan Steam Pot Chicken (page 177), but can also be used to steam vegetables, rice, and fruit.

Accessories

福   The following are some useful accessories that make particular tasks easier. They are ones that I like to use.

Cutting Board. With all the cutting that is necessary for Chinese cooking, a good cutting board is essential. Traditionally, the Chinese used thick slices of hardwood tree trunks. They were often bulky and very heavy, about six inches thick and fifteen inches across. Many Chinese markets and restaurants use these, but they are not practical for home use. A fourteen-inch round or at least a twelve-inch rectangular board is sufficient. The material can be wood or plastic.

The item that started Joyce Chen Products was a solid polyethylene cutting board, which we called The Cutting Slab. It is nonporous so it won't absorb moisture or odors; it has the same density as wood, so it won't dull knives; it has a textured surface, so food won't slip and dough won't stick; and it is dishwasher-safe.

Spatula and Ladle. Because large restaurant woks are too heavy to lift, professional chefs use long-handled spatulas and ladles to stir and scoop food in and out. At home, a shorter spatula and shorter ladle are adequate for stirring and scooping sauces and soups.

I use a bamboo spatula that is well shaped and comfortable in the hand. Bamboo, unlike the softer beechwood popular in European wooden tools, is very strong and long-lasting and can go right into the dishwasher. Choose a twelve- to fifteen-inch spatula that is rounded to match the contour of a rounded pan. Be sure it is stiff and rigid, you cannot stir-fry properly with a flexible spatula. I find that inexpensive plastic spatulas become soft when heated and are awkward to use. A metal spatula with a sturdy handle is fine for carbon-steel pans but can damage nonstick cookware.

Ladles are usually made of metal, because bamboo is not thick or wide enough to make into a ladle. Be careful not to scratch your nonstick pans. To be on the safe side, I use a plastic ladle on my nonstick cookware.

Wire Skimmer or Strainer. This utensil, with its long bamboo handle and wire mesh basket, is handy for lifting foods out of deep-fry oil and for blanching vegetables. A five- or six-inch wire basket is the most useful size for home use. Look for strainers that have strong, well-formed baskets made of either brass or copper wire.

Rolling Pin. The Chinese use a small rolling pin with no handles. It offers more control for rolling out scallion cakes, Mandarin Pancakes, or Peking Ravioli skins. A Chinese rolling pin is eleven to twelve inches long and one inch or slightly less in diameter. I purchased a beautiful professional pin in Hong Kong, but my mother used to make her own from wooden dowels available at almost any hardware store.

Kitchen Scissors. Every kitchen should have a pair of good scissors. I use scissors all the time, for such tasks as deveining shrimp, cutting off the stems from dried black mushrooms, trimming the fat from poultry, and cutting up a whole chicken or lobster. Joyce Chen Products distributes a unique, powerful pair of kitchen scissors called Joyce Chen Unlimited Scissors®. The handles are soft and flexible. And because the scissors have large loop handles, even hands slippery with chicken fat can't easily slip out. The scissors can be used right or left handed and are dishwasher-safe.

Ginger Grater. Ginger graters have raised teeth that separate the pulp from the root. They are made from a variety of materials from stainless steel to porcelain to bamboo. The best in my opinion are the porcelain ones.

Steamer Tongs. These look very much like canning jar lifters, but they open wider. They help you lift a plate from a tight steamer or place a plate or bowl into a hot steamer without burning your fingers.

Chopsticks. Bamboo cooking chopsticks are longer and thicker than chopsticks for table use. They are perfect for stirring green vegetables like spinach, for lifting noodles, and for plucking morsels out of hot oil. Bamboo is relatively inexpensive; when the tips get scorched, the chopsticks can be replaced.

How to Use Chopsticks
筷子

The Chinese call chopsticks "quick brothers" (*kwai zi*); they are the universal eating implement in China. They are very versatile, and you'll find them in the kitchen as well as on the dining table. Chopsticks are usually made of a nonconductive material such as bamboo, plastic, or wood but can also be made from silver, ivory, lacquer, enamel, or even jade and gold. I have two pairs of slim silver chopsticks intricately engraved and held together at the far end with silver chains. These were given to me by a Chinese friend as wedding chopsticks and are almost too beautiful to use. Chinese chopsticks have blunt ends; Japanese chopsticks are pointed. As a rule, the top end of the chopstick is square (so it won't roll off the table) and the eating end is round. Bamboo or wood chopsticks are inexpensive and good for beginners since they are not too slippery.

Adults should hold the chopsticks at the middle. It is easier for children to hold chopsticks lower down. Keep the ends of the chopsticks even and parallel; they must not cross. Every once in a while you can tap the eating ends on a plate if the chopsticks start to slip. This is not considered bad manners.

Some large foods or meat on the bone offer a special challenge to the uninitiated. The Chinese eat chicken and sparerib nuggets by holding the food with chopsticks and nibbling around the bone. After the meat is nibbled away, the bone is transferred by chopstick to a bone dish. To eat egg rolls, Peking Ravioli, or anything else that is not bite-size, you pick up the food with chopsticks and bite off pieces; return the rest to your bowl or plate or continue to hold it with the chopsticks.

Techniques in a Chinese Kitchen

Cutting Techniques

Since there are no forks and knives at the Chinese table, virtually all ingredients must be cut into bite-size pieces. Not only can they be eaten easily with chopsticks, they also cook evenly and look appealing. Although home cooking, unlike elaborate restaurant cuisine, does not utilize some of the fancier garnishing cuts, it does require many basic cutting techniques. Western cooks often seem afraid of preparing to cook a Chinese meal. There may be more cutting than you're used to, but with a good knife and a little instruction, you'll find it easier than you first thought.

First is the knife. Use either a sharp Chinese knife, the best choice, or an eight-inch chef's knife. Because of its shape and weight, a Chinese knife helps you cut quickly, evenly, and cleanly. It is surprisingly versatile. See pages 32–33 for a description of a Chinese knife and what to look for when buying one.

The rectangular shape of the Chinese knife may make it seem a bit front heavy and awkward at first, but it is held differently than a Western-style knife. Grip the Chinese knife at the bolster, firmly like a good handshake, with your bent forefinger resting on one side of the blade and thumb on the other. In this way, the center of balance is further forward, providing more control and less fatigue.

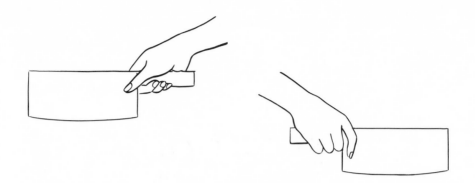

Your other hand should be relaxed with the fingers bent so that the fingertips are slightly behind the knuckles. In this way the knuckles guide the knife, while the fingertips hold down the food. Cut slowly and deliberately. Speed will come later as you develop strength, dexterity, and coordination. When cutting don't raise the knife above your knuckles, just lift the blade enough to move to the next clean cut. Since your fingertips are under and behind the knuckles, you can't cut yourself.

When you cut up ingredients for stir-frying, uniform shape and size is the rule. Tiny pieces of vegetables with large chunks of meat are not esthetically pleasing nor will the ingredients cook evenly. Sometimes you cannot change the shape and size of an ingredient. Bean sprouts, for example, are long, thin, and stringy. Since you can't make them larger, other ingredients should be made smaller — shredded instead of roll-cut or sliced.

How to Slice

The three slicing techniques that follow are the ones I use in this book. Although they are used for a variety of foods, I have focused on their use in my recipes.

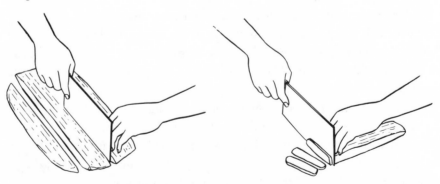

The Straight Slice. The straight slice is commonly used to cut meat and vegetables. This is the one to use when a recipe calls for sliced flank steak, for example. Meat cut this way cooks up very tender.

Trim the fat from the meat. With your knife vertical to the cutting board, cut *with* the grain along the full length of the meat. Cut it into long strips about 2 inches wide. Slice the long pieces *across* the grain into ⅛-inch-thick slices.

The Diagonal Slice. As with the straight slice, the blade is vertical to the cutting board, but at an angle. The more acute the angle, the longer the pieces. Cut each piece at the same angle for uniform size. This slice is most frequently used for cylindrical vegetables such as carrots, celery, cucumbers, and zucchini.

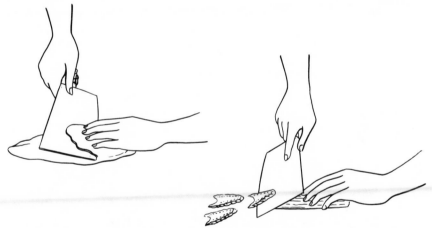

The Horizontal Slice. Horizontal slicing gives you thin wide pieces. In this book, I use this technique to slice chicken breasts and as the first step to shredding beef (page 44). To do this, it is easier to work with meat that has been partially frozen, and it is imperative to have a sharp knife. Wet the blade with water to help it glide smoothly.

Move the cutting board to the edge of the counter so your knuckles don't press on the counter as you work. Place your knife almost horizontal to, but angled down toward, the cutting board. Gently press down on the chicken. Slowly cut the chicken with a sawing motion into thin 2-inch-square pieces.

To cut vegetables, position your knife so you are cutting away from yourself.

How to Shred

Chinese shredding is done by hand, and the results are quite different from what you get using a box grater. Shredding with a knife gives a matchstick shape about the size and shape of a bean sprout. It is easier to shred meat if it is partially frozen.

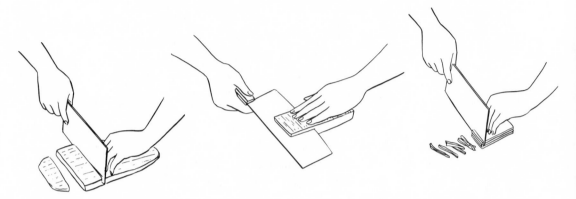

To Shred Flank Steak. Slice the flank steak *against* the grain into 2-inch-wide pieces. Using the horizontal slice, cut the meat into three or four pieces. Pile up the pieces and cut the meat into ⅛-inch shreds along the grain of the meat. Beef cut this way will be fairly chewy.

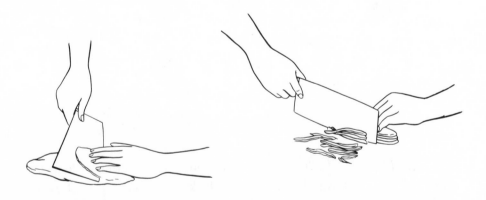

To Shred Pork and Chicken. For pork, I prefer to use thin-cut boneless chops. Thicker chops can be split and shred in the same manner as flank steak. Be sure to trim off the fat first.

For chicken breast, remove the bone and skin. With the blade angled down, slice the meat into wide thin pieces. Pile the pieces on top of each other and cut across into shreds.

To shred pork tenderloin, partially freeze the meat for easier cutting. Cut thin slices, then stack them up and cut across into shreds.

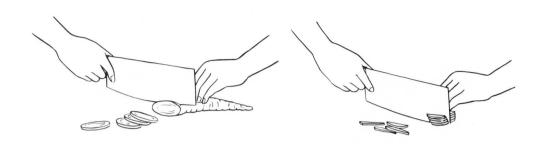

To Shred Vegetables. For carrots, daikons, and other root vegetables, use the diagonal slice to make thin flat pieces. Stack these pieces up and cut across with a straight slice into shreds.

When shredding large amounts of celery for fillings, where the appearance of the celery is not important, as for egg rolls, I save a lot of time by using the diagonal cut and slicing into very thin pieces.

For vegetables like cabbage and onions that are naturally layered, cut into thin pieces using the straight slice.

A convenient tool for shredding vegetables is a mandoline. You may be able to find a Japanese-style mandoline at a Japanese grocery store. You could also use a good-quality plastic slicer. The shred may be a little larger than you get with hand shredding, but you save an enormous amount of time. A mandoline works well with firm vegetables, like carrots and daikon, but does a poor job on celery and leaf cabbages.

To Shred Gingerroot. Peel and cut into thin slices. Stack the slices and cut across into fine shreds.

To Shred Snow Peas. Stack the snow peas and use the diagonal slice across the length of the snow peas to make long shreds.

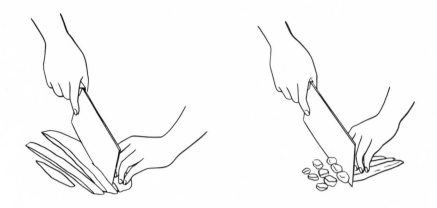

How to Dice or Cube

For dicing, split the item as thick as the size of the dice desired. Stack the slices, cut into like-size strips, and cut across into dice.

Cubing (¾- to 1-inch pieces) is used mainly for meats. Most of the stir-fried chicken breast in this book is cubed. Lay a trimmed chicken breast on the cutting board. Cut it lengthwise into ¾-inch-wide strips. Cut across the strips with a straight slice into ¾-inch cubes.

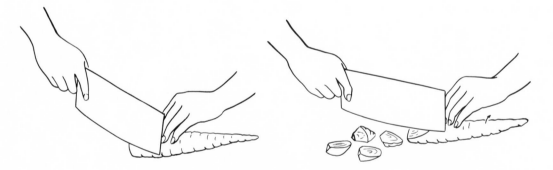

How to Roll-cut

The roll-cut is a useful and pretty cut for cylindrical vegetables such as carrots, zucchini, and parsnips. It is a way to get uniform pieces from vegetables that are not naturally uniform in shape. Roll-cut pieces have more surface area, move around the pan freely, cook evenly, and look attractive.

To roll-cut, place the vegetable horizontally on the cutting board. Starting at the thick end, slice off a section with a diagonal cut. The angle you use will determine the ultimate thickness and length of the piece. After the first cut, roll the vegetable toward you a quarter of a turn, then cut again at the same angle. Continue until you reach the end of the vegetable. If this is done correctly, you should not be able to distinguish the skinny-end pieces from fat-end pieces.

How to Mince

For a regular mince, first slice the ingredients to a smaller size, then rock the knife from stem to stern while pivoting it from left to right (using the tip of the knife as the pivot point), pushing the pieces to the center every so often so that they are cut over and over again. This rocking mince cut is great for harder ingredients, like nuts, as it keeps them from flying this way and that. The number of times the knife is rocked across the ingredients determines how fine the mince is.

For a very fine mince (the Chinese do this when they need ground meat — since in general they do not have such modern conveniences as meat grinders, much less food processors), use two knives of equal size and weight. Hold the knife the way a Western knife is held, by the handle. With a knife in each hand, chop up and down across the pile, keeping the knives parallel with each other. Scrape the knives and scrape the ingredients toward the center occasionally so that every scrap is chopped until the proper consistency is achieved. This technique, by the way, results in a very different consistency from ground meat. Since the meat is actually cut into tiny pieces, the texture tends to be firmer. This fine mince technique is also useful for mincing cabbage for Peking Ravioli filling.

How to Crush

This is a neat way to peel garlic as well as to crush garlic cloves, knobs of ginger, or scallion bulbs to help release more aromatic flavor. If you want to peel a garlic clove, crush it first with the broad side of a Chinese knife, just enough to break the skin, then peel it away.

Knobs of ginger can be crushed with a more forceful blow. Be careful when you strike with the knife that the blade is perfectly flat and not angled. Otherwise you may damage your knife. And be sure to bring your cutting board to the edge of the counter so you don't bang your knuckles.

Peeled garlic and scallion bulbs are lightly crushed just to break the skin. You will have better control if you place the flat side of the knife against the ingredient and press down with your other hand.

How to Tenderize

Even the blunt edge of the Chinese knife is useful. My mother often used it to tenderize meat. Pound the meat first in one direction and then the opposite in a cross-hatch pattern. Do this on both sides. You can also use the crushing technique and slap the meat with the flat side of the blade to loosen and break up the meat fiber.

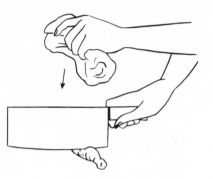

How to Chop

People always seem to want to chop big, heavy things with the Chinese knife, probably because of its relatively great size and weight. Chopping must be done properly, with care and with the proper knife (pages 32–33). More good Chinese knives are destroyed with this cut than any other.

Chop only light chicken or duck bones, not beef or pork. Use the back third of the blade, *never* the tip. Instead of using the knife as an axe, I prefer this safer, quieter, and more precise technique.

Place the knife in position on top of what is to be chopped. Wrap your other fist in a kitchen towel and use it like a hammer on the portion of the blade that is doing the chopping. The cloth will soften the blow to your hand. Do not twist the knife as it may damage or chip the blade. Instead of your fist, you can also use a rubber mallet.

Cooking Techniques

壽 For the most part the Chinese home cook relies on five cooking techniques: stir-frying, deep-frying, steaming, boiling, and stewing. Smoking has a limited home application and roasting and baking are relegated to commercial establishments since the Chinese do not have ovens. Since ovens are commonplace in this country, however, I have included a few recipes for dishes that can be easily prepared in a home oven. Pickled and preserved foods are very popular in the Far East, but with the increasing availability of good commercial products, they are being done less and less at home.

The five basic techniques, which are the ones most often used in this book, are not difficult. It is the nuances within each that contribute to the subtle delicacy, incredible variety, and vast culinary panorama of Chinese cuisine.

How to Stir-fry

Stir-frying has become almost synonymous with Chinese cooking. It is believed that it began during the Han Dynasty over two thousand years ago in response to the lack of adequate fuel. Stir-frying requires quick, intense heat and short, rapid cooking. This not only conserved valuable fuel but also retained the natural nutrients and vitamins of the food.

In stir-frying, uniform, bite-size pieces of food are cooked in small amounts of oil over high heat. Sound easy? It is, but there are a few things to keep in mind, starting with a good-quality wok or stir-fry pan (pages 33–35). Put out of your mind any notion that stir-frying involves pushing food up the sides of the wok while cooking in the center. This is incorrect, and no Chinese I know cooks this way.

The Oil. You do not need a great deal of oil to stir-fry, especially if you are using a good quality nonstick pan. Generally I recommend using about three tablespoons of oil for a dish that serves four. A little oil does not, however, mean you can use a cooking-oil spray. That's not enough oil, not even in a nonstick pan.

To test the oil temperature for stir-frying I use this simple technique: Place the tip of a wooden or bamboo spatula in the oil; bubbles will form if the oil is hot enough. I sometimes dip the bamboo spatula in the moist ingredients; then the spatula not only bubbles but sizzles too. The intensity of the sizzle will indicate how hot the oil is. Most ingredients are added to hot oil, although delicate or dry ingredients may be added to warm oil.

I do not recommend that the pan be preheated before adding the oil as some cooks do. With nonstick cookware, heating up an empty pan may damage the coating. If you are using a carbon-steel wok, you may preheat the pan if you like, but it is not necessary.

The Heat. Many people think Chinese cooking requires high, searing heat. This is true to a certain extent but with certain cautions and exceptions. High heat does not mean blasting away at the highest setting on your stove irrelevant of what is happening in the pan. Some recipes actually require lower heat to keep dry or delicate ingredients from burning. As with any cooking technique, control is the most important concept here.

Most of the stir-fry recipes in this book call for medium-high or high temperatures. The rule of thumb is to start at medium-high and adjust up or down accordingly. If the food appears to be cooking too rapidly or is beginning to stick, scorch, or burn, turn down the heat or remove the pan to a cool burner. I often add some water or broth, which brings down the temperature immediately.

If the food is cooking too fast on an electric stove, lift the pan right off the heat and replace it when more heat is needed. This up-and-down motion is easier and more efficient than constantly trying to adjust the heat. You may also move the pan to a cool burner, where you can continue stirring while the pan cools.

The Preparation. Have all the ingredients prepared and ready for cooking. Stir-frying goes very fast and demands a well-organized and efficient cook. As much as possible premix the sauces and organize cut ingredients in small dishes or bowls so that everything is within your reach. When I cook for a dinner party, I set out different trays or baking pans with the ingredients for each dish organized on its own tray in the order in which they will be used. This way, the cooking is choreographed and moves smoothly from one dish to the next.

The Cooking. Put food in the pan according to which ingredient takes longest to cook. Root vegetables and cabbage, for example, are put in first, while the more delicate fast cooking ingredients such as snow peas and bean sprouts are added in last. The first ingredients added to the hot oil should be as dry as possible to prevent spattering.

Do not overload your pan. A pan with too much food in it will cool down rapidly and never quite recover for proper stir-frying. A six- or eight-inch stir-fry pan is too small to cook a whole recipe; if that's what you have, you may have to cook in batches. Even with a fourteen-inch wok, you have to be careful when you double a recipe. The pan may be larger, but the heat source has not changed.

You will notice that in some recipes the salt is added to the oil before the ingredients. My mother told me that this helps keep spattering down, and the salt is evenly distributed throughout the dish. Because storebought ingredients, such as soy sauce, oyster sauce, hoisin sauce, and so on, vary in saltiness, I sometimes find it is more convenient to add the salt to taste at the end.

The Serving. Most stir-fried foods should be removed from the pan and served immediately. The people should wait for the food, not the food for the people. When my mother prepared dinner, we had to be at the table when she brought the dishes out of the kitchen. That way, each one could be enjoyed at its peak. Nor should guests wait for the cook. The person cooking is always the last to come to the table.

How to Deep-fry

Deep-frying calls for ingredients to be submerged in a bath of hot fat. Traditionally the Chinese used lard, but because of concern about cholesterol in the diet, vegetable oil — soy, corn, peanut, or the more recently favored canola — is used. I don't deep-fry frequently at home because, in addition to the health issue, there is the inconvenience of handling large amounts of cooking oil. When this method is called for, however, keep the following in mind.

The Temperature. Oil that is either too hot or not hot enough will give you food that is burnt or, on the other hand, soggy and soaked with oil. Bring the oil to a temperature of 350°F. to 375°F. Test the oil by dropping in a small piece of bread, gingerroot, or wonton skin. The oil is ready if it foams actively along the edge. Use a deep-fat thermometer, especially if you are inexperienced.

Keep in mind that hot oil quickly drops in temperature once food is introduced. When deep-frying a second batch, be sure to allow the oil to return to temperature before adding food again. Be alert as well to oil that is too hot. If the food is scorching, turn down the heat. Regulate the temperature by turning the heat up and down as needed so that oil temperature remains as constant as possible.

The Cooking. Never crowd the pan when deep-frying. Crowding not only reduces the oil temperature rapidly and leads to greasy food but also makes the food cook unevenly. For even cooking, also be sure the oil is deep enough for the food to be submerged and to swim around freely.

Shallow-frying. For some dishes, such as Lemon Chicken, I use a home-style method of shallow-frying, which takes a smaller amount of oil, only one cup instead of the four or five needed for regular deep-frying.

Double-frying. Some recipes call for ingredients to be fried twice, Sweet and Sour Pork, Cantonese Style, for instance. The first frying is to cook the ingredient and the second to make the coating crisp. This method is often employed by restaurants. At home, you can plan such recipes ahead and deep-fry the first time, cool the ingredients, and refrigerate them until they are to be fried a second time and glazed with sauce.

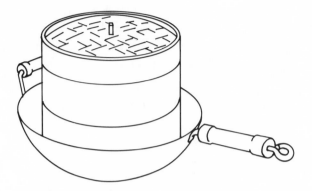

How to Steam in a Wok

Steaming is a common Chinese home-cooking technique. In most Chinese kitchens, the ubiquitous bamboo steamer is set in a wok or pan of boiling water to cook meats, seafood, and breads. In general the Chinese do not steam vegetables, which are parboiled or stir-fried. An exception is the recipe for Steamed Eggplant Salad. The steam that enters the covered steamer is trapped and cooks the food gently with moist heat. Although you can't burn food in a steamer, you can overcook it, so watch the timing. Here are some other points to keep in mind:

- Be sure the bamboo steamer fits into your wok. If your wok is fourteen inches in diameter, a ten- to 12-inch steamer will fit. The water should touch the bamboo steamer's bottom edge but still be at least one inch from the bottom tier. The food being steamed should never touch the boiling water.

- I'm often asked how to clean a bamboo steamer. I thought that a curious question until I realized that many people didn't understand that food is never placed directly on the steamer trays. Seafood and meat are steamed on dishes so the juices are not lost. Bread is steamed on small pieces of paper so they don't stick to the steamer.

- Have the water actively boiling before putting in the food. Keep the water at a constant boil over medium-high heat until the cooking is done. An exception to this is Steamed Egg Custard Soup which starts in a cold steamer so the eggs cook gently. Add more boiling water as necessary.

Constructing a Makeshift Steamer. If you don't have a Chinese steamer, you can create a makeshift steamer using a wok, stir-fry pan, or large stockpot. (Many wok sets come with steaming racks.) Be sure the pan is large enough to hold the dish used for steaming. It must have at least two inches of headroom and enough room around it so that it can be easily removed when hot. Remove the top and bottom of an empty tuna-fish can to make a stand

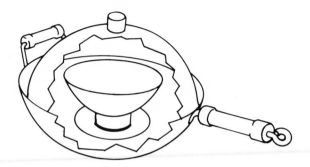

and place it in the bottom of your pan. Bring water to a boil. Put the plate or bowl containing the food on the stand, cover the wok with a lid, and steam.

If you plan to steam food often, you should buy a bamboo or metal steamer. Frequent steaming in a carbon-steel wok means you will have to reseason your wok often, and boiling water in a nonstick carbon-steel wok may shorten the life of the coating.

How to Boil

The Chinese employ boiling in specific ways. Sometimes they parboil vegetables to shorten the final cooking time, especially for multicourse banquets and at restaurants, where speed is essential. At home, this technique is useful when you cook for a dinner party.

To parboil vegetables, cut and wash them first, then stir them into enough boiling water for them to swim around freely. As soon as they are added to the water, the boiling will stop. Continue stirring for even cooking. If the vegetables are tender or you want them to remain very crisp, drain them after fifteen to thirty seconds, or just before the water looks as if it's going to return to a boil. Some harder vegetables such as carrots and green beans may require a little longer cooking; leave them in the water until it boils again. After draining, refresh the vegetables in cold water to stop the cooking and set the bright colors. If not using right away, store covered in the refrigerator.

Chinese cooks also use boiling water to sear meats and poultry, immersing them in a large pot of boiling water. Good examples are Shanghai Red-cooked Duck and Shanghai Red-cooked Ham. As soon as the water returns to a boil, the bird or meat is taken out and rinsed in cold water.

White-cooked meat is cooked only in hot water, without soy sauce or other flavorings. Simmering keeps the meat tender and seals in the natural flavor instead of washing it out into the water. The simmer must be slow and gentle with only one or two bubbles appearing at a time. Such meats are almost always served cold with a table dip for seasoning. This process is used frequently for larger pieces of meat such as a whole chicken (White-cooked Chicken), duck and ham (White-cooked Pork).

How to Stew

Stewing is slow cooking over low heat in a liquid, like braising. When stewing large pieces of meat, be sure your pot has a tight-fitting lid. After cooking, remove the lid and reduce the liquid over high heat while basting the meat constantly for even color and flavor. Many "red-cooked" dishes use this technique — Shanghai Red-cooked Duck and Shanghai Red-cooked Ham, for example.

Menu Planning and Serving Chinese Food

M enu planning plays a large and significant role in Chinese life, all the more since many foods are symbolic of good luck, prosperity, long life, and happiness. The arrangements and combinations of food fulfill a sense of harmony and completeness. Banquets celebrating marriages, births, birthdays, festivals, and the lunar New Year call for special foods and ingredients served in a particular manner.

The Chinese concept of menu planning is quite different from the American notion of a main dish accompanied by a side dish or two and followed by dessert. Chinese meals consist of a number of entrees with rice and a soup. Dessert is rarely served, except on special occasions. The number of entrees depends on how many people are eating. The more people there are at the table, the more variety there will be. It stands to reason that Chinese dinners are more fun with a crowd.

There are no rules about how many dishes to serve since much depends upon the number of people, individual appetites, and so on. Generally speaking, prepare two or three dishes plus a soup for four adults, four or five dishes plus soup for six. For only two people a single dish that combines meat and vegetables plus a soup, if desired, would be fine. White rice is served at all meals.

How to Pair Dishes

The Chinese seem to have an innate ability to choose dishes that provide a well-balanced and complementary meal that incorporates the ancient Chinese principles of yin and yang. It isn't that we are all versed in this concept, but experience has taught us what tastes and looks good together. Yin stands for cold, dark, and moist; yang stands for hot, bright, and dry. The balanced tension of these opposites creates a harmony that infiltrates all aspects of life.

When we plan our meals, we look for contrasts — hot and sour, warm and cold, crisp and soft, spicy and bland, etc. We would not serve a meal with two beef dishes or two spicy dishes. My mother was especially well versed in pairing, and whenever we went out, everyone turned to her to do the ordering. We were never disappointed.

For a multicourse meal, prepare a variety of dishes, choosing from meat, poultry, seafood, vegetables, and soup. For a Chinese family the soup is often the only beverage, so it is an important part of the meal. You may choose to leave it out when serving Westerners. Remember, what makes the meal interesting is not only the taste but the *contrast* and *balance* of taste, texture, temperature, and color of different dishes. Serve Chinese food the way it was meant to be served, with lots of steamed rice.

The number of servings indicated in each recipe in the book is the approximate number served Western style and Chinese style, that is, as part of a multicourse meal.

The sample menus on pages 60–61 will give you a good balance of taste, texture, color, and nutrition.

How to Serve Chinese Food

Family-style meals and banquets are served differently. For casual dinners at home all the dishes, including the soup and rice, are served at once at the center of the table. People use their own chopsticks to take food from the serving dish to their rice bowls. The dishes served at family meals are straightforward and simple. When we invite friends over to share a casual family meal, we humbly refer to it as *bian fan,* or simple rice.

At formal banquets, each dish is presented with its own serving spoon or serving chopsticks, and served alone so that the full enjoyment of its taste and appearance may be savored. Formal banquets offer as many as twelve different dishes. Sometimes in southern China strong tea is served in tiny cups as a palate cleanser. Rice is not served during the meal but at the end, and only as a polite gesture for those desiring it. It is considered a filler and is not served earlier so that guests will not fill up on rice and not be able to enjoy all the dishes to come. Dessert is often served in the form of fresh fruit, sweet soup, or steamed rice pudding, depending upon the season.

The Chinese like to use round tables, which make the serving dishes easily accessible to everyone and are conducive to conversation. Banquet tables usually seat eight, ten, or twelve — the Chinese prefer to set the table with an even number of places. The guest of honor is always seated facing the door and the host is seated across from the place of honor. There is traditionally much commotion before everyone is seated, with the guest of honor coyly refusing the place of honor and the host insisting. This is all part of Chinese ritual and good manners and is performed, and expected, at almost every social function.

To set the table Chinese style you will need a pair of chopsticks for each diner, a porcelain spoon and bowl for soup, a small dipping dish for bones, an eight-inch plate for holding food, and a rice bowl.

What to Drink with Chinese Food

禄 Many Westerners assume, incorrectly, that all Chinese drink tea at mealtimes. Only the southern Chinese, namely the Cantonese, drink tea at the dining table; everyone else has tea after meals. Most Chinese restaurants in America, however, do serve tea since the early groups of Chinese in the United States were from Canton (Quangzhou). Northern Chinese like to have soup, preferably a clear broth, as the beverage. Tea is then served after meals to cleanse the palate and to aid digestion.

There are hundreds, if not thousands, of types of tea drunk in China. They fall into three main categories — black (the Chinese call it red, since the color black is considered unlucky), green, and flower. One of the most famous green teas comes from my father's hometown of Hangchow (Hangzhou) and is called *lung ching* or dragon well. Most Westerners are familiar with oolong tea, which is the one most often served at Chinese-American restaurants. Translated as black dragon, oolong is a semifermented black tea. At home after meals, our family always drank the green or flower-infused tea, such as jasmine, which are preferred by northern Chinese. These teas are not fermented and they brew up into a light amber or yellow color. Their delicate aroma and flavor should not be adulterated with sugar, milk, or cream.

Chinese tea should always be brewed with water that has boiled for only a few seconds. If you are using loose tea, sprinkle it into the pot and then pour the boiling water over the leaves. Cover and let steep for two to three minutes. Use about one teaspoon of tea leaves per cup of boiling water. The same tea may be used a second time for another pot of tea. We do the same thing if we are making it by the glass. Tea is best served in porcelain or glass cups; it is said that metal cups will spoil the flavor and color of tea. The Chinese don't mind the tea leaves, as good tea has whole tea leaves (not tea dust) that unfurl and sink to the bottom of the glass, out of the way. Many Chinese teas are

Pairing Wines with Chinese Food

酒

Pairing Western wines with Chinese food presents a bit of a challenge. Since the typical Chinese meal may consist of meat, fish, and poultry, the wine choice should be based on the seasonings and not the main ingredients. My friend, Bob Bradford, a photojournalist and wine expert, shared his thoughts and suggestions on what wines best complement Chinese foods.

Bob suggests keeping a few basic principles in mind: How a wine's lively acidity, for example, can be like a squeeze of lemon, adding zest to food; or how white wines with big body and sweetness are often well suited to rich, spicy foods.

One of the most successful and versatile of assertive white wines for Asian dishes is a full-bodied Gewürztraminer, of which there are several good affordable selections from domestic producers. This perfumy, German-Alsatian grape has a pleasant spiciness that complements and enhances the intricate, sometimes exotic, flavors of Asia.

There are also many styles of Johannesburg Riesling that go well with Chinese food. Try a crisp, acidic dry version or one with a fresh, but full, sweeter big fruit character that can stand up to heavy seasonings and Szechuan specialties or a rich, honeylike late-harvest Riesling. Bob has been pleased with all three styles with Chinese food.

One of the most popular wines sold in Chinese restaurants is a full-style Chardonnay, and although Bob finds it agreeable, he doesn't find it the most interesting selection. He does find that full-bodied sparkling wines are excellent companions to most Asian dishes. Do not pair them with foods that are too heavy or sweet, however, since they can thin out and become a little bitter.

With delicate and lightly seasoned foods try a medium-bodied Chenin Blanc with its floral bouquet and crisp acid or a medium-style, fruity Semillon. Also worth trying are deep, black muscat wines or American berry wines such as raspberry and Bartlett pear.

Many assertive and robust young wines such as Chianti, Pinot Noir, the Cabernets, and Zinfandel also match up perfectly with many Chinese dishes.

Last, Bob suggests that you keep on tasting with an open mind and let your palate be the last word.

now also available in tea bags, but the finest teas are always purchased loose so that the quality and beauty of the leaves may be confirmed and enjoyed.

Beer and wine are also enjoyed by the Chinese, but usually only at a banquet setting. Chinese beers are beginning to appear in America. One of the earliest imports to America is the famous Tsingtao beer, named after the Shangdong port city of Tsingtao (Qingdao), occupied by the Germans in the late 1890s as a treaty port. It is said that Tsingtao beer is brewed according to an old German method. Many people enjoy beer with Chinese food. My husband enjoys fine beer and tells me that Tsingtao, as well as a number of Japanese beers, is excellent with Chinese food.

The Chinese have never developed a strong viticulture tradition. Instead of grapes, most Chinese wines are made from rice (*shiaoxing* is famous). Stronger spirits are distilled from grains such as millet (*mao tai*) and sorghum (*gaoliang*). The Chinese usually reserve alcoholic beverages only for celebratory meals.

Home-style meal for six

APPETIZER
Drunken Chicken (optional)

SOUP
Crab and Asparagus Soup

ENTREES
Mushrooms with Bean Curd
Sweet and Sour Shrimp
Spicy Beef with Carrots and Celery
Red-mouthed Green Parrot

RICE
White Rice

健康

Home-style meal for six

APPETIZER
Pickled Carrots and Daikon

SOUP
Mandarin Cucumber Soup

ENTREES
Chicken with Mushrooms
Kan Shao Green Beans
Coral and Jade
Stir-fried Asparagus

RICE
White Rice or Yangchow Fried Rice

Home-style meal for four

SOUP

Steamed Egg Custard Soup

ENTREES

Stir-fried Watercress with Fu Ru
Sweet and Sour Spareribs, Shanghai Style
Stir-fried Cauliflower and Broccoli

RICE

White Rice

Home-style meal for four

SOUP

Watercress and Shredded Pork Soup

ENTREES

Stir-fried Green Beans
Steamed Salmon with Black Beans
Egg Foo Yung, Family Style

RICE

White Rice

Eating the Chinese Way

吃

Chinese food is best when eaten the way the Chinese do, that is, with a bowl of rice as the mainstay of the meal. I find, however, that most Westerners are uncomfortable eating rice from a bowl the way the Chinese do. The problem seems to be in lifting the rice bowl to their lips; yet it is practically impossible to eat rice from a flat plate with chopsticks. Besides, when rice is put on a plate with other foods, it becomes an insignificant side dish instead of the substantial base of the meal, as it is intended to be.

Hold the rice bowl in one hand by the top and bottom edges. (The Chinese rice bowl has a foot on the bottom so you can hold it without burning your fingers on the heat from the rice.) Use your chopsticks to bring food from the serving dish to the bowl or, in some cases, directly to your mouth. The food is brought to the rice bowl so that it can rest lightly on the rice, allowing excess gravy or sauce to drip onto the rice.

To eat the rice, raise the bowl and push the rice gently into your mouth with the chopsticks. With practice, you'll soon be able to accomplish this movement with dexterity. In between courses or during conversation, place your chopsticks on chopstick rests or, as we do at home, across the top of the rice bowl.

Soup

At Chinese family meals, soup is considered the beverage. Cold water, soft drinks, and mineral water are not served. In fact, it is an old wives' tale that you'll get a stomachache from drinking ice water with meals. As a child, I always liked a glass of water with my meals, but I was the only one at the table who had one.

In home-style eating, the soup and all the other main dishes are served at one time. This way the soup can be enjoyed throughout the meal to quench one's thirst. I like to add soup to my rice, although my mother always told me that this was a custom only for home eating and not appropriate for more formal occasions.

Since the soup is mainly a beverage and palate refresher, it is more common to serve clear soups made with a light broth base than thick soups. Most Chinese soups are based on chicken broth; sometimes pork bones are used to make broth, but never beef or lamb bones as the flavor would be too strong for Chinese tastes. Chinese Chicken Broth is much lighter than most chicken stocks and I always dilute canned chicken broth with water to approximate the chicken broth made at home.

Some more substantial soups, such as Wonton Soup, are served as snacks. Thick soups, such as Crab and Asparagus Soup and Chicken Velvet Corn Soup, are served on special occasions, when thinner, lighter soups would be considered too ordinary.

Chinese Chicken Broth

Makes about 10 cups

*C*hinese restaurants keep a large vat of chicken broth cooking at all times. It is used for soup and in stir-fry dishes instead of water for a richer flavor.

Instead of cooking a whole chicken for broth, I freeze chicken bones left over from other dishes. When I have enough bones saved up, I make my broth. I have to admit, though, that I do not always have homemade chicken broth on hand and sometimes substitute canned broth for convenience. Since the Chinese broth is made without salt and is quite light, I suggest you mix canned broth with water and not add salt to the recipe. Then you can adjust the salt later to your taste.

福

3 to 4 pounds chicken bones, such as backs, necks, wings, ribs, feet
2 tablespoons dry sherry
3 slices unpeeled gingerroot, 1 × ⅛ inch each
1 scallion

1. Bring a large amount of water to a boil in a stockpot large enough to hold all the bones and enough water to cover them. Blanch the bones by dropping them in the boiling water. When the water returns to a boil, about 3 to 5 minutes, drain the bones in a colander and rinse with cold water. This blanching ensures a clearer broth.

2. Rinse and scrub out any clinging scum from the stockpot. Put the chicken bones back into the pot with just enough cold water to cover them. Add the sherry, gingerroot, and scallion, bring the water to a boil over high heat, and immediately turn the heat down to maintain a simmer. Do not cover the pot.

3. Skim off any foam or impurities and discard. Simmer, uncovered, for 1½ to 2 hours, or until the chicken is tender and the bones fall apart easily. Remember, it's the slow simmering that makes a good broth, so don't rush this process.

4. Skim off the fat that is on the surface and remove any large bones. Strain the broth through a fine mesh strainer or through 2 layers of damp cheesecloth spread over a colander. Cool, uncovered, then refrigerate the broth in a sealed container until ready to use. (Remove any congealed fat before using.) Refrigerated, the stock will keep for about 5 days to 1 week. You may also freeze the broth in 1- or 2-cup containers for easier use. Serve the broth alone, salted to taste and garnished with chopped scallion, as a base for other soup recipes, or in stir-fry dishes in place of water.

Note   In China, where refrigeration is not available to everyone, people boil their stock each time before using it to kill any bacteria. It's still a good idea.

Variation   Pork bones may be added to the chicken bones to make a richer broth. To coax flavor out of the pork bone marrow, disjoint bones or crush them before cooking. Trim away all excess fat. The Chinese do not use beef or lamb bones, as the stronger flavor of these bones are not suitable for Chinese-style stock. For a clear stock, do not mix raw and cooked bones.

壽

Wonton Soup

Serves 2, or 4 to 6 as part of a
multicourse meal

*I*n Chinese, the word wonton means "swallowing clouds." This fanciful name refers not to the crispy, deep-fried wontons but to the wontons cooked in soup. They are fluffy and float in the clear broth like clouds.

The Chinese eat Wonton Soup as a main course, not as the first course it has become in Chinese-American restaurants. It is usually served in large noodle bowls as a snack or lunch or at family get-togethers when all the family members help fold the wontons.

禄

4 cups Chinese Chicken Broth (page 64) plus 1 teaspoon salt or
  1 (13¾-ounce) can chicken broth and enough water to make 4 cups
1 slice unpeeled gingerroot, 1 × ⅛ inch
16 to 24 pork or turkey wontons, boiled and drained (pages 293–294)
Salt to taste
2 tablespoons thinly sliced scallions
4 tablespoons minced Szechuan vegetable (optional)
4 tablespoons finely shredded Egg Garnish (page 255) (optional)
1 teaspoon sesame seed oil

1. Bring the chicken broth with the gingerroot to a boil and add additional salt to taste. Place 4 to 6 wontons in individual soup bowls. Sprinkle the wontons in each bowl with some scallion and 1 tablespoon each Szechuan vegetable and shredded egg, if desired.

2. Pour the boiling soup over the wontons and drizzle with sesame seed oil. Serve immediately.

壽

Variation Instead of the Chinese-style garnishes of Szechuan vegetable and shredded egg, add 4 ounces spinach leaves, which have been thoroughly washed, to the boiling broth just before serving. Cook the spinach leaves only as long as it takes to wilt them.

Steamed Egg Custard Soup

Serves 3 to 4

This smooth family-style soup requires the simplest of ingredients and very little atten-tion. I like to prepare them when I'm in a hurry because once it's mixed and put in a steamer, it doesn't need to be watched. If you don't have a proper steamer, use a wok with a lid and place a low metal stand inside so the bowl doesn't touch the bottom of the wok. Fashion the stand from a tuna-fish can with both ends removed.

In China littleneck clams, still in their shells, are often added to this soup before steaming. The clams, a symbol of wealth, give it lots of flavor.

禧

3 eggs
1 teaspoon dry sherry
3 cups cold Chinese Chicken Broth (page 64) plus 1 teaspoon salt or
  1 (13¾-ounce) can chicken broth and enough water to make 3 cups
2 teaspoons thinly sliced scallions or chives
½ teaspoon light soy sauce, for garnish

1.   Lightly beat the eggs with the sherry in a 1½-quart heatproof bowl, using a fork or a pair of chopsticks. The eggs should be completely blended but not frothy or there will be bubbles in the soup.

2.   Stir the cold broth into the eggs. Mix thoroughly to get rid of lumps, which would cook up hard. Sprinkle the scallions over the mixture.

3.   Place the bowl in a steamer filled with 2 inches of water as described on page 52. Cover the pan and steam over medium-high heat for 20 minutes, or until the liquid becomes firm, like a soft custard. (The soup will keep hot in the covered steamer off the heat for 15 to 20 minutes.) Drizzle soy sauce over the soup. Serve hot in the same bowl.

Egg Drop Soup

Serves 4, or 6 as part of a multicourse meal

*F*or many people this soup with its delicate swirls of beaten eggs is the first soup they remember trying in a Chinese-American restaurant. This home-style version, not thickened with any starch, is lighter than its restaurant counterpart. The size of the egg swirls depends upon how fast you stir the eggs into the hot soup — the slower you stir, the bigger the pieces.

健康

4 cups Chinese Chicken Broth (page 64) plus 1 teaspoon salt or
    1 (13¾-ounce) can chicken broth and enough water to make 4 cups
2 slices unpeeled gingerroot, 1 × ⅛ inch each
2 eggs
½ teaspoon dry sherry
1 tablespoon thinly sliced scallions
Salt to taste

1. Combine the chicken broth and gingerroot in a medium saucepan and bring to a boil over medium-high heat.

2. While the broth is coming to a boil, beat the eggs with the sherry in a small bowl or measuring cup. When the broth is boiling, remove the gingerroot. Pour a thin, steady stream of egg into the liquid while stirring constantly. Remove the pan from the heat as soon as all the eggs are added. Salt to taste, and sprinkle the minced scallions over the top. Serve hot.

Meatballs with Crystal Noodle Soup

his easy soup makes a satisfying meal by itself, as well as a hearty soup course in a lighter multicourse meal of stir-fried vegetables and bean curd. Add the bean thread only when you're ready to serve. It overcooks easily and can become soft and gluey.

福

½ pound ground lean pork or beef (1 cup)

¼ teaspoon grated peeled gingerroot

1 tablespoon light soy sauce

½ teaspoon dry sherry

1½ teaspoons cornstarch

½ teaspoon salt, and additional to taste

2 ounces bean thread

5 cups Chinese Chicken Broth (page 64) plus 1 teaspoon salt or
  1 (13¾-ounce) can chicken broth and enough water to make 5 cups

1. Mix the ground meat with the gingerroot, soy sauce, sherry, cornstarch, and ¼ teaspoon salt. Set aside.

2. Soak the bean thread in warm water for a few minutes until soft. Drain carefully, keeping the strands together, and with scissors, cut into 6-inch lengths. Set aside.

3. Bring the chicken broth and ¼ teaspoon of salt to a boil in a medium saucepan over medium heat. Scoop up one tablespoon of the meat mixture at a time and form about 16 to 18 smooth, small balls using your fingertips. Drop the meatballs into the boiling broth. Reduce the heat to low and simmer, covered, for 10 minutes. (You can cook the meatballs ahead and keep them warm or reheat them.) Just before serving, add the bean thread and stir a few times. Serve immediately.

Add additional salt to taste if desired.

Shredded Pork and
Mustard Greens Soup

**Serves 4, or 6 as part of a
multicourse meal**

*C*hinese mustard greens are appreciated for their thick, green curved stems and distinctive, slightly bitter taste. They are available in Chinese markets and often have their
leaves severely trimmed, leaving a rather ragged looking loose cabbage heart. Add
mustard greens to soup only just before serving, or they will overcook and turn yellow.

禄

1/3 cup shredded lean pork (3 ounces) (page 44)
2 teaspoons light soy sauce
1 teaspoon cornstarch
1/2 teaspoon dry sherry
1/4 pound Chinese mustard greens
5 cups Chinese Chicken Broth (page 64) plus 1 teaspoon salt or
    1 (13¾-ounce) can chicken broth and enough water to make 5 cups
2 slices unpeeled gingerroot, 1 × 1/8 inch each
1/4 teaspoon salt, or to taste

1. Mix the pork, soy sauce, cornstarch, and sherry together. Set aside.

2. Wash the mustard greens under running water and shake off the
excess water. Cut the leaves and stems into 1-inch pieces. You should have
about 1 cup.

3. Bring the chicken broth and gingerroot to a boil in a 2-quart saucepan over medium-high heat. Stir in the pork and bring the broth back to a
boil. Stir in the mustard greens and cook for 1 minute. Salt to taste. Serve hot.

Snow Cabbage with Shredded Pork Soup

Serves 4, or 6 as part of a multicourse meal

*S*now cabbage (page 25), sold in cans in Asian markets, is a handy ingredient to keep in your pantry for flavoring otherwise simple dishes like soup noodles or stir-fry. A small dish of pickled snow cabbage is sometimes served as a condiment with breakfast rice gruel, known as congee. You can substitute shredded chicken for the pork in this recipe.

壽

½ cup shredded lean pork (4 ounces) (page 44)

1 teaspoon cornstarch

1 teaspoon light soy sauce

½ teaspoon dry sherry

4 cups Chinese Chicken Broth (page 64) plus ½ teaspoon salt or
    1 (13¾-ounce) can chicken broth and enough water to make 4 cups

2 slices unpeeled gingerroot, 1 × ⅛ inch each

¼ cup canned snow cabbage, coarsely chopped

¾ cup shredded firm tofu (bean curd) (optional)

Salt to taste

1. Place the pork in a bowl, stir in the cornstarch, soy sauce, and sherry, and mix well. Set aside.

2. Combine the chicken broth and gingerroot in a medium saucepan and bring to a boil over medium-high heat. Add the pork mixture and stir to cook the meat evenly and to keep the shreds separate.

3. When the pork shreds change color and separate, add the snow cabbage and the bean curd, if using. Stir gently. Bring the soup back to a boil, then remove from the heat. Add additional salt to taste. Serve hot.

Peking Hot and Sour Soup

Serves 4, or 6 as part of a multicourse meal

*T*his is one of mother's best-loved recipes, which she made famous in the 1950s at our first restaurant on Concord Avenue in Cambridge. What makes the soup sour is vinegar, what makes it hot is white pepper. If you like your soup extra hot, just add more pepper. In China, this soup is never served at banquets because the ingredients are considered too ordinary!

禧

¼ cup shredded lean pork (2 ounces) (page 44)

1 teaspoon dry sherry

3 tablespoons cornstarch

¼ cup dried golden needles, soaked in 2 cups hot water for 15 minutes and drained

¼ cup dried wood ears, soaked in 2 cups hot water for 15 minutes and drained

3½ cups Chinese Chicken Broth (page 64) and 1 teaspoon salt or
    1 (13¾-ounce) can chicken broth and enough water to make 3½ cups

1 tablespoon light soy sauce

½ cup shredded firm tofu (bean curd)

1 medium egg, beaten

2 tablespoons cider vinegar

¼ teaspoon ground white pepper

Salt to taste

1 teaspoon sesame seed oil

1 tablespoon thinly sliced scallions

1.   Stir the pork, sherry, and 1 teaspoon of the cornstarch together in a bowl. Set aside. Dissolve the remaining cornstarch in ½ cup cold water. Set aside.

2.   Cut off the tough stems from the golden needles and woody pieces from the wood ears, if any. Cut the golden needles in half and the wood ears into ½-inch pieces. Rinse, drain, and squeeze out excess liquid from both.

3.   Put the vinegar and pepper in a large serving bowl.

4.   Combine the chicken broth and soy sauce in a medium saucepan and bring to a boil. When the broth is boiling, stir in the pork. After 1 minute, stir in all the wood ears and golden needles. Bring back to a boil and boil for

Soup

72

1 minute. Add the bean curd. As soon as soup comes back to a boil again, mix the cornstarch mixture and stir it in. Stir until soup thickens.

5.   Pour a stream of beaten egg into the hot soup while constantly stirring. Remove from the heat immediately and pour the soup into the serving bowl with the vinegar and pepper. Add salt to taste and garnish with sesame seed oil and scallions. Serve hot.

Watercress and Shredded Pork Soup

Serves 4, or 6 as part of a multicourse meal

W atercress is a popular green vegetable among the Cantonese. It is often served stir-fried or in soups.

健康

2 cups watercress sprigs (about 3 ounces)
⅓ cup shredded lean pork (about 3 ounces) (page 44)
½ teaspoon dry sherry
1 teaspoon cornstarch
4 cups Chinese Chicken Broth (page 64) plus 1 teaspoon salt or
        1 (13¾-ounce) can chicken broth and enough water to make 4 cups
2 slices unpeeled gingerroot, 1 × ⅛ inch each
Salt to taste

1.   Wash the watercress and discard any wilted or yellowed leaves. Drain and cut the sprigs into 3-inch pieces. Set aside.

2.   Place the pork in a bowl, add the sherry and cornstarch, and stir together well. Set aside.

3.   Combine the chicken broth and gingerroot in a medium saucepan and place over medium-high heat. When the broth comes to a boil, mix up the pork again, stir it into the broth, and bring back to a boil. Add the watercress and stir for about 30 seconds, or just until the watercress is wilted. Remove from the heat and discard the gingerroot. Salt to taste. Serve immediately.

Soup

Frozen Bean Curd and Black Mushroom Soup

**Serves 4, or 6 as part of a
multicourse meal**

*T*his is a light, subtly flavored soup. I like the texture of frozen tofu. It soaks up the broth like a sponge and has a tender, yet chewy consistency.

福

½ cup dried black mushrooms, soaked in hot water for 15 minutes
½ pound frozen tofu (bean curd), thawed and squeezed dry
4 cups Chinese Chicken Broth (page 64) plus 1 teaspoon salt or
 1 (13¾-ounce) can chicken broth and enough water to make 4 cups
1 slice unpeeled gingerroot, 1 × ⅛ inch
1 (8-ounce) can sliced bamboo shoots, drained (1 cup)
Salt to taste

1. Remove the mushrooms from the soaking liquid, rinse, and drain. Squeeze out excess liquid, discard woody stems, and cut into quarters. Set aside. Slice the bean curd into 1-inch squares, ½ inch thick.

2. Pour the chicken broth into a saucepan. Add the gingerroot and bring to a boil over medium heat.

3. Add the mushrooms, bean curd, and bamboo shoots. Return to a boil, reduce the heat, and simmer for about 10 minutes until the mushrooms impart their flavor to the soup and the ingredients are heated. Correct the seasoning. Serve hot.

Bean Curd and Daikon Soup

Serves 4

*T*ypical of clear soups served at family meals, this one combines two ordinary ingredients in a quick and easy way.

禄

1 daikon or Chinese icicle radish (about ½ pound)
4 cups Chinese Chicken Broth (page 64) plus 1 teaspoon salt or
    1 (13¾-ounce) can chicken broth and enough water to make 4 cups
2 slices unpeeled gingerroot, 1 × ⅛ inch each
½ pound firm tofu (bean curd), drained and cut into slivers
Salt to taste

1. Trim away the ends of the daikon, pare, and shred through the large holes of a box grater. Squeeze the shreds in your hands to remove the excess water. You should have about 1 cup. Set aside.

2. Combine the broth and gingerroot in a medium saucepan and place over medium-high heat. When the liquid comes to a boil, add the daikon and simmer for 15 minutes, or until it turns translucent.

3. Add the tofu and stir gently until the broth returns to a boil. Taste for salt. Serve hot.

Mandarin Cucumber Soup

**Serves 4, or 6 as part of a
multicourse meal**

My mother liked to prepare this soup because it reminded her of her childhood in Beijing. There was a small town nearby called Feng Tai 豐台 that once supplied the
palace with both flowers and vegetables. The vendors at the Feng Tai train station
sold tiny cucumbers, six inches long, from small woven trays. The cucumbers were too
expensive to buy enough for a dish to feed a large family, so people bought just
enough to make this special soup.

Both my mother and I use the young, thin cucumbers that are available during
the summer at local produce stands. English seedless cucumbers that are wrapped in
plastic and sold at most supermarkets can also be used. Since the skin of these cucumbers is tender and not coated with wax, you don't have to peel them. If you use
regular cucumbers, peel them, leaving alternate strips of green skin behind.

壽

1 long seedless cucumber or 1 pound very young cucumbers
¼ cup thinly sliced lean pork (about 1 boneless pork chop)
½ teaspoon dry sherry
1 teaspoon cornstarch
4 cups Chinese Chicken Broth (page 64) and 1 teaspoon salt or
    1 (13¾-ounce can) chicken broth and enough water to make 4 cups
1 teaspoon sesame seed oil
Salt to taste

1. Cut the cucumbers in half lengthwise, remove seeds, if any, and slice
on the diagonal ¼ inch thick. You should have 2 cups. Set aside.

2. Place the pork in a bowl, add the sherry and cornstarch, and stir
together well. Set aside.

3. Bring the chicken broth to a boil in a medium saucepan. Add the
pork and stir until the broth returns to a boil.

4. Just before serving, add the cucumber slices, stir 2 or 3 times, and
remove from the heat. Drizzle with sesame seed oil. Salt to taste as desired.
Serve immediately.

Note The cucumbers cook very quickly and can overcook easily by just sitting in the hot broth.

Ham and Winter Melon Soup

Serves 4, or 6 as part of a multicourse meal

*I*n China, the most famous ham comes from Jinhua. When we traveled by train in China on our first visit after the country became open to foreigners, we stopped briefly at Jinhua. Vendors were selling the hams at the station, and many people got on the train with whole hams tucked under their arms.

In this soup, a very acceptable substitute for Chinese ham is Smithfield ham. It is so heavily salted and well aged that even a little bit imparts a rich taste and fragrance to the soup. Be sure to cook the winter melon until tender and soft. It's almost impossible to overcook it.

禧

1 slice winter melon (1 pound)
¼ pound Smithfield ham
2 cups Chinese Chicken Broth (page 64) plus ½ teaspoon of salt or
    1 (13¾-ounce) can chicken broth and enough water to make 2 cups
2 slices unpeeled gingerroot, 1 × ⅛ inch each
Salt (optional)

1. Cut the green skin off the winter melon and remove the seeds and soft, pulpy interior. Rinse, drain, and cut into ½ × 2-inch slices. Place the slices in 2 cups of water in a medium saucepan and bring to a boil over medium heat. Reduce the heat to low and simmer until the melon becomes translucent and tender, 15 to 20 minutes.

2. Cut off and discard the dark skin and fat from the ham. Slice the meat into 2 × 1 × ⅛-inch pieces.

3. Add the ham, broth, and gingerroot to the simmering melon and cook for 15 minutes over low heat. (The soup may be kept warm over very low heat or cooled and reheated until ready to serve.) Taste and add salt if desired. Serve hot.

Soup

Chicken Velvet Corn Soup

**Serves 4 to 6, or 8 as part of a
multicourse meal**

F or this thick soup made with pureed chicken breast and creamed corn, I find that a
good-quality canned cream-style corn — Del Monte is the brand I prefer — gives
excellent results in a fraction of the time it would take to make it from scratch.

健康

½ pound skinless boneless chicken breast

½ cup water

1 teaspoon dry sherry

4¼ cups Chinese Chicken Broth (page 64) plus 1 teaspoon salt or
    1 (13¾-ounce) can chicken broth and enough water to make 4¼ cups

1 (16½-ounce) can cream-style corn

½ teaspoon salt, or to taste

Dash white pepper

2 slices unpeeled gingerroot, 1 × ⅛ inch each

2 tablespoons thinly sliced scallions

1 tablespoon cornstarch, dissolved in 2 tablespoons water

2 egg whites, lightly beaten but not frothy

1 teaspoon sesame seed oil

1.   Cut the chicken into 2-inch chunks and put into the workbowl of
a food processor fitted with the metal blade. Add the water and sherry. Process
for about 15 seconds, pulsing 2 or 3 times, until the meat is a smooth puree.
Transfer to a small bowl. Set aside. (Or puree in a blender and discard any
gristle that becomes lodged in the blades.)

2.   Place the chicken broth, salt, pepper, corn, and gingerroot in a 2-
quart saucepan, stir together, and bring to a boil over medium heat.

3.   Add the chicken puree and stir so that the meat breaks up into small
bits. The chicken will quickly turn white, indicating that it is cooked. Add
the scallions, stir a few times, and taste. Add more salt as desired. Mix up the
cornstarch solution again and pour it into the soup, stirring constantly until
the soup thickens.

4.   Remove from the heat, discard the gingerroot, and pour the egg
whites in a thin stream from about 6 inches above the saucepan. Stir gently a
few times so that thin threads of egg white rise to the surface. Drizzle with
sesame seed oil and give a few last stirs. Serve hot.

Crab and Asparagus Soup

*R*ather than hearty chowders, Chinese seafood soups are generally light, and the fresh taste of the seafood comes through. This soup is thickened with cornstarch to keep the bits of crabmeat suspended in the broth.

福

8 spears asparagus

1 (6-ounce) can crabmeat, drained (about ¾ cup)

1 teaspoon dry sherry

4 cups Chinese Chicken Broth (page 64) plus 1 teaspoon salt or
    1 (13¾-ounce) can chicken broth and enough water to make 4 cups

1 slice unpeeled gingerroot, 1 × ⅛ inch each

2 tablespoons cornstarch, dissolved in ½ cup water

1 egg, beaten

Dash white pepper

1 teaspoon sesame seed oil

Salt to taste

1.   Clean the asparagus, snap off the tough ends, and trim the leaves off the lower stalk. Cut on the diagonal into 1½-inch pieces. Set aside.

2.   Flake the crabmeat, removing any cartilage, and mix with the sherry. Set aside.

3.   Combine the chicken broth and gingerroot in a saucepan and bring to a boil over medium heat. Stir in the asparagus and crabmeat. As soon as the soup returns to a boil, add the cornstarch mixture and stir until the broth thickens and comes back to a boil. Stir in the egg and immediately remove from heat. Remove the gingerroot. Drizzle with sesame seed oil and adjust seasoning. Serve immediately.

Chinese Celery Cabbage and Dried Shrimp Soup

Serves 6 to 8

*T*his is comfort soup for me. It always reminds me of those childhood "hot and noisy" get-togethers — as the Chinese would call them — when my mother would cook all day. Traditionally this soup, served with Moo Shi Pork (page 192) and Mandarin Pancakes (page 118), made up a whole meal. Sometimes my mother used Smithfield ham in place of the dried shrimp. Don't use fresh shrimp, though; they are not suitable.

¼ cup dried shrimp
1 teaspoon dry sherry
1 pound Chinese celery or napa cabbage
2 ounces bean thread
2 tablespoons canola, corn, or peanut oil
½ teaspoon salt
2 slices unpeeled gingerroot, 1 × ⅛ inch each
6 cups Chinese Chicken Broth (page 64) plus 1 teaspoon salt or
    1 (13¾-ounce) can chicken broth and enough water to make 6 cups

1. Place the shrimp in a small bowl or measuring cup and pour on the sherry and 3 tablespoons water. Set aside.

2. Discard the tough outer leaves of the cabbage and cut it into quarters lengthwise. Cut out the core and slice the cabbage quarters into 1½-inch chunks. Set aside.

3. Soak the bean thread in warm water for 3 to 5 minutes until soft. Drain carefully so that the strands stay together as much as possible. Cut into 6- to 8-inch lengths with scissors. Set aside.

4. Heat the oil in a stockpot. When the oil is hot but not smoking, add the salt, gingerroot, and cabbage chunks; the ingredients should sizzle. Stir and cook until the cabbage is wilted.

5. Pour in the chicken broth, add the dried shrimp with the soaking liquid, and bring to a boil. Cover and simmer until the cabbage is transparent and tender.

6. Just before serving, bring the soup to a boil, add the bean thread, and remove soup from the heat and check seasoning. Serve immediately.

Peking Fish Soup

Serves 6 to 8

*T*his is a surprisingly quick soup to prepare and cook. The complex flavors and appearance with clouds of egg white belie its simplicity. The fish in this soup cooks very quickly. If you turn off the heat just before the fish looks completely done, it will continue to cook in the soup and be just perfect when you are ready to serve.

½ pound white fish fillets, such as cod or haddock

1½ teaspoons cornstarch

1 tablespoon dry sherry

1 egg white

5 cups Chinese Chicken Broth (page 64) plus 1 teaspoon salt or

    1 (13¾-ounce) can chicken broth and enough water to make 5 cups

½ teaspoon salt

½ teaspoon white pepper

3 tablespoons cider vinegar

1 tablespoon peeled, finely shredded gingerroot (page 45)

1 scallion, white and green parts, thinly sliced

2 sprigs cilantro, cut into 1-inch lengths

1. Slice the fish fillets into 1½-inch wide pieces. If necessary, cut the pieces crosswise so they are no longer than 2 inches. Mix the cornstarch, sherry, and egg white together until well blended. Add the fish and mix thoroughly. Set aside.

2. Bring the chicken broth to a boil in a 2-quart saucepan. Reduce the heat to medium and add the fish pieces. Stir gently for about 10 seconds.

3. Immediately stir the salt, pepper, vinegar, gingerroot, and scallion into the soup and simmer just until the fish turns white. Be careful not to overcook. Turn off the heat. Adjust salt to taste and add cilantro. Stir a few times and serve without delay.

Rice, Noodles, and Bread

A mericans refer to wheat as the staff of life, but to Asians, the staff of life is rice. For the Chinese, there is nothing more comforting than the warm fragrance of rice cooking. It is as compelling as the aroma of fresh bread baking in the oven. The rice bowl is ubiquitous. Even in the wheat-growing North, rice is eaten at just about every meal, including breakfast. When Chinese greet each other they often say, "Have you eaten rice yet?" instead of "Hello."

My mother cooked long-grain rice for the dinner table and general eating but preferred short-grain rice to make congee, a thin rice gruel served at breakfast, for a late night snack, and to the elderly. At every lunar New Year, my mother made *nien gao,* a sticky cake made from glutinous rice, sweetened with sugar, and flavored with candied sweet olive blossoms from the *Osmanthus fragrans* tree. Following the Shanghai tradition, she often tinted the cake light green or pink. This special dessert symbolized the sticking together of the family and good luck for the new year in general.

In northern China, noodles, leavened and unleavened breads, and dumplings made predominately from wheat flour are the staple starch at meals. There are many varieties and types of noodles from thin, wispy noodles called dragon's beard to thick wide ribbons. Instead of birthday cakes we serve long noodles to symbolize long life.

My mother used to make birthday noodles by hand for each of us on our Chinese birthdays, which was based on the lunar calendar (our Western birthday was based on the Gregorian calendar). As a child I would brag to my amazed friends that I had *two* birthdays! We always had cake on our Western birthdays, but long-life noodles were traditional on our Chinese birthdays. The birthday person did not have to help, but everyone else was involved. Mother used to joke that she would make our birthday noodles so long that we would have to eat them from a ladder!

When I was growing up, Chinese noodles were available only at noodle shops in Chinatown. Fresh Chinese noodles are delicious, but noodle dishes can also be made successfully with packaged dried spaghetti or vermicelli. We often made noodle dishes with packaged spaghetti, and I still do. Noodles are served as a snack, lunch, or as a one-dish meal.

Other wheat dishes especially popular in the North are *man tou* (steamed bread) and *bing* (flatbread), such as scallion cakes (page 303) and Mandarin Pancakes. *Man tou,* the most common family-style steamed bread, is traditionally eaten with dishes cooked with a savory gravy. Various filled steamed breads are served mainly by street vendors or restaurants and not usually made at home.

Rice

福 The Chinese prefer plain white rice that has been cooked with water. The concept is that the rice serves as a blank canvas upon which the flavors and textures of the food play. Although not traditional, you may substitute chicken or beef broth for water if you like. Jade Rice, Onion and Garlic Rice, and Confetti Rice, all made with broth, are rice dishes that best accompany Western-style meals.

Fried rice is a way the Chinese use up leftover rice and pieces of cooked meat. Fresh rice would never be cooked just to make fried rice. Fresh rice is too soft and tender for stir-frying and gets mushy from the constant stirring. For the best fried rice, always use day-old rice, preferably day-old long-grain rice, which is firmer and will stand up to a second cooking better than short-grain rice. I store leftover rice in a plastic bag in the refrigerator and loosen the rice right in the bag. The two kinds of fried rice my mother made most often at home are Shanghai Golden Fried Rice and Choo Choo Train Fried Rice — both very easy and quick and neither of them brown. The brown color that is so popular in America comes from adding a little thick soy sauce to the rice.

Proportions and Preparation

Two cups of raw rice will yield about five cups of fluffed cooked rice. This will serve three to four people with average appetites. The Chinese, in general, consume twice as much rice as Westerners. My theory about the complaint, "After eating Chinese food, you're hungry again an hour later," is that Westerners eat far too little rice. For the Chinese, rice is used not only as a palate cleanser and accompaniment to savory foods, but as a filler.

The Chinese wash and rinse the rice many times before cooking. This is a habit that just about every Chinese continues to practice, even though raw rice is cleaner than it used to be and sometimes enriched with vitamins that are washed away. I still wash and rinse the rice in cold water just as my mother did. I believe this not only rinses away any impurities but also helps to make the rice cook up whiter and fluffier and taste fresher. You can decide for yourself.

You will need 2¼ cups of water to cook two cups of washed and rinsed rice. If you like a harder, drier rice, reduce the water to 2 cups, an equal amount of water to rice. For short-grain rice, use two cups water. If you do not wash your rice, increase the water by four tablespoons.

Washing and Measuring Rice the Traditional Chinese Way The Chinese don't use calibrated measuring tools when they cook. It is a matter of feel and experience rather than strict proportions. This is especially the case when it comes to cooking rice. Since cooking perfect rice seems to elude many non-Asian cooks, it may come as a surprise that the Chinese approximate the correct amount of rice and water with only two fingers.

As you cook more and more rice, you'll get a sense of what a cup of rice looks like, so you'll eventually be able to pour rice directly into the cooking pot without measuring it. The Chinese usually use the same pot to cook rice, so after a while it really does become second nature. It's so simple even children can do it. Here's how to use this age-old method:

- Select a saucepan with straight sides. This works in automatic electric rice cookers, which usually have straight-sided inner pots.

- Add the raw rice to the pan, pouring in the approximate amount you think you'll need. If you are inexperienced, you may wish to measure the rice at first.

- Wash and rinse the rice three or four times right in the saucepan. After the last rinse, drain as much water out as you can by tipping the saucepan carefully without spilling the rice. You should proceed with the recipe immediately after washing since the rice will begin to absorb moisture. If allowed to sit in even a small amount of water for any length of time, the rice may cook up softer than desired.

Rice,

Noodles,

and Bread

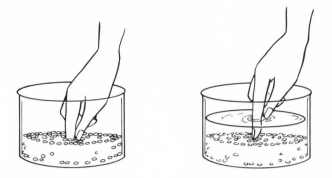

- Smooth and level the surface of the rice with the back of your fingers. Then insert your index finger straight into the rice and touch the bottom of the pan lightly *(above left)*. Hold your index finger straight when measuring. Mark the depth of the rice by putting your thumb on the side of your index finger where the top of the rice touches it. Keep your thumb in place until all the water is measured.

- Pour warm or cold water into the pan just to the top of the rice. Then, with the tip of your index finger touching the top of the rice (not down into the rice), add water until it touches the tip of your thumb where it meets the index finger *(above right)*. If you like your rice harder or are using short-grain rice, use a little less water. If you like a softer, moister rice measure the water to slightly above the tip of your thumb.

Keeping Rice Warm The Chinese seem to know instinctively just when to start cooking the rice so that it will be ready when the meal is brought to the table. However, if you have to hold the rice for any reason, here are a few suggestions.

Saucepan rice will keep warm, as long as it is covered, for about thirty minutes, depending upon the temperature in the room, without extra attention. If you need to hold it for a longer time, turn off the heat and keep it covered. If necessary, you can give it some gentle heat later, sprinkling it first with a few tablespoons of water and turning the heat to very low. Cook for ten to fifteen minutes, being careful not to burn the rice.

Even the very basic electric rice cookers often have a "keep warm" feature. I find that it works well for about half an hour but if left on longer it sometimes browns the rice on the bottom of the pan. Even turned completely off, my basic, uninsulated rice cooker keeps the rice satisfactorily hot for up to an hour. Some deluxe models have a host of features that cook the rice as well as keep it warm for up to twelve hours. These cookers are bulky and expensive.

Rice that is cooked in a steam pot need only be left in the boiling water. The hot water surrounding the pot will keep the rice warm for up to forty minutes. If it needs reheating, simply turn the heat on and let the water boil again.

Reheating Leftover rice should always be wrapped and stored in the refrigerator to keep it from drying out. Cold rice reheats surprisingly well in the microwave oven. I generally transfer the amount of cold rice I want into a microwave-safe container and cover it with a lid or plastic wrap. Two cups of cold rice will reheat in about three minutes on high. There is no need to sprinkle any water on the rice as the moisture in the rice itself seems to be enough.

If you have an electric rice cooker, simply add three to four tablespoons of water to the cold rice in the cooker's inner pot and turn the machine on. It will turn itself off when the rice is ready.

You can also reheat cold rice successfully in a steamer. The steam keeps the rice from drying out. Place the cold rice in a heatproof bowl or dish, allowing for room on top of the rice to let the steam circulate freely. Steam for five to eight minutes, or until the rice is hot.

Serving

Freshly cooked rice is compact and should be fluffed with a pair of moistened chopsticks or a fork before serving. The Chinese eat their rice directly from a rice bowl. The family style is to serve everyone a bowl of rice. If people want seconds, they go to the rice pot and serve themselves another bowl.

If you are having a dinner party, you can transfer the cooked rice to a covered casserole of a contrasting color and let your guests serve themselves to a bowl or plate. The Japanese make heavy plastic rice servers that look like lacquerware with matching rice paddles. These handsome servers not only help keep the rice warm but are an attractive way to serve rice at the table.

Saucepan Rice

Makes about 5 cups cooked rice, enough to serve 3 to 4 people

Y ou can make excellent rice in a regular kitchen saucepan. Be sure to read the notes on rice on pages 84–87. Watch the rice carefully so it does not boil over.

2 cups long-grain rice
2¼ cups water

1.   Pour the rice into a heavy-bottomed 2-quart saucepan. Cover the rice with plenty of cold water and gently rub the grains between your hands. Wash and drain the rice 3 or 4 times tipping the saucepan carefully to pour out as much water as possible without spilling the rice or drain in a strainer. Add the water and cover the pan.

2.   Bring to a boil over medium-high heat. Immediately reduce the heat to medium-low and stir the rice with a wooden spoon from the bottom up and around the sides of the pan. Scrape down the grains from the sides. Cover and cook until there is no visible liquid on top of the rice and there are holes on the surface of the rice, about 5 minutes. If the rice begins to boil over, place the cover askew until step 3.

3.   Immediately turn the heat down to very low, as low as you can, and cook for 20 to 30 minutes, or until the rice is tender and a grain no longer has a hard core when pressed between the fingers.

福

Note   If you inadvertently scorch the rice, use my mother's trick. Uncover the pan for a few minutes to release the steam, place a piece of bread over the rice, and put the lid back on. The bread absorbs much of the burnt flavor. Discard the bread before serving.

Rice,

Noodles,

and Bread

Electric Rice Cooker Rice

Makes about 5 cups cooked rice, enough to serve 3 to 4 people

Electric rice cookers make such good rice and are so easy to use that the Chinese hardly cook rice in a saucepan anymore. I have been using a rice cooker for years, and it always makes perfect rice that does not have to be watched or monitored at all.

There are many models of electric rice cookers. The most convenient and popular size is the five-cup rice cooker. If you have a large family or need to cook lots of rice, though, you might want to consider the eight-cup size. In general, all rice cookers perform equally well; some newer models have special features that are nice but not imperative. My twenty-year-old Hitachi basic model is still used every day and has never missed a beat!

2 cups long-grain rice
2¼ cups water

Wash the rice 3 or 4 times in plenty of cold water in a bowl or the inner cooking pot of the electric rice cooker. Tip the bowl or pot to drain as much water as possible without spilling the rice or drain in a strainer. Add the water, cover, and follow the manufacturer's directions. In my electric cooker, 2 cups of rice cook in about 20 minutes.

Steam Pot Steamed Rice

Makes about 5 cups cooked rice, enough to serve 3 to 4 people

lthough the Yunnan steam pot is designed especially for cooking the famed Yunnan Steam Pot Chicken (page 177), I've found that it also makes perfect rice without any worry of burning or need to observe the different stages of cooking rice on the stove. What's more, the hard-fired clay retains heat and keeps the rice warm. The attractive and interesting design makes it a perfect serving dish as well.

2 cups long-grain rice
2¼ cups water

1. Place the rice in a bowl and cover with cold water. Rub the grains between your hands and then drain. Wash and drain 3 or 4 times. Drain by tipping the bowl carefully to pour out as much water as possible without spilling the grains or drain in a strainer.

2. Transfer the rice to a steam pot and pour in the water. Be sure all the grains are totally submerged and the surface of the rice is smooth and even. Cover the steam pot and place in a wok, stockpot, or roaster. Be sure there is enough room around the pot for you to lift it out when the rice is cooked. Add water so that the steam pot is sitting in water up to the bottom or middle of the handles. Do not overfill or the water will boil into the steam pot through the inner chimney or the lid. Cover the wok or pot and bring the water to a boil.

3. When the water reaches a boil, reduce the heat until the water maintains a slow boil. Cook for 30 to 40 minutes, or until a grain of rice is totally smooth when pressed between the finger tips. It is not necessary to stir the rice or check it during the cooking procedure. Just be sure that the water in the pot in which the steam pot is sitting does not boil away. Replenish with more boiling water as needed.

Onion and Garlic Rice

Serves 3 to 4 as a side dish

ice is a wonderful accompaniment for Western-style beef or chicken stews. Instead of plain steamed rice, I often make flavored rice.

禧

2 tablespoons canola, corn, or peanut oil

1 medium onion, chopped

2 garlic cloves, pureed or put through a garlic press

2 cups long-grain rice

2 cups Chinese Chicken Broth (page 64) plus 1 teaspoon salt or

  1 (13¾-ounce) can chicken broth and enough water to make 2 cups

3 tablespoons minced parsley

1.   Heat the oil in a skillet over medium heat and brown the onion. Add the garlic and stir a few times. Remove the pan from the heat and transfer the onion and garlic to a 2-quart saucepan.

2.   Add the rice and broth to the saucepan. Stir, cover the pan, and bring to a boil over medium heat. Reduce the heat to medium-low and cook until the surface of the rice is marked with holes and all the visible liquid has been absorbed, about 5 minutes.

3.   Gently stir the rice, scraping down the sides. Immediately turn the heat down to very low. Cook, covered, for 20 to 30 minutes, or until the rice is cooked through and tender. Remove from the heat.

4.   When ready to serve, transfer the rice to a covered serving dish and sprinkle with parsley. Serve immediately.

Rice Skin

鍋巴

Sometimes rice that has been cooked too long in a saucepan forms a brown crust on the bottom and sides. The Chinese call this "rice skin." My mother liked to cook it with lots of water to make a smoky rice porridge.

At the restaurant, the cooks dried the rice skin by placing the pan over very low heat. Once it had dried and shrunk, it could be removed easily from the pan. It was broken into smaller pieces and stored in a dry place. The chefs would deep-fry the rice skin in hot oil to make a crispy rice that crackled and sizzled when it was added to soups or covered with sauce in the Peking fashion. The hot sizzling rice, called *guo ba,* has to be served as soon as possible after frying for the most explosive sizzle. When someone ordered a dish with sizzling rice, the waiters were instructed to stand by as the chef dropped the skin into the hot fat. As a child I loved sizzling rice with sugar sprinkled on top, so the chefs would often fry a little extra for me.

Jade Rice

Serves 3 to 4 as a side dish

M y mother used to make this Shanghai steamed rice with chopped dark green bok choy leaves for the family. She would often pick through the trimmed bok choy leaves at our favorite Chinatown market to come up with a handful for her rice. She hated to see good food go to waste! I use pureed spinach leaves instead; they provide a uniform green color.

健康

¼ pound spinach leaves
2 cups Chinese Chicken Broth (page 64) plus 1 teaspoon salt or
    1 (13¾-ounce) can chicken broth and enough water to make 2 cups
2 cups long-grain rice
2 Chinese sausages, finely chopped

1. Wash the spinach thoroughly and parboil for 30 seconds. Rinse in cold water, drain, and squeeze out the water. Coarsely chop the leaves and combine with the broth in a blender or food processor. Blend or process until completely pureed.

2. Combine the rice, spinach puree, and sausage in a 2-quart saucepan. Stir together, scraping down the sides of the saucepan. Cover the pan and bring to a boil over medium heat. Cook until the liquid is almost absorbed and the top of the rice has small holes, about 5 minutes. Stir gently and scrape any grains from the side of the pan. Reduce the heat to very low and cook, covered, for 20 to 30 minutes, or until the rice has absorbed all the moisture and is cooked through. Serve hot.

Confetti Rice

Serves 4 to 5

*T*his dish gets its name from the riot of color created by the vegetables. It's a great alternative to fried rice since the chicken broth imparts a delicate flavor without any added oil. I have given directions for making the rice in a steam pot or saucepan. If you are using an electric rice cooker, follow the manufacturer's instructions and add the peas halfway through the cooking.

福

2 cups long-grain rice

2 cups Chinese Chicken Broth (page 64) plus 1 teaspoon salt or

   1 (13¾-ounce) can chicken broth and enough water to make 2 cups

½ cup diced fresh carrots or thawed frozen carrots

½ cup diced red bell pepper (about ½ pepper)

½ cup corn, fresh or frozen

⅓ cup thinly sliced scallions or diced red onion

½ cup fresh peas, parboiled, or thawed frozen peas

2 tablespoons minced parsley

1. Place the rice in a large bowl and cover it with cold water. Swish the rice around with your hands and then drain. Repeat 2 times and drain.

2. Place the rice in a 2-quart steam pot or in a 2-quart saucepan. Add the broth, 3 tablespoons water, carrots, red pepper, corn, and scallions. Mix well and smooth the surface flat so that every grain of rice is submerged in the broth. Put a lid on the steam pot or saucepan.

3. Place the steam pot in a bath of water in a wok, stir-fry pan, or other shallow pan wide enough to hold the pot comfortably. The water level should not come up any higher than 2 inches from the lid. Cover the pan holding the steam pot with a lid and bring the water to a boil. Reduce the heat to medium or medium-low and simmer for 20 minutes. Add more boiling water to the pan as necessary so it does not ever evaporate completely. (Or place the saucepan over medium heat. When the water boils, stir the rice, turn the heat to medium-low, and cook until there is no visible liquid over the rice and the surface of the rice forms holes, about 5 minutes.)

4. Uncover the steam pot or saucepan and stir in the peas. Re-cover the steam pot and the wok and cook for 20 minutes. (Or re-cover the saucepan, turn the heat as low as possible, and cook for 15 to 20 minutes.) The rice should be tender and no longer have a hard core.

5.   Remove the steam pot from the water or the saucepan from the heat. Fluff up the rice with a pair of wet chopsticks or a bamboo rice paddle. If using the steam pot, sprinkle the parsley over the top and serve directly from the pot. Transfer the saucepan rice to a covered serving dish and sprinkle with parsley. Serve immediately.

健康

Shanghai Golden
Fried Rice

Serves 3 to 5

When we were children, my mother often made this simple fried rice for us at home. The light color might surprise you, but actually the Chinese are not used to the dark fried rice so familiar in Chinese-American restaurants. If you'd like a meatless version, simply omit the ham and, if desired, increase the salt slightly to adjust for the change.

4 cups cold cooked rice

2 large eggs

½ teaspoon dry sherry

3 to 5 tablespoons thinly sliced scallions, green and white parts, or minced onion

1 teaspoon salt, or to taste

4 tablespoons canola, corn, or peanut oil

½ cup chopped ham, bacon, or Chinese sausage (optional)

1. Place the cold rice in a large bowl and use your fingers to break up any lumps. Break the eggs directly onto the rice and add the sherry, scallions, and salt. Mix together thoroughly with your hands or with a wooden spoon.

2. Pour the oil into a wok or stir-fry pan and place the pan over medium-high heat. Heat until the oil is hot but not smoking. Test by dipping a spatula into the rice mixture and then into the oil; it should sizzle. If using the meat, add it to the hot oil and stir for about 30 seconds.

3. Turn the rice mixture into the pan, increase temperature to high, and stir constantly for 8 to 10 minutes, breaking up any lumps with the back of the spatula. The grains will be loose and fluffy and the rice heated through. Taste for seasoning. Serve hot.

Rice,

Noodles,

and Bread

Choo Choo Train
Fried Rice

E very Chinese person who travels a lot knows what train fried rice is — it's the type of fried rice usually served in dining cars in China. My mother coined this name when we were children because she thought we would find the dish more appealing. I guess she was right, because this was one of our favorite dishes.

禧

4 cups cold cooked rice
2 large eggs
½ teaspoon dry sherry
4 tablespoons canola, corn, or peanut oil
2 tablespoons minced onion
1½ teaspoons salt
½ cup diced baked ham
½ cup fresh peas, parboiled, or thawed frozen peas

1. Place the rice in a mixing bowl and use your fingers to separate the grains until they are loose. Set aside. Lightly beat the eggs and sherry together with a fork or chopsticks. Set aside.

2. Heat the oil in a wok or stir-fry pan over high heat. When the oil is hot, stir in the onions and the eggs. Scramble until the eggs are dry and break into small pieces.

3. Add the rice, salt, ham, and peas and stir constantly until the ingredients are well blended and heated, about 8 to 10 minutes. Serve hot.

Yangchow Fried Rice

Serves 3 to 5

*F*rom the Shanghai region, this attractive rice, flecked with yellow, green, orange, and pink is a popular snack since almost every kind of ingredient can be found in it.

健康

4 cups cold cooked rice

2 eggs

1 teaspoon sherry

4 tablespoons canola, corn, or peanut oil

½ cup diced cooked chicken

1 cup cooked small shrimp (6 ounces)

½ cup diced baked ham

1 cup diced carrots, parboiled, or thawed frozen carrots

1 cup fresh peas, parboiled, or thawed frozen peas

½ cup thinly sliced scallions

1 teaspoon salt, or to taste

Dash ground pepper, or to taste

1.   Place the rice in a bowl and use your hands to break up and separate the grains. Set aside. Lightly beat the eggs and sherry together with a fork or chopsticks. Set aside.

2.   Heat the oil in a wok or stir-fry pan over medium-high heat. When the oil is hot, add the eggs and scramble until they puff lightly but are still loose. Immediately stir in the rice and stir for about 2 minutes so that the rice heats up and the eggs are completely mixed in.

3.   Raise the heat to high and add the remaining ingredients and stir vigorously until they are well mixed into the rice and heated through. Correct seasoning as desired. Serve hot.

福

Note   This is a good recipe for leftover meat and shrimp. If you don't have all 3 kinds listed above, you can leave one out, but increase the other two so you have 1½ cups total. Fried rice heats up well in the microwave or in a stir-fry pan.

Rice,

Noodles,

and Bread

Fried Rice with Ham

Serves 3 to 5

*T*hick soy sauce gives this rice its brown color. If it's unavailable, you can omit it or use dark soy sauce, but the same amount will not color the rice. Add more gradually, taking care that the rice does not become too wet or salty.

禄

4 cups cold cooked rice
2 large eggs
1 teaspoon salt
½ teaspoon pepper
4 tablespoons canola, corn, or peanut oil
½ cup thinly sliced scallions or diced onion
1 teaspoon thick soy sauce (optional)
1 cup fresh peas, parboiled, or thawed frozen peas
1 cup diced carrots, parboiled, or thawed frozen carrots
½ cup diced cooked ham, chicken, turkey, or pork
1 cup fresh bean sprouts

1. Place the rice in a large bowl and use your fingers to break up any lumps. Set aside. Beat the eggs in a separate bowl with the salt and pepper. Set aside.

2. Pour the oil into a wok or stir-fry pan and place the pan over medium-high heat. When the oil is hot but not smoking, add the scallions; they should sizzle. Stir for about 15 seconds. Stir the beaten eggs into the pan with a spatula and scramble until the eggs are dry and separate.

3. Add the rice to the eggs and mix thoroughly. Pour the soy sauce evenly over the mixture. Add the peas, carrots, ham, and bean sprouts. Stir constantly until all the ingredients are well mixed and heated through. Serve immediately.

Oyster Sauce Fried Rice

Serves 6 to 8

My mother developed this fried rice to use as a stuffing in our Thanksgiving turkey. The giblets and oyster sauce give a wonderful savory flavor to the big bird. Even when we're having a traditional bread stuffing—at the request of my American husband—I like to make this rice as a side dish. It is tasty enough to stand alone and is even better the next day when the flavors have mellowed and blended. It warms up beautifully in the microwave. This dish may be prepared with or without the giblets and livers.

Giblets (liver, heart, and gizzard) from a turkey or 1/2 cup chicken giblets or
    livers (optional)
6 cups cold cooked rice
1/2 cup dried black mushrooms, softened in hot water for 15 minutes (optional)
4 tablespoons canola, corn, or peanut oil
1 onion, chopped (about 1/2 cup)
2 teaspoons minced garlic
1 cup chopped celery
1/4 teaspoon black pepper
1/2 cup oyster sauce
Salt to taste
1/2 cup minced parsley

1. Chop the giblets or livers into small pieces. If you are using the gizzard, peel off and discard the thick membrane. Set aside. Put the rice in a mixing bowl and break up any lumps with your hands. Set aside.

2. Squeeze the water from the mushrooms, if using, and trim off the stems with a pair of scissors. Shred the caps and set aside.

3. Heat the oil in a wok or stir-fry pan over high heat until hot but not smoking. Test with a piece of onion; it should sizzle when added to the oil. Add the onions and stir-fry until lightly browned. Add the giblets, garlic, celery, and mushrooms. Stir constantly until the giblets change color and are separated.

Rice,

Noodles,

and Bread

4. Season with black pepper and oyster sauce and stir until well mixed. Add the rice. Stir constantly with a spatula until the rice is evenly mixed into the gravy and heated through. Taste and adjust seasoning as desired by adding more oyster sauce, 1 tablespoon at a time. Do not allow rice to become too wet; add salt if oyster sauce does not provide enough seasoning. Remove from the heat and stir in the parsley. If not ready to serve immediately, place in a covered casserole in a low oven. Serve hot.

Variation   To use as stuffing for a turkey, rinse the turkey and dry inside and out with a paper towel. Stuff the cavity with the rice mixture only when you are ready to roast. Stuff lightly so the rice can expand during roasting. Any extras can be heated separately and served in a casserole. This recipe is enough for a 10- to 12-pound bird.

健康

Shredded Pork with Stir-fried Noodles

Serves 3 to 4

Stir-fried noodles are a favorite snack food or lunch dish for the Chinese. We sometimes add vinegar or even ketchup to the individual servings. It may sound unconventional, but it's really quite good. Try it.

½ pound dried Chinese noodles, thin spaghetti, or linguine

1 teaspoon sesame seed oil

½ pound lean pork or beef, shredded (about 1 cup)

2 tablespoons light soy sauce

2 teaspoons cornstarch

1 teaspoon dry sherry

½ teaspoon sugar

1 cup dried black mushrooms, softened in hot water for 15 minutes

2 tablespoons canola, corn, or peanut oil

1 slice unpeeled gingerroot, 1 × ⅛ inch

2 cups shredded napa, Chinese celery cabbage, or bok choy

½ cup shredded carrots

½ cup thinly sliced scallions, white and green parts

1 teaspoon dark soy sauce

1. Cook the noodles in a large amount of boiling water until a little more tender than al dente. Drain, rinse in cold water, and toss with the sesame seed oil to keep them from sticking together. Set aside.

2. Place the pork in a bowl and add the light soy sauce, cornstarch, sherry, and sugar. Stir together well. Set aside.

3. Drain the softened mushrooms, reserving 2 tablespoons of the soaking liquid. Strain the liquid through a fine sieve. Set aside. Snip off the stems of the mushrooms with scissors and discard. Cut the caps into thin shreds. Set aside.

4.   Pour the oil into a wok or stir-fry pan and place it over high heat. Add the gingerroot and stir around the pan until the oil is hot but not smoking; the gingerroot will sizzle. Stir up the pork again and add it to the pan. Stir for about 2 minutes, or until there is no pink left in the meat. Add the cabbage, carrots, mushrooms, and scallions. Stir for about 2 to 3 minutes, or until the vegetables are tender-crisp.

5.   Add the reserved mushroom liquid and stir a few times to mix. Add the noodles and stir thoroughly until the noodles are heated through. Stir in the dark soy sauce until the noodles are evenly colored. Turn out onto a large serving platter. Serve immediately.

福

Note See pages 44–45 for a description of how to shred meat and vegetables.

禄

Both Sides Brown Noodles

Serves 6 to 8

Professional Chinese chefs brown these noodles at the same time as they are preparing
the sauce. It is not always practical to do this at home, so I've suggested you brown
the noodles first and keep them warm in a low oven while you make the sauce.
Eat the noodles as soon as you can after browning while they are still hot and crisp.

1 pound Chinese egg noodles, fresh or dried, or fettuccine or linguine

8 tablespoons canola, corn, or peanut oil

½ pound lean pork or beef, shredded (about 1 cup)

1 teaspoon dry sherry

7 teaspoons cornstarch

1½ cups Chinese Chicken Broth (page 64) or canned broth

1 slice unpeeled gingerroot, 1 × ⅛ inch

3 cups shredded green, napa, or bok choy cabbage (½ pound)

1 (8-ounce) can sliced bamboo shoots, drained (1 cup)

1 cup dried black mushrooms, softened in hot water for 15 minutes, drained,
     stems removed, and caps shredded or sliced fresh mushrooms

3 scallions, white and green parts, cut into 2-inch lengths

2 teaspoons salt

1. Stir the noodles into a large amount of boiling water and boil until
a little more tender than al dente. Be sure not to overcook since the noodles
will be cooked again. If the noodles are fresh they will cook in a very short
time. Taste often as they cook. When tender, drain and rinse in cold water.
Drain thoroughly and mix with 2 tablespoons of the oil to prevent them from
sticking together. Set aside.

2. Mix the meat with the sherry and 2 teaspoons of the cornstarch in
a bowl and stir together well. Set aside. Dissolve the remaining 5 teaspoons of
cornstarch in ½ cup of the broth and set aside.

3. Heat 4 tablespoons of the oil in a large nonstick skillet or other flat-
bottomed heavy pan over medium-high heat. Add the noodles and spread
them out to the edges of the pan. Fry until the noodles are golden brown, 7
to 10 minutes on each side. Lift and peek every so often to see how they are
browning. When the first side has browned, flip the noodles over and fry the

other side. Remove from the pan and place on a serving platter in a warm oven. (If a large skillet is unavailable, cook the noodles in batches in a smaller pan.)

4.   To make the sauce, pour the remaining 2 tablespoons of oil into a wok or stir-fry pan and place the pan over high heat. Add the gingerroot and stir around the pan until it begins to sizzle. Mix up the meat again, pour it into the pan, and stir for about 2 minutes. Stir the cabbage, bamboo shoots, mushrooms, and scallions into the pan. Add the remaining 1 cup of broth and the salt. Reduce the heat to medium, cover the pan, and cook until the cabbage is tender, 3 to 5 minutes, stirring occasionally. Add the cornstarch slurry to the pan and cook until the sauce thickens.

5.   Remove the noodles from the oven and pour the sauce over them. Serve hot.

健康

Note   See pages 44–45 for a description of how to shred meat and vegetables.

福

Noodles with
Peking Meat Sauce

Serves 6 to 8

My mother often used packaged spaghetti or vermicelli for this dish because in the early 1950s using Chinese egg noodles meant a special trip to Chinatown. When we had this dish in China, it was at a tiny restaurant that had a "noodle stretcher," a man who stretched noodles by hand. After he stretched the noodles, helpers immediately dropped them into a large vat of boiling water, then strained them right into a large noodle bowl. They scooped up a large ladle of sauce, poured it on, and added a crunchy vegetable garnish. People were lined up waiting to lunch on a plate of those Peking noodles! They were delicious, but I've always liked my mother's better.

禄

½ pound ground pork (about 1 cup)

1 teaspoon dry sherry

1 teaspoon cornstarch

½ cup bean paste, preferably Japanese miso

2 tablespoons hoisin sauce

1 tablespoon sugar

2 tablespoons dark soy sauce

1 tablespoon canola, corn, or peanut oil

1 teaspoon minced garlic

1 medium onion, minced

½ cup thinly sliced scallions, green and white parts

1 cup water

1 pound spaghetti, thin or regular

10 radishes, shredded, for garnish

1 medium cucumber, partially peeled, seeded, and shredded, for garnish

2 cups bean sprouts, parboiled for 15 to 20 seconds and drained well, for garnish

10 ounces fresh spinach, washed, parboiled for 15 to 20 seconds, squeezed dry, and minced, for garnish

5 garlic cloves, peeled and finely minced, for garnish (optional)

1. Mix the pork with the sherry and cornstarch in a small bowl and set aside. Stir the bean paste, hoisin sauce, sugar, and soy sauce together in another small bowl. Set aside.

2. Heat the oil in a wok or stir-fry pan over high heat. When the oil is hot, stir in the pork and cook for 2 minutes, or until the meat changes color and separates. Add the garlic and onion and stir for 1 minute. Add the scallions and stir constantly for 1 minute, or until the scallions are soft but not browned.

3. Stir in the bean paste mixture and water and mix thoroughly with the meat. Turn the heat to low and simmer for 3 to 4 minutes, stirring occasionally. You will have a thin sauce.

4. Bring 5 quarts of water to a boil in a large pot. Stir in the spaghetti and boil until a little more tender than al dente. Drain and rinse in hot water; immediately divide the noodles among 6 or 8 individual noodle bowls. Place the meat sauce in a serving bowl on the table. Set the vegetable garnishes out in individual bowls and let people sauce and garnish their own noodles.

壽

Note   Shred the radishes and cucumber as described on page 45.

Variation   For a spicy version, substitute ½ cup Szechuan-style hot bean paste for the miso and add 1 tablespoon Chinkiang vinegar and 1 teaspoon toasted and ground Szechuan peppercorns.

Noodles with Bean Curd Sauce

Serves 6

*P*reviously frozen bean curd with its open, spongy texture works very well in this sauce. It has a firmer texture than fresh bean curd, holds up to stirring and mixing, and soaks up the wonderful bean sauce flavor. Serve the dish with the same vegetable garnish as for Noodles with Peking Meat Sauce (page 106).

1 pound firm bean curd, previously frozen
½ cup plus 2 tablespoons bean paste, preferably Japanese miso
2 tablespoons hoisin sauce
1 tablespoon sugar
2 tablespoons dark soy sauce
1 pound thin spaghetti
2 tablespoons canola, corn, or peanut oil
½ cup chopped onion
1½ teaspoons minced garlic
2 teaspoons minced peeled gingerroot
½ cup thinly sliced scallions, green and white parts
1½ cups water
1 tablespoon cornstarch, dissolved in 2 tablespoons water

1.   Thaw the bean curd by placing it in a bowl of hot water. When it is completely thawed, gently squeeze out the excess water and cut the cake into ½-inch or smaller cubes. Set aside.

2.   Blend together the bean paste, hoisin sauce, sugar, and soy sauce in a small bowl. Set aside.

3.   Bring 5 quarts of water to a boil in a large pot. Stir the spaghetti into the boiling water and cook until tender.

4.   While the spaghetti is cooking, heat the oil in a wok, stir-fry pan, or heavy saucepan over high heat until hot but not smoking. Test by dipping a piece of onion into the oil; it should sizzle. Add the onion to the hot oil and stir for about 1 minute. Add the garlic and gingerroot and stir for 30 seconds. Add the scallions and stir until they wilt. Stir in the bean curd and mix a few times. Add the bean paste mixture and the water. Blend well with the spatula. Reduce the heat to medium and simmer for about 1 minute. Pour in the cornstarch slurry and stir constantly until the sauce thickens.

5. Drain the spaghetti, rinse with hot water, and divide among 6 individual noodle bowls. Serve the bean sauce and vegetable garnish in separate bowls alongside the noodles and let people help themselves to sauce and garnish.

健康

Note Bean paste, depending on the brand, can be very salty; a little bit goes a long way. In step 4, start by spooning on a small amount of sauce, mix and taste, and add more if desired.

福

Cold Noodles, Szechuan Style

Serves 6 to 8

*T*he second time Keith, then my husband-to-be, met my mother it was her birthday. *We had planned a family picnic, a sort of birthday potluck so my mother wouldn't have to cook. In honor of the special day Keith, who is not Chinese, decided to make cold Chinese noodles to symbolize long life. He was very brave—or very foolish—to try this, but everyone loved his noodles, including my mother.*

Since these noodles are served at room temperature, they are ideal for picnics. Try them sometime instead of potato salad.

1 pound thin spaghetti
4 tablespoons sesame seed oil
1 whole chicken breast (about 1 pound) or about 2 cups shredded, cooked chicken
¼ cup sesame seed paste (tahini)
2 teaspoons grated peeled gingerroot
3 teaspoons finely minced garlic
1 heaping teaspoon Szechuan peppercorns, toasted and ground
1 tablespoon rice vinegar
1 tablespoon chili oil
3 tablespoons light soy sauce
2 teaspoons sugar
½ cup thinly sliced scallions, green and white parts
3 tablespoons sesame seeds, toasted (optional)
Cilantro or parsley sprigs, for garnish (optional)

1.   Bring 5 quarts of water to a boil and stir in the spaghetti. Boil until tender. Do not overcook or the noodles will be mushy. Drain and rinse under cold water. Drain thoroughly, transfer to a serving platter, not a bowl, and mix in 2 tablespoons of the sesame seed oil to the keep the noodles from sticking together. Set aside.

2.   If using a whole chicken breast, put the chicken breast in a pot of boiling water. When the water returns to a boil, turn the heat down to a

simmer. Simmer partly covered, for 20 to 25 minutes, or until the chicken is cooked through. Drain and set out on a plate to cool. When the chicken is cool enough to handle, remove and discard the skin and bones. Shred the meat by hand and spread over the noodles.

3.   Mix the sesame seed paste with the remaining 2 tablespoons of sesame seed oil and the gingerroot, garlic, Szechuan peppercorns, vinegar, chili oil, soy sauce, and sugar. Blend into a smooth thin paste. Pour the paste over the noodles. Reserve 2 tablespoons of scallions and 1 tablespoon of sesame seeds, if using, and sprinkle the remainder over the noodles. Toss together well. I find the best way to get the ingredients evenly mixed is to use my hands. Sprinkle the reserved scallions and sesame seeds, if using, over the top of the noodles and serve. (Or cover and refrigerate until ready to use. Bring back to room temperature and serve decorated with sprigs of parsley or cilantro.)

壽

Dan Dan Noodles

飯 麵 饅 頭

Serve 6 to 8

D an Dan Noodles are Szechuan street food at its most traditional. Dan dan *refers to the thumping sound made by the pails of noodles and sauce at the ends of bamboo panniers as they are carried through the streets in a sort of traveling fast food restaurant.*

The noodles are served cold or tepid. Once assembled, the dish holds well, although the noodles absorb the sauce after an hour. If you like saucier noodles, dress them just before serving. I sometimes add blanched and shredded snow peas or blanched bean sprouts along with the scallions for texture.

1 pound thin spaghetti

2 tablespoons sesame seed oil

¾ cup creamy peanut butter

¾ cup Chinese Chicken Broth (page 64) or canned chicken broth

2 tablespoons light soy sauce

2 teaspoons chili oil, or to taste

¼ teaspoon cayenne, or to taste

1 heaping teaspoon Szechuan peppercorns, toasted and ground

3 scallions, white and green parts, thinly sliced

1.   Bring 4 to 5 quarts of water to a boil in a large pot. Add the noodles and cook uncovered, until a little more tender than al dente. Avoid overcooking, or the noodles will be mushy. Stir occasionally to keep the noodles from sticking together. When done, drain and rinse with cold water until thoroughly cool. Drain well, transfer to a large serving bowl, and gently toss with 1 tablespoon of the sesame seed oil (hands work best). Set aside.

2.   While the noodles are cooking, blend the peanut butter and broth together in a bowl until smooth and creamy. Add the soy sauce, chili oil, the remaining 1 tablespoon of sesame seed oil, the cayenne, and Szechuan peppercorns and mix thoroughly. If you have the time, let the sauce sit for 30 minutes or more to allow the spices to develop.

3.   Pour the peanut paste over the cooked noodles and add the scallions. I use my hands to toss the noodles because they mix the ingredients more evenly and the noodles don't break. Serve cool.

Rice,

Noodles,

and Bread

Variation   For a vegetable garnish, blanch snow peas and bean sprouts in the boiling water that will be used to cook the noodles. For snow peas, snap off both ends and string ¼ pound of snow peas. Blanch for 10 to 15 seconds. Remove with a wire skimmer and rinse in cold water to refresh and drain. Cut on the diagonal into shreds. For bean sprouts, blanch 2 cups of bean sprouts in boiling water for 15 seconds. Remove with a wire skimmer and rinse in cold water. Drain well. Add the vegetables to the noodles with the scallions in step 3.

福

Chicken Soup with Noodles

Serves 3 to 4

N oodles are most popular in the wheat-growing north of China, but all Chinese enjoy a steaming bowl of noodles as a light meal or midnight snack. In Asia, noodle shops or noodle vendors with their carts are everywhere.

禄

½ pound Chinese dried noodles, thin spaghetti, or vermicelli

4 cups Chinese Chicken Broth (page 64) plus 1 teaspoon salt or

    1 (13¾-ounce) can chicken broth and enough water to make 4 cups

2 slices unpeeled gingerroot, 1 × ⅛ inch each

½ teaspoon salt, or to taste

⅛ teaspoon ground white pepper

1 pound skinless boneless chicken breast, shredded (page 44)

½ teaspoon cornstarch

1 teaspoon dry sherry

4 cups spinach, watercress, or napa cabbage, washed and cut into 2-inch pieces

Sesame seed oil, for garnish

1. Bring 3 quarts of water to a boil in a large pot. Add the noodles and cook until a little more tender than al dente but not mushy. Stir occasionally to keep the noodles from sticking together. When done, drain, rinse thoroughly with cold water, and drain well. Set aside.

2. While the noodles are cooking, mix the chicken broth, gingerroot, salt, and pepper together in a saucepan and heat to boiling.

3. Mix the chicken, cornstarch, and sherry together in a bowl. When the broth is boiling, add the chicken mixture, stirring constantly until the chicken shreds are separated and white, about 1 minute. Stir in the greens and cook just until they are wilted. If using napa cabbage, cook for about 2 minutes, or until the white parts are translucent.

4. When ready to serve, reheat the noodles by rinsing in hot water. Drain well and divide among 4 individual bowls. Spoon the hot soup over the noodles and top with pieces of chicken and vegetable. (Or put the noodles in the soup until they are hot, spoon them into the bowls with chicken and vegetables, and pour on the hot broth.) Drizzle ½ teaspoon sesame seed oil into each bowl. Serve hot.

Shredded Pork with Szechuan Vegetable and Noodles in Soup

Serves 3 to 4

I *have found that people who are not adept with chopsticks find soup noodles difficult to eat. The noodles slip off a spoon and a fork won't pick up the soup! Chopsticks and a Chinese porcelain spoon are really the best and most efficient tools for eating soup noodles.*

½ pound Chinese dried noodles or thin spaghetti

½ pound lean pork, shredded, about 1 cup (page 44)

2 teaspoons cornstarch

2 teaspoons dry sherry

2 teaspoons light soy sauce

2 tablespoons canola, corn, or peanut oil

2 slices unpeeled gingerroot, 1 × ⅛ inch each

½ cup shredded Szechuan vegetable, rinsed and drained

4½ cups Chinese Chicken Broth (page 64) plus 1¼ teaspoons salt or
     1 (13¾-ounce) can chicken broth and enough water to make 4½ cups

1 teaspoon sesame seed oil

1. Cook the noodles in a large amount of boiling water until a little more tender than al dente. Stir a few times to prevent sticking. Be careful not to overcook. Drain in a colander and rinse thoroughly in cold water. Set aside.

2. Place the pork in a small bowl. Add the cornstarch, sherry, and soy sauce and stir together until well mixed. Set aside.

3. Pour the oil into a wok or stir-fry pan and place the pan over medium–high heat. Add the gingerroot and stir around the pan until the gingerroot begins to sizzle. Stir up the pork again, pour it into the pan, and cook for 1 minute, stirring constantly. Add the Szechuan vegetable and stir for 1 minute, or until the pork has changed color and is cooked through.

(continued)

4. Add the chicken broth. Bring to a boil and stir in the sesame seed oil. Discard the gingerroot. Taste and adjust the seasoning, adding more salt if desired.

5. When ready to serve, add the cooked noodles and let the soup return to a boil. Remove from the heat and divide noodles, soup, pork, and vegetable among individual bowls. Serve immediately.

禧

Variation Add 2 cups shredded Chinese cabbage (celery cabbage, bok choy, or napa) when adding the Szechuan vegetable in step 3. Stir until cabbage is wilted. Add the chicken broth and proceed as directed.

Snow Cabbage and Shredded Chicken Soup with Noodles

Serves 3 to 4

*T*he leafy greens and stems of the snow cabbage (page 25) are chopped and pickled in brine for a handy ingredient. It is especially popular in the provinces of Zhejiang and Jiangsu. My father was from the former and my mother grew up in the latter, so it's no wonder that cans of snow cabbage were always kept in the pantry.

  You may substitute shredded lean pork for the chicken as well as rice sticks for the wheat noodles.

½ pound Chinese dried noodles, thin spaghetti, or vermicelli
¼ pound chicken breast, shredded (page 44)
1 teaspoon dry sherry
1 teaspoon cornstarch
1 tablespoon canola, corn, or peanut oil
1 slice unpeeled gingerroot, 1 × ⅛ inch
½ cup canned shredded bamboo shoots, drained
½ cup snow cabbage, drained
4½ cups Chinese Chicken Broth (page 64) plus 1¼ teaspoons salt or
    1 (13¾-ounce) can chicken broth and enough water to make 4½ cups

    1. Bring 3 quarts of water to a boil in a large pot. Add the noodles and cook until a little more tender than al dente, but not soft. Stir occasionally to keep the noodles from sticking together. When done, drain, rinse thoroughly with cold water, and drain well. Set aside.

    2. While the noodles are cooking, mix the chicken with the sherry and cornstarch in a small bowl. Set aside.

    3. Pour the oil into a wok or stir-fry pan and place the pan over medium-high heat. Add the gingerroot and stir until it sizzles and becomes fragrant. Stir up the chicken mixture again. Add and cook for about 1 minute, or until the meat has turned white. Add the bamboo shoots and snow cabbage, stir about 30 seconds, and pour in the chicken broth. Bring the liquid to a boil. Taste and add salt if desired.

    4. When ready to serve, add the noodles to the boiling soup and cook just until they are heated through. Divide the noodles evenly among individual soup bowls. Ladle the soup with pieces of meat and vegetable into each bowl. There should be enough soup to come up to the level of the noodles, but not submerge them. Serve hot.

福

Variation Substitute shredded lean pork for the chicken as well as thin dried rice noodles—also called rice sticks—for the wheat noodles. Soak the rice sticks in warm water until they are tender, then add them to the boiling broth in step 3 and heat through.

Rice,

Noodles,

and Bread

Mandarin Pancakes

飯麵饅頭

Makes twelve 7-inch pancakes

Mandarin pancakes, called bao bing *in Chinese, one of the most popular foods in Pe-king, are the traditional accompaniment to Moo Shi Pork (page 192) and Peking Duck. It takes a fair amount of handwork to make Mandarin pancakes, but we used to make them by hand in our restaurant all the time. Once a week the entire kitchen crew—chefs, sous chefs, choppers, everyone—would congregate and roll out Manda-rin pancakes on an assembly line. The dough was made in a huge commercial mixer, but the pancakes were formed one by one. It took all afternoon to make enough to last the week. The way to get them so thin is to roll two pancakes together. They come apart easily after being cooked because the sesame seed oil keeps them from fusing together. I would help separate the hot pancakes as they came off the griddle. The secret is to slap them between your hands, as if applauding, then find a loose spot and pull the pancakes apart with your fingers. After a while I had to exchange duties with the people rolling the pancakes because my fingers would get so hot!*

With the high cost of labor and advent of pancake-making machines, restaurants eventually turned to frozen machinemade pancakes from Chinatown. The packaged pancakes are very thin and quite excellent, but nothing will take the place of the memory of the sight, smell, and sound of everyone working together in the kitchen to make Mandarin pancakes.

禄

1¾ cups unbleached all purpose flour
¾ cup boiling water
1 teaspoon sesame seed oil

1. Mix the flour and boiling water in a bowl with a wooden spoon or chopsticks. As soon as your hands can tolerate the heat, knead the hot dough together until smooth. Knead for 3 minutes, then cover the dough with a damp towel and set aside for at least 30 minutes. The Chinese say this "wakes" the dough.

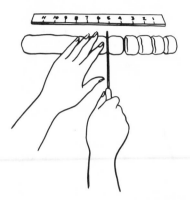

2.   Roll the dough on a lightly floured board under the palms of your hands into a rope exactly 12 inches long. Using a ruler as a guide, cut the rope into 1-inch pieces.

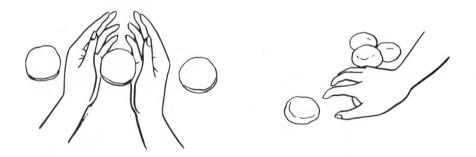

3.   Turn a piece of dough on end and roll it between the palms of your hands into a cylinder. Flatten the cylinder with the palm of your hand into a circle. Continue until all are done.

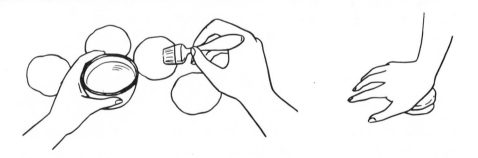

4.   Brush 1 side of each cake lightly with the sesame seed oil. Place 1 cake on top of another, oiled sides together, and flatten the 2 cakes out with the heel of your hand, pressing evenly to keep the pancakes from sliding apart.

(continued)

Rice,

Noodles,

and Bread

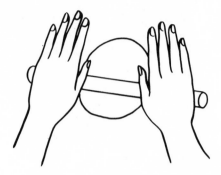

5.　With a rolling pin, roll the pairs of cakes to about 7 inches in diameter. Roll lightly and evenly to maintain a uniform thickness and even diameter of both pancakes. Rotate and turn over the pair of pancakes frequently, checking that the edges don't get too thick and the center doesn't get too thin. This will take some practice. Cover the pancakes with a dry cloth to keep them from drying out.

6.　Fry each pair of pancakes in an ungreased heavy-bottomed skillet or on a griddle over medium-low heat until light brown spots appear, less than 1 minute. Turn over to brown the other side for about 30 seconds. Check the heat frequently to be sure it doesn't get too high or too low. Be careful not to overcook the pancakes or they will become brittle and crack.

7.　Remove the pancakes and slap them a couple of times between your hands. This cools them a bit and forces any air bubbles out, creating an opening from which you can pull the pancakes apart. Pull them apart gently and slowly as soon as they are cooked. Once they cool, it's difficult to separate them without tearing. Pile the separated pancakes with the exposed side up. Keep them covered with a dry cloth to keep the edges from drying.

8.　Just before serving, reheat by steaming for 10 minutes, being careful that they don't touch the water. (Or reheat the Chinese home-style way: Place the pancakes on aluminum foil over simmering rice. The steam from the rice provides enough heat to warm the pancakes and the foil keeps them from sticking to the rice.) Serve the pancakes in a covered dish.

壽

Note　For longer storage, stack the cooked pancakes in a plastic bag, seal securely, and refrigerate or freeze. When ready to reheat, thaw the pancakes and steam.

Variation　If you are planning to serve the pancakes with Peking Duck, make them smaller. Instead of one 12-inch rope, make two 12-inch ropes. You will have 2 dozen 5-inch pancakes.

Eating Mandarin Pancakes

People often seem to have trouble eating Mandarin Pancakes, but it's really very simple. Spread a pancake on a *clean* plate — it's very important that the outside remain dry. With a scallion brush, brush the pancake down the middle with a little Hoisin Sauce Dip (page 326), if desired. Put 2 to 3 tablespoons of Moo Shi Pork or 2 pieces of Peking Duck skin in the center. (The scallion brush is usually placed in the pancake with the meat.) Be careful not to overfill, or you won't be able to pick it up after rolling. Roll the pancake up, cigar style.

Place the roll in your left hand, supporting the ends with your thumb and little finger. Keep the little finger slightly raised and pressed against your ring finger to form a seal to prevent gravy or oil from dripping. Even so, it's best to eat over your plate since no matter how expert you are, gravy sometimes ends up dripping on your lap.

Chinese Steamed Bread
Man Tou

Makes twelve 3-inch buns, serves 4 to 6 when not serving rice

*T*here are many different types of bread in China, and because Chinese homes traditionally do not have ovens, the breads are steamed instead of baked. Some are plain, others are stuffed with sweet or savory fillings, but almost all use the same basic yeast dough. In the north of China, plain, unfilled bread, called man tou, is served in place of rice. My mother particularly liked to make plain steamed buns to serve with red-cooked dishes notably, Shanghai duck (page 187) and Shanghai Red-cooked Ham (page 217). The buns are great for soaking up the rich soy sauce gravy.

Because the bread is steamed, there is no crust and no browning; the bread is totally white. The Chinese in general prefer snowy white steamed breads and do not use whole wheat or any whole grain flour. In fact, when I was testing various types of flour for this recipe, my Chinese friends definitely preferred the whiter buns made from bleached flour even though the taste and texture of the unbleached flour buns were the same.

Man tou are easy to make at home, where they are formed in simple shapes. Because my mother was born in Beijing (Peking) and grew up in Shanghai, she made the buns round, which my Number One Aunt from Shanghai tells me is typical in that region. The Fujian chefs in our Cambridge restaurant like their steamed bread in a larger oblong loaf. You can do either, although I think the round shape is more delicate and attractive at the table.

2 tablespoons sugar

1 teaspoon active dry yeast

1 cup plus 3 tablespoons warm water (105°F. to 110°F.)

3½ cups all-purpose flour plus additional for kneading (1 pound)

1½ teaspoons canola, corn, or peanut oil

1 teaspoon baking powder

1. Dissolve the sugar and yeast in the water in a measuring cup or small bowl. Place in a warm, draftfree place for about 10 minutes, or until it develops a head of foam.

2. To make the dough in a food processor, place the flour in the work-bowl fitted with the steel blade. With the machine running, pour in the yeast solution in a thin stream. Be sure to scrape in all the foam too. Process for about 15 seconds, or until a rough ball forms. If the dough appears very dry and does not form a ball, stop the machine and look. Sometimes the dough just needs a few more seconds. If you are sure the dough is too dry, add small amounts of warm water (¼ teaspoon or less at a time) until a rough ball forms. Transfer the dough to a lightly floured surface.

3. To make the dough by hand, place the flour in a large mixing bowl and add the yeast solution. Stir until it forms a coarse, lumpy dough. Use additional warm water, a little at a time, if the dough appears too dry. Turn the dough onto a lightly floured surface.

4. Knead for 5 to 7 minutes, or until the dough is smooth, firm, and elastic. After the first minute of kneading, the dough should not stick to either your hands or the work surface. If it is sticky, knead in more flour, a little at a time. Form the dough into a ball.

5. With a paper towel, spread ½ teaspoon of the oil in a bowl large enough to hold 3 times the bulk of the dough. Turn the dough around in the bowl a few times to cover it with a light film of oil. Cover the bowl tightly with plastic wrap and place in a warm, draft-free place to rise to double its volume. This will take from 1 to 2 hours.

6. While the dough is rising, cut out 12 pieces of wax paper or parchment, 3½ inches square for individual rolls. For loaves, cut out 8 pieces 5 × 3 inches. Pour the remaining 1 teaspoon of oil into a small dish. Set aside.

7. After the first rise, punch down the dough. Cover the dough and allow it to rise a second time to double its volume (30 minutes to 1 hour). Punch it down again. (The second rise is not necessary, but I have found that it seems to provide a smoother, finer texture.) If you are unable to proceed with the dough right away, you may refrigerate it at this point or after the first rise.

8. Sprinkle the baking powder over the work surface and knead the dough for 5 minutes, or until all the baking powder is well incorporated. Lightly flour the surface if necessary to keep the dough from sticking.

9. Roll the dough into a 12-inch-long rope. For Shanghai-style buns, cut the dough into 1-inch pieces, using a ruler as a guide. Pull each piece away as you cut it or the pieces will stick together. Roll each piece of dough into a ball. Using your fingertips, lightly oil one of the papers with oil and place a bun in the center. (For loaf-shaped buns, cut 1½-inch pieces of dough and place on the oiled paper without reshaping.)

(continued)

Rice,

Noodles,

and Bread

10.   Place all the buns on a baking sheet or on the work surface and cover with a dry cloth. Allow the buns to rest in a draft-free place for 15 to 20 minutes, or until the dough slowly springs back when lightly pressed with a finger. The buns will not double in bulk but will be about 50 percent larger.

11.   Prepare the steamer and have water boiling over high heat (page 52). Place the buns, with the paper liners, on each tier, leaving at least 1 inch between and above each bun to allow for expansion. (If you have only 1 tier or a small steamer, steam the buns in batches.) Stack the tiers over the boiling water, cover, and steam over high enough heat to maintain a steady stream of steam. If you are using a metal steamer, wrap the lid with a dish towel to prevent condensation from dripping on the buns and disfiguring them. Steam for 15 minutes, or until the buns are puffed up. Have boiling water in a kettle on hand to replenish the water in the steamer as necessary.

12.   When the buns are ready, turn off the heat and allow them to sit in the covered steamer for a few seconds to avoid a sudden temperature change, which would wrinkle the surface. To serve, remove the buns to a plate or serve directly from the steamer. For casual family meals, leave the paper on the buns; for dinner parties, remove the paper before serving. To eat, bite or break off a section of the bun and eat it like rice between bites of braised or deep-fried meats or use it to soak up gravies, sauces, and soups.

健康

Note   Don't bring all the steamed buns to the table at once, especially if it is a cold day or the air-conditioner is on. Keep them warm in the steamer. You can also refresh the buns or reheat ones that were made earlier in the day by steaming them for a few minutes before serving.

Extra buns may be cooled and packed in a plastic bag. Tightly sealed, they will keep well in the refrigerator for about 1 week to 10 days or in the freezer for a couple of months. Reheat for 10 minutes in a steamer just the way they were cooked. Frozen buns may be placed directly in the steamer without defrosting; they will need 15 minutes of steaming to heat through.

Leftover buns are also delicious as a breakfast bread or snack in a typical family-style way my mother often used. Slice a cold bun ⅝ inch thick and pan-fry in ½ inch of hot oil, turning so that both sides are browned and crisp while the inside remains soft and white. Sprinkle with light brown sugar. Or toast the slices and sprinkle lightly with a thin covering of brown sugar. I like these so much that I purposely make extra *man tou* so I'll definitely have some left over.

Seafood 海鮮

Most Chinese meals have at least one seafood dish and no banquet is complete without a whole fish. The Chinese love of seafood and the special care and skill they give to its final presentation have made them experts at seafood preparation.

When it comes to fresh seafood, the Chinese are fanatics. If it's not alive, it's not fresh. In almost every restaurant in Hong Kong and Taiwan, there are aquariums with all kinds of fish and shrimp swimming around. Even land-locked areas of China have fish farms where freshwater fish are raised.

Once my husband, Keith, and I were in a Hong Kong seafood restaurant sitting next to an open tank holding live eels. Suddenly one large eel got out of the tank and squirmed under our table. We leapt up and watched with horror as this snakelike creature slithered around. No one else in the restaurant seemed the least bit upset. Then a cook appeared with a net, scooped up the eel, dropped it unceremoniously back into the tank, covered the tank with a screen, and walked back to the kitchen. We sat back down and ordered our meal as though nothing out of the ordinary had happened.

Goldfish or fancy colored carp, known as *koi* in Japan, are kept for decoration and good luck, not for eating. Many businesses have a large fish tank as part of the office decor for good luck. The Chinese word for fish is *yu,* which is a homonym for abundance. So whenever there is fish, on the dining table or in a tank, it symbolizes prosperity and having more than one needs. Certainly an important notion in a country where food was scarce and famine common.

Some larger Chinatown markets carry live freshwater fish in tanks. Other fish are usually displayed whole on a bed of ice, to be cleaned and filleted if you wish. To give you an idea of the variety of seafood the Chinese have at their disposal, I listed the number of different seafood I found on one day in a Boston Chinatown market. Eight varieties of live freshwater fish were swimming in tanks. Sitting on ice were butterfish, smelts, whiting, pomfret, grouper, squid, yellow croaker, hybrid striped bass, sea bass, bigmouth bass, scup (porgie), belt fish, gray sole, white perch, bighead carp, buffalo carp, grass carp, tilapia. Wiggling about in baskets were live blue crab and rock crab. Now that's quite a choice!

To get the best seafood, you should go to a market specializing in seafood if you can. The quality will be higher, and many fishmongers will order whole fish or a particular kind for you if you let them know in advance. The Chinese almost always buy a whole fish, unless of course the fish is so large that they have to buy portions of it. If you are buying a whole fish look for clear, smooth eyes, not sunken or cloudy; bright red gills; firm, smooth flesh without a trace of sliminess; and a fresh smell without a hint of fishiness. If you are buying fillets, use the last two tests.

Crustaceans and mollusks must be live. No Chinese will buy a dead lobster, crab, or clam. In the Far East all the shrimp are alive and swimming about seconds before they are cooked and brought to the table. A specialty in Hong Kong is freshly steamed shrimp with the heads still on. A dramatic dish in the Far East is something called Drunken Shrimp. Live jumbo shrimp are brought to the table in a clear heatproof bowl. The maitre d' pours in a vodkalike liquor, inebriating and flavoring the shrimp and flambés them, tossing them in the flames until they're cooked. The taste is incredible.

Dried seafood is commonly available in Chinese markets and sometimes, as in the case of dried scallops, they command a very high price. Since there is no refrigeration, salting, drying, and curing are ways to preserve seafood. Fish, shrimp, scallops, oysters, and squid are used in both the fresh and dried forms. Although the preference is always for fresh, the Chinese would rather use good dried seafood than seafood that is not fresh. Many recipes in this book use dried shrimp as a flavoring.

Steamed Whole Fish, Cantonese Style

Serves 2 to 3, or 4 to 6 as part of a multicourse meal

A whole fish, with head, tail, and fins intact, is a symbol of prosperity and good luck. The Chinese word for fish is a homonym for the word abundance, and whole fish is always served on special occasions like the lunar New Year, birthdays, and weddings. The eyes and cheeks are particularly prized, and these are saved for the guest of honor or the eldest at the table.

Since the fish is cooked with the skin on, I always scale the fish again even if it has been scaled at the market to make certain the skin is smooth and scaleless.

If you can't get flounder, substitute sea bass, striped bass, rock cod, trout, or red snapper.

健康

1 to 1½ pounds whole flounder, cleaned and scaled
½ teaspoon salt
1 teaspoon dry sherry
2 tablespoons light soy sauce
2 scallions, shredded
2 tablespoons finely shredded peeled gingerroot (page 45)
Dash white pepper
1½ tablespoons canola, corn, or peanut oil
1 teaspoon sesame seed oil
3 tablespoons coarsely chopped cilantro

1. Rinse the fish, inside and out, and pat dry. It is not necessary to score flatfish like flounder, but if the fish you are using is thick, score both sides with long, parallel cuts almost to the bone. Scoring allows the flavors to penetrate and the fish to cook evenly. Place the fish dark skin up on a heatproof plate or platter and sprinkle with salt, sherry, and soy sauce. Scatter the scallions and gingerroot on top.

2. Bring water in a steamer to a full boil and place the plate with the fish in the steamer. Cover and cook over medium-high heat for 10 to 15

(continued)

Seafood

minutes, or until the flesh at the thickest part is white. Be careful not to overcook. Remove the fish from the steamer, being careful not to spill the juices from the platter. Sprinkle pepper over the fish.

3.   Heat the cooking oil and sesame seed oil in a small saucepan until just smoking. Pour the hot oil over the fish and garnish with cilantro. Serve immediately.

福

Note   Restaurants use huge steamers that hold a number of dishes all at once, including a whole fish on an oval platter. I use a 12-inch steamer and put the flounder on a 9-inch glass pie plate. The head and tail extend a bit over the edges, but most of the fish is in the dish. After steaming, I carefully slip the fish with all of its juices onto a 14-inch porcelain oval platter for presentation. This works with flounder because it is more round than long. If your fish is too long for your steamer, cut it in half and reassemble it on an oval platter before finishing it with the hot oil.

West Lake Fish

Serves 3 to 4, or 6 to 8 as part of a multicourse meal

My father was born in Hangzhou (Hangchow), a small town on the outskirts of Shanghai. It is a famous place, not only for the scenic beauty of its mountains and the West Lake but also for its food. The Chen family tomb is still in Hangzhou and is tended by my late fifth aunt's son. It is a Chinese tradition for children to say they are from the place where their father was born rather than where they were actually born. And so although I have never lived in Hangzhou, I feel a special bond to my father's home.

The first time we went to Hangzhou, in 1972, we traveled with my sixth aunt on my father's side and two first cousins. One of the first things my mother did was to take us to one of those big restaurants by West Lake to have West Lake Fish. She had often told us how a chef's helper would bring the fish to the table and slam it on the floor to kill it in front of you so you would know it was fresh. Fortunately, they no longer did this, but the fish was delicious and even more so with the view of West Lake in front of us.

After our fish lunch we spent the rest of the day walking on trails in the mountains, stopping at teahouses to drink Hangzhou's celebrated Dragon Well green tea

brewed with mountain spring water from the famous Tiger Run spring. We had
bowls of hot sweet soup made with the starch of lotus root gathered from West Lake
and flavored with chestnut bits and flowers from the sweet olive tree (Osmanthus
fragrans), which grows in abundance there.

My mother wrote this recipe in honor of my father's birthplace. Note that the
fish is soaked in boiled — not boiling — water. That way it cooks gently and does
not dry out. You need a fine-textured freshwater fish for this recipe. That was never a
problem for us because my father loved to fish. He would bring the fish home live,
and we would keep it in the extra bathtub until ready to cook it.

禄

1 freshwater bigmouth or smallmouth bass, cleaned and scaled (1½ to 2 pounds)
    (If unavailable, use any firm, white-fleshed fish such as striped bass, cod, or
    red snapper.)
1 tablespoon dry sherry
5 slices unpeeled gingerroot, 1 × ⅛ inch each
½ cup sugar
⅓ cup cider vinegar
1 tablespoon light soy sauce
1 garlic clove, crushed and peeled
2 tablespoons cornstarch

1.   Rinse the fish in cold water and drain. Make 3 slashes, crosswise, on
the meatiest part of each side of the fish for even cooking.

2.   Bring water to a boil in a fish poacher or oval roaster large enough
to submerge the whole fish. Slide the whole fish into the boiling water and
add the sherry and 3 of the gingerroot slices. Cover the pan tightly and immediately remove from the heat. Let the fish soak in the hot water for 15 to
20 minutes, or until cooked through.

3.   While the fish is soaking, chop up the remaining 2 slices of gingerroot and put it into a garlic press and squeeze to extract the juices. You should
have about ¼ teaspoon. Mix the gingerroot juices with the sugar, vinegar, soy
sauce, garlic, and cornstarch in a small saucepan. Heat the mixture over medium heat and stir constantly until it thickens. Discard the garlic.

4.   Remove the fish from the roaster with a big spatula and flat plate
held underneath. Drain off the water carefully. Place the fish on a large oval
serving platter and pour the sauce over it. Serve immediately.

Soy Sauce Fish,
Shanghai Style

Serves 2 to 3, or 4 to 6 as part of a
multicourse meal

I've known Anna Ku Lau since kindergarten, longer than any other friend. Anna and her family are originally from Wu Xi, near Shanghai, where sweet soy-sauce dishes, known as "red-cooked," are popular. She told me that her favorite recipe from my mother's cookbook is this one.

In winter, especially around the lunar New Year, Soy Sauce Fish is cooked in large quantities and served cold as a side dish or with drinks. Sometimes instead of a whole fish, a large fish head is cooked; this is considered a real delicacy.

壽

1 whole fish, such as sea bass, perch, or scup, cleaned and scaled (1¼ to 1½
     pounds)
¼ teaspoon salt
6 scallions, roots trimmed and cut in half
⅓ cup canned sliced bamboo shoots, drained
⅓ cup dried black mushrooms, softened in hot water for 15 minutes, stems
     removed and caps sliced
1 tablespoon dry sherry
¼ cup plus 1 tablespoon dark soy sauce
2 tablespoons light brown sugar
½ cup canola, corn, or peanut oil
2 slices unpeeled gingerroot, 1 × ⅛ inch each

1.   Rinse the fish in cold water and dry both inside and out with paper towels. Make 3 equal diagonal cuts on each side for even cooking. If the fish is too large to fit into your pan, cut it in half. Sprinkle both sides with ¼ teaspoon of the salt. Let stand for 10 minutes.

2.   Combine the scallions, bamboo shoots, and mushrooms in a bowl. Set aside. In another small bowl, mix together the sherry, soy sauce, sugar, and ¾ cup water. Set aside.

3.   Pour the oil into a large wok over high heat. Add the gingerroot and stir around the pan until the oil is hot; the gingerroot will sizzle.

Seafood

130

4.　Slide the fish into the hot oil head first and fry over medium-high heat on 1 side for 3 or 4 minutes, or until golden brown. Cover the wok to keep the oil from spattering. When the first side is golden brown, remove the pan from the heat. Loosen the fish with a spatula and turn it over. Add the scallions, bamboo shoots, and mushrooms. Return the pan to the heat. Cook about 3 minutes or until the second side is lightly browned.

5.　When the fish is golden brown on both sides, remove from the heat. Pour off or ladle out the excess oil. Add the soy sauce mixture, cover, and bring to a boil. Boil slowly over low heat for 3 minutes, remove the lid, and raise the heat to medium-high. Baste the fish until a little more than ½ cup of the liquid remains. Transfer the fish and liquid to a platter. Serve hot or cold.

禧

Note　If you have cut the fish in half, reassemble the pieces on the serving platter and use the vegetables to cover the division.

Steamed Fish Fillets

Serves 2 to 3, or 4 to 6 as part of a
multicourse meal

*T*he Chinese are experts with seafood, and steaming is a favorite way to cook fish. It is fast and retains the natural flavor of fresh fish. The natural juices are nutritious and very good over rice. My mother always steamed whole fish, but I often use fresh fillets for convenience.

1 pound whitefish fillets, such as haddock, flounder, or bass, skin removed

½ scant teaspoon salt, or less to taste

3 medium dried black mushrooms, softened in hot water for 15 minutes

1 teaspoon dry sherry

1 tablespoon light soy sauce

⅓ cup shredded bamboo shoots

2 ounces Smithfield ham, shredded

1 scallion, white and green parts cut into 2-inch pieces, and finely shredded

1 teaspoon finely shredded peeled gingerroot

1.   Place the fish fillets on a heatproof platter with a rim or pie plate that will fit into your steamer. Sprinkle both sides with salt. Let stand for 10 minutes.

2.   Drain the mushrooms, rinse and squeeze dry. Cut off and discard the stems and shred the caps. Set aside.

3.   Sprinkle the sherry and soy sauce on the fish, then spread the mushrooms, bamboo shoots, ham, scallion, and gingerroot evenly over the fish.

4.   Bring the water in the steamer to a fast boil. Place the plate with the fish in the steamer. Cover and steam over medium-high heat for 6 to 8 minutes for flounder and 10 to 12 minutes for thicker fish, or until the flesh is white all the way through. Do not overcook. Check the fish at the thickest part after the shorter cooking time. If the flesh is not white, then cook another 2 minutes. If the uncooked area is very small, turn off the heat and keep the steamer covered. The remaining steam in the steamer will finish cooking the fish by serving time.

5. As soon as the fish is ready, it should be served without delay. Serve directly from the steaming dish, or transfer to a serving platter with the juices.

福

Variation In the traditional Chinese manner a whole fish may be cooked the same way; a 1½- to 2-pound sea bass, striped bass, flounder, red snapper, rock cod, or perch are good choices. Scale and clean the fish thoroughly. Rinse and score both sides of the fish, if thick on the diagonal, with long parallel cuts almost to the bone. This allows flavors to penetrate fish and cook more evenly. If the fish is too long for your steamer, you may have to cut it in half. Then follow the procedure above. Cook a whole fish for about 10 to 15 minutes.

禄

Steamed Salmon
with Black Beans

Serves 2 to 3, or 4 to 5 as part of a
multicourse meal

The deep ebony of black beans against the coral of the salmon makes this a very beautiful dish. The steaming time is very fast, so plan accordingly. The salmon should be served straight from the steamer to the table, at the peak of perfection. You can prepare bass or flounder fillets the same way.

1 pound salmon fillet or steaks

3 teaspoons dry sherry

1 teaspoon grated peeled gingerroot

¼ teaspoon salt

1 garlic clove, pureed

2 tablespoons thinly sliced scallions

1 tablespoon fermented black beans, coarsely chopped

1 teaspoon sesame seed oil

Cilantro or parsley sprigs, for garnish

1. Place the fish in a heatproof dish at least 1 inch deep, such as a glass pie plate. Stir together the sherry, gingerroot, salt, and garlic in a small bowl. Pour this mixture onto the fish and rub generously on both sides. Let stand for at least 15 minutes.

2. If you are using a fillet, turn it skin side down. Spread the scallions and black beans evenly on top. Drizzle with sesame seed oil.

3. Bring the water in the steamer to a vigorous boil. Place the pie plate on the steamer tray and cover. Steam for about 10 minutes, checking for doneness at about 8 minutes. The fish will look opaque and feel springy to the touch. It is better to slightly undercook than overcook since the heat in the fish itself will finish the cooking for you.

4. Serve directly from the steaming dish or transfer to a warm platter with the juices.

Kan Shao Scallops

Serves 3 to 4, or 5 to 6 as part of a multicourse meal

*T*he Szechuan kan shao *or dry-cooked method intensifies the natural flavor of scallops. You can use either bay scallops or sea scallops; if you use bay scallops, reduce the cooking time.*

禧

1 pound sea scallops

1 tablespoon minced peeled gingerroot

1 tablespoon dry sherry

⅓ cup fermented black beans, coarsely chopped

2 garlic cloves, minced

1 tablespoon crushed red pepper, or to taste

3 tablespoons canola, corn, or peanut oil

3 tablespoons dark soy sauce

1 teaspoon sugar

1. Rinse the scallops quickly and cut in half horizontally if they are very large. Drain thoroughly and pull off the tough outer muscle. Place the scallops in a bowl, add the gingerroot and sherry, and stir to mix. Set aside.

2. Combine the black beans, garlic, and red pepper in a small dish. Pour the oil into a wok or stir-fry pan and place over medium-high heat. Add the black bean mixture to the oil and stir until the oil is hot and the spices fragrant; they will begin to sizzle. Don't let the garlic burn or it will become bitter.

3. Add the scallops to the pan and stir-fry until they turn opaque, about 1 to 2 minutes. Add the soy sauce and sugar and stir for another 30 seconds to 1 minute, or until thoroughly cooked. All the liquid will have evaporated. Serve hot.

Stir-fried Fish
with Vegetables

**Serves 4, or 6 as part of a
multicourse meal**

*U*se a firm whitefish for stir-frying and stir gently to avoid breaking up the pieces.

健康

1 cup dried black mushrooms, softened in hot water for 15 minutes

2 ounces snow peas (about 1 cup)

1 pound firm whitefish fillets, such as cod, haddock, mahimahi, carp, hake, or
     pollack

2 teaspoons dry sherry

¼ teaspoon grated peeled gingerroot

½ to 1 teaspoon salt, or to taste

5 tablespoons canola, corn, or peanut oil

2 slices unpeeled gingerroot, 1 × ⅛ inch each

1 garlic clove, crushed and peeled

½ pound napa or Chinese celery cabbage, quartered lengthwise, cored and cut
     into 1½-inch chunks

½ cup Chinese Chicken Broth (page 64) or canned chicken broth

1 (8-ounce) can sliced bamboo shoots, drained (1 cup)

2 teaspoons cornstarch, dissolved in 1 tablespoon water

1. Drain the mushrooms, rinse, and squeeze dry. Cut off the stems with
scissors and discard. Slice the caps in halves or quarters so the pieces are fairly
uniform in size. Set aside.

2. Rinse the snow peas and snap and string both ends. Cut the larger
snow peas in half on the diagonal so the peas are of fairly uniform size. Set
aside.

3. Cut the fish into 2-inch square pieces and place in a bowl. Add the
sherry, grated gingerroot, and ½ teaspoon of the salt. Mix together well.

4. Pour 3 tablespoons of the oil into a wok or stir-fry pan and heat
over high heat until the oil is hot but not smoking. Test by dipping the tip of
a spatula into the fish mixture and then into the pan; it should sizzle. Stir up

the fish again and add to the hot oil. Stir gently for about 30 seconds, or until the fish is partially done. Remove to a platter.

5. Add the remaining 2 tablespoons of oil to the same pan and add the gingerroot slices, garlic, and remaining ½ teaspoon of salt if using homemade broth. Stir around the pan until they sizzle. Add the cabbage and broth, stir, and cook, covered, for about 1 minute. Remove the lid and add the mushrooms, snow peas, and bamboo shoots. Stir-fry until the snow peas turn bright green.

6. Return the fish to the pan and stir gently. Add the cornstarch slurry and stir until the sauce thickens. Taste and add salt, if needed. Discard the gingerroot and garlic, if desired. Serve immediately.

Sea Scallops
with Snow Peas

Serves 3 to 4, or 5 to 6 as part of a
multicourse meal

*F*ermented black beans give a rich yet not overpowering flavor to this delicate scallop *dish, which is perfect for a dinner party. The snow peas lend a colorful and crunchy contrast.*

福

1 pound sea scallops

1 teaspoon sherry

1 teaspoon cornstarch

½ pound snow peas

1 (8-ounce) can sliced water chestnuts, drained (1 cup)

4 tablespoons fermented black beans, coarsely chopped

2 teaspoons light soy sauce

1 teaspoon sugar

3 tablespoons canola, corn, or peanut oil

1 garlic clove, thinly sliced

2 slices unpeeled gingerroot, 1 × ⅛ inch each

2 to 3 tablespoons broth or water (optional)

(continued)   *Seafood*

1. Rinse and drain the scallops. Remove the crescent-shaped muscle and discard. Cut larger pieces in half horizontally so all the scallops are about the same size. Place the scallops in a bowl, stir in the sherry and cornstarch, and mix well. Set aside.

2. Snap and string both ends of the snow peas. If desired, cut larger ones in half on the diagonal. Rinse and drain. Set aside. Place the black beans in a small bowl and add the soy sauce, sugar, and 2 tablespoons water. Set aside.

3. Pour the oil into a wok or stir-fry pan and place over high heat. Add the garlic and gingerroot and stir around the pan until the oil is hot but not smoking; the garlic and gingerroot will sizzle. Add the scallops and stir briskly for 1 to 1½ minutes, or until the scallops just begin to turn opaque and are partially cooked. Be careful not to overcook at this stage, since the scallops will continue to cook after the vegetables are added.

4. Add the black bean mixture and continue stirring for 15 seconds. Add the water chestnuts and snow peas. Add broth or water for more gravy, if desired. Stir constantly for another minute until the snow peas turn darker green. Discard the gingerroot, if desired, and transfer the scallops to a serving platter. Serve immediately.

Celery and Dried Shrimp Salad

Serves 4 to 5 as part of a
multicourse meal

*D*ried shrimp have a long shelf life and are extremely versatile — my brother Henry especially enjoyed snacking on dried shrimp when he was a teenager. I always have them on hand to use in fried rice or soups or to stir-fry with vegetables. A little goes a long way.

4 cups shredded celery (about 8 stalks) (page 45)
1 cup shredded carrot (about 1 medium) (page 45)
¼ cup dried shrimp
1 tablespoon plus 1 teaspoon light soy sauce
2 tablespoons rice vinegar
1 tablespoon sugar
½ teaspoon grated peeled gingerroot
1 teaspoon sesame seed oil

1.   Blanch the celery and carrots in boiling water for 30 seconds. Drain and refresh under cold water until completely cool. Drain thoroughly and place in a covered bowl in the refrigerator until ready to use.

2.   Place the dried shrimp in a bowl and pour on 1 cup water to soften and to remove the excess salt. Soak for 15 minutes or more. Drain.

3.   When ready to serve, mix the soy sauce with the vinegar, sugar, and gingerroot. Combine the celery, carrots, and shrimp and toss with the soy sauce dressing. Garnish with sesame seed oil. Serve immediately.

Note   Although traditionally the Chinese do not eat raw vegetables, I have prepared this dish very successfully with unblanched carrots and celery.

Sweet and Sour Shrimp

Most restaurant-style sweet and sour shrimp is coated in a thick batter, fried in lots of oil, and served in a cloying sauce — completely unappealing and nothing like my version. The shrimp here are lightly coated in a thin cornstarch paste, shallow-fried, and served in a light tart sauce that does not overwhelm their delicate flavor.

1 pound large shrimp, shelled

1 tablespoon dry sherry

3 tablespoons light soy sauce

5 tablespoons cornstarch

$\frac{1}{2}$ teaspoon salt

1 medium red bell pepper, cored, seeded, and cut into 1-inch cubes

1 medium green bell pepper, cored, seeded, and cut into 1-inch cubes

1 cup canned pineapple chunks, well drained, syrup reserved

1 garlic clove, crushed and peeled

$\frac{1}{3}$ cup cider vinegar

$\frac{1}{3}$ cup plus 1 tablespoon sugar

$\frac{1}{3}$ cup syrup from the canned pineapple

$\frac{1}{4}$ cup ketchup

1 cup plus 1 tablespoon canola, corn, or peanut oil

1.   Cut a slit along the back of the shrimp and pull out and discard the vein. Rinse in cold water and drain thoroughly. Combine the sherry, 1 tablespoon soy sauce, 3 tablespoons cornstarch, and salt in a bowl and stir until you have a smooth paste. Add the shrimp and mix. Let stand for 20 minutes or more.

2.   In the meantime, add the peppers to a small saucepan of boiling water. As soon as it comes to a boil, drain and rinse in cold water to stop cooking. Add the pineapple to the peppers and set aside.

3.   Combine the garlic, vinegar, sugar, syrup, ketchup, 2 tablespoons soy sauce, and 2 tablespoons cornstarch dissolved in $\frac{1}{3}$ cup water in a bowl. Set aside.

4.   Heat 1 cup oil in a wok or stir-fry pan over medium-high heat. When the oil is hot (350°F. to 375°F.), drop half of the shrimp, one at a time, into the pan. Stir and turn the shrimp carefully and slowly with a slotted spoon or wire skimmer. Cook for 2 to 3 minutes, or until the shrimp turns opaque and pink and are lightly crisp along the edges. Transfer to a dish lined with paper towels. Continue with the rest of the shrimp until all are cooked. Keep in a warm oven while you make the sauce.

5.   Pour out the oil in the wok and wipe with paper towels. Pour the sauce mixture into the pan and heat over medium heat, stirring constantly, until the mixture comes to a boil. Stir in the cornstarch slurry and continue stirring until the sauce thickens and becomes translucent. Discard the garlic and stir in 1 tablespoon oil. Add the pineapple chunks, peppers, and shrimp. Give a few big turns with a spatula to coat the shrimp. Transfer to a platter and serve immediately.

Soy Sauce Shrimp in the Shell

Serves 3 to 4, or 5 to 6 as part of a multicourse meal

W hen the Chinese cook shrimp in the shell, they leave the shell on when they serve it because that's where the sauce is. Some people are quite adept at shelling the shrimp in their mouth. My mother was a real artist at this. The shrimp never touched her fingers as she gracefully lifted it to her mouth with chopsticks and after a few barely noticeable swishings, delicately spit the shell into the discard dish.

1 teaspoon dry sherry

1 tablespoon dark soy sauce

1 tablespoon light soy sauce

3 teaspoons brown sugar

1 pound large shrimp in the shell, deveined

1 cup canola, corn, or peanut oil

1 garlic clove, crushed and peeled

1 slice unpeeled gingerroot, 1 × ⅛ inch

2 tablespoons thinly sliced scallions, white and green parts

1. Stir the sherry, both soy sauces, brown sugar, and 2 tablespoons water together in a small bowl until the sugar is dissolved. Set aside.

2. Devein the shrimp by cutting through the back of the shell with scissors. Do not remove the shell. Pull out and discard the vein. Rinse and drain thoroughly and pat dry with paper towels.

3. Heat the oil in a wok or stir-fry pan over medium-high heat to 375°F. Dip an end of a shrimp into the oil; it should sizzle. Carefully, so not to make the fat spatter, add all the shrimp to the hot oil and fry for no more than 1 minute, stirring with a wire skimmer so each shrimp cooks evenly. When all the shrimp turn pink, remove them to a plate lined with paper towels. Reserve 2 tablespoons of the oil and discard the rest.

4. Heat the reserved oil in the wok or stir-fry pan over medium-high heat. Add the garlic, gingerroot, and scallions to the pan and stir until fragrant, about 30 seconds. Do not burn. Pour in the soy sauce mixture and return the fried shrimp to the pan. Stir briskly until all the shrimp are coated. Transfer to a platter. Serve immediately.

Crystal Shrimp

Serves 3 to 4, or 5 to 6 as part of a multicourse meal

*T*here is no soy sauce to darken the clear white sauce in this Shanghai dish. That's why the shrimp are described as crystal. The original recipe calls for deep-frying the shrimp, but I prefer this version.

福

1 pound medium shrimp, shelled

¼ teaspoon grated peeled gingerroot

1 teaspoon dry sherry

1 teaspoon cornstarch

1 scant teaspoon salt

1 scallion, green and white parts, cut into 2-inch pieces

4 tablespoons canola, corn, or peanut oil

1.   Cut a slit along the back of the shrimp and pull out and discard the vein. Rinse the shrimp in cold water, drain and place in a bowl. Add the gingerroot, sherry, cornstarch, and salt. Stir until the shrimp is well coated, then mix in the scallions. Set aside.

2.   Heat the oil in a wok or stir-fry pan over high heat until hot but not smoking. Test by dipping a spatula into the shrimp and then into the oil; it should sizzle. Stir up the shrimp mixture again and pour it all into the hot oil. Stir briskly until the shrimp turn opaque, about 1 to 2 minutes. Transfer the shrimp to a platter with a slotted spoon. Discard the scallion if desired. Serve immediately.

Seafood

Coral and Jade

M y mother coined this name for a popular shrimp dish that we serve at our restaurant. The shrimp is stir-fried in a light tomato sauce, which accentuates the pink color of the cooked shrimp and makes it resemble coral. Snow peas when cooked take on the green color of imperial jade, so prized by the Chinese. What lovely imagery for a lovely dish!

1 pound large or medium shrimp, shelled

1 teaspoon grated peeled gingerroot

1 teaspoon dry sherry

1 teaspoon cornstarch

½ to 1 teaspoon salt, or to taste

3 tablespoons canola, corn, or peanut oil

¼ pound snow peas, ends snapped off and strings removed, cut in half on the
    diagonal

2 tablespoons ketchup

1 (8-ounce) can sliced water chestnuts, drained (1 cup)

1. Cut a slit along the back of the shrimp and pull out and discard the intestinal vein. Rinse the shrimp in cold water, drain, and place in a bowl. Stir in the gingerroot, sherry, cornstarch, and ¼ teaspoon salt and mix well. Set aside.

2. Heat 1 tablespoon of the oil in a wok or stir-fry pan over medium heat until hot but not smoking. Dip an end of a snow pea into the pan; it should sizzle. Add the snow peas and stir just until they turn a darker green, about 30 seconds. Do not scorch the tender snow peas inadvertently by heating the oil too hot. Remove the snow peas and spread out on a plate. Set aside.

3. Pour the remaining 2 tablespoons of oil into the same pan and heat over high heat. Stir up the shrimp mixture again, pour into the pan and cook, stirring constantly, for 1 to 2 minutes, or until the shrimp just turn pink and opaque. Stir in the ketchup, water chestnuts, and remaining ¼ teaspoon salt and stir-fry for about 30 seconds. Return the snow peas to the pan and mix together for 30 seconds to 1 minute. Remove from the heat and taste, adding more salt if desired. Transfer to a serving dish. Serve immediately.

Seafood

壽

Note Use large or medium shrimp depending on the number of people you are serving; medium shrimp will serve more people.

Shrimp with Peas

Serves 3 to 4, or 5 to 6 as part of a multicourse meal

*P*eas go nicely with shrimp, complimenting but not overpowering them, and their bright green color is pretty against the pink of cooked shrimp.

禧

1 pound medium shrimp, shelled

¼ teaspoon grated peeled gingerroot

1 teaspoon dry sherry

1 teaspoon cornstarch

1 teaspoon salt

1 cup green peas, fresh or frozen and thawed

1 scallion, green and white parts, cut into 2-inch pieces

3 tablespoons canola, corn, or peanut oil

1. Cut a slit along the back of the shrimp and pull out and discard the intestinal vein. Rinse the shrimp in cold water, drain, and place in a bowl. Add the gingerroot, sherry, cornstarch, and salt and stir to coat the shrimp. Set aside.

2. If using fresh peas, drop them into boiling water and boil for 1 minute. Drain immediately and run under cold water to stop the cooking. Set aside.

3. Heat the oil in a wok over medium-high heat. When the oil is hot, add the scallion pieces; they should sizzle. Stir a few times. Add the peas and stir for 1 minute. Stir up the shrimp mixture again and pour it all into the pan. Stir for another minute, or until the shrimp turn opaque and pink. Transfer the shrimp and peas to a platter. Discard the scallions if desired. Serve immediately.

Seafood

Shrimp in Tomato Sauce

**Serves 3 to 4, or 5 to 6 as part of a
multicourse meal**

lthough ketchup is a commonplace American staple, this sauce is anything but mundane. Many people don't realize that ketchup originated in Asia.

健康

1 tablespoon dry sherry

1 tablespoon cider vinegar

4 tablespoons ketchup

1 teaspoon light or dark soy sauce

½ teaspoon salt

2 teaspoons sugar

1 teaspoon grated peeled gingerroot

1 pound medium shrimp, shelled

2 teaspoons cornstarch

2 teaspoons dry sherry

3 tablespoons canola, corn, or peanut oil

2 garlic cloves, crushed and peeled

1 slice unpeeled gingerroot, 1 × ⅛ inch

3 tablespoons thinly sliced scallions, green and white parts

1. Stir the sherry, vinegar, ketchup, soy sauce, salt, sugar, and gingerroot together in a bowl and set aside.

2. Cut a slit along the back of the shrimp and pull out and discard the vein. Rinse the shrimp in cold water, drain, and place in a bowl. Add the cornstarch and sherry and stir to coat well. Set aside.

3. Pour the oil into a wok and place the pan over high heat. Add the garlic and gingerroot and push them around the pan until the oil is hot; they will sizzle. Stir the shrimp up again and turn it all into the hot oil. Stir-fry for 1 minute, or until the shrimp are opaque and pink. Pour the sauce mixture into the pan and stir until the shrimp are evenly coated. Sprinkle the minced scallions over the shrimp, mix with a couple of big turns of a spatula, and transfer to a platter. Discard the gingerroot and garlic if desired and serve immediately.

Shrimp with Black Beans

Serves 3 to 4, or 5 to 6 as part of a multicourse meal

Seafood and fermented black beans are commonly combined in Cantonese-style dishes. It's amazing how everyday ingredients take on a whole new character with just a little of this extraordinary seasoning. This family-style dish is not usually served at banquets. It is not considered elegant enough because the dark sauce covers the coral shrimp. At home it is enjoyed with great relish.

福

1 pound large shrimp, shelled
1 teaspoon dry sherry
1 teaspoon cornstarch
3 tablespoons canola, corn, or peanut oil
1 tablespoon thinly sliced scallions
1 tablespoon minced peeled gingerroot
1 garlic clove, crushed and peeled
3 tablespoons fermented black beans, chopped
Salt to taste (optional)

1.   Cut a slit along the back of the shrimp and pull out and discard the intestinal vein. Rinse the shrimp in cold water, drain, and place in a bowl. Mix well with the sherry and cornstarch. Set aside.

2.   Heat the oil in a wok or stir-fry pan over high heat until hot but not smoking. Dip a spatula into the shrimp and then into the oil; it should sizzle. Add the scallions, gingerroot, garlic, and black beans and stir a few times. Mix up the shrimp again and add it to the pan. Stir constantly. Add 2 tablespoons of water and cook until the shrimp is opaque, about 2 minutes. Taste the sauce and add salt, if desired. Serve immediately.

Shrimp in Lobster Sauce

**Serves 3 to 4, or 5 to 6 as part of a
multicourse meal**

*T*his has always been a popular American-Chinese dish, and it was a favorite in our
original restaurant in Cambridge, Massachusetts. There is no lobster in the dish at
all. Rather, the shrimp is cooked in the type of sauce the Cantonese use for lobster.
You can omit the pork if you wish.

1 pound medium or large shrimp, shelled

2 teaspoons dry sherry

3 tablespoons cornstarch

1¼ cups water

¼ pound ground lean pork (about ½ cup)

2 tablespoons dark soy sauce

¼ teaspoon sugar

3 tablespoons canola, corn, or peanut oil

2 slices unpeeled gingerroot, 1 × ⅛ inch each

2 garlic cloves, crushed and peeled

2 tablespoons fermented black beans, minced

Salt

1 egg, beaten

1. Cut a slit along the back of the shrimp and pull out and discard the
vein. Rinse the shrimp in cold water, drain, and place in a bowl. Stir in 1
teaspoon of the sherry and 1 tablespoon of the cornstarch and mix well. Set
aside.

2. Mix the remaining 2 tablespoons of cornstarch with ¼ cup of the
water. Set aside. Mix the pork with the remaining teaspoon sherry, the soy
sauce, and sugar in a small bowl. Set aside.

3. Heat the oil in a wok or stir-fry pan over medium-high heat until hot but not smoking. Test by dipping the end of a shrimp into the oil;
it should sizzle. Stir up the shrimp mixture again, pour it into the pan, and
cook, stirring constantly, until the shrimp is just pink. Remove the shrimp
from the pan with a slotted spoon, leaving as much oil as you can in
the pan.

4.   Add the gingerroot, garlic, and black beans to the same pan and stir a few times. Add the pork mixture. Stir about 30 seconds. Add 1 cup of water. Bring to a boil, cover the pan, and lower the heat. Simmer for 2 minutes and taste carefully for seasoning. Add a small amount salt, if needed.

5.   Uncover the pan and return the shrimp to the pan. Discard the gingerroot and garlic, if desired. Add the cornstarch slurry and stir until thickened. Pour the beaten egg into the pan in a thin stream. Give 2 big stirs. Serve hot.

壽

Lobster, Cantonese Style

Serves 2, or 4 as part of a
multicourse meal

The Chinese like to cook lobster — as well as crab and shrimp — in the shell because it holds the moisture in and because it makes a beautiful presentation. For the fullest enjoyment of this dish, dispense with table manners and use your fingers. Suck the sauce from the lobster pieces, then remove the meat from the shell.

My mother always insisted on getting an active live lobster; it had to be flapping vigorously when she picked it up. Some people are a bit squeamish when it comes to chopping up a live lobster. The first cut, which splits the lobster in two, kills it instantly, but if this bothers you, plunge the lobster in boiling water first. I do not recommend buying ready cooked lobster because the meat is usually dry and overcooked. Be sure to cook the lobster as soon as it is chopped.

禧

1 live lobster (1½ to 2 pounds)
¼ pound ground pork (about ½ cup)
2 slices unpeeled gingerroot, 1 × ⅛ inch each
2 garlic cloves, crushed and peeled
1½ tablespoons fermented black beans, coarsely chopped
2 teaspoons dry sherry
½ teaspoon salt
1½ tablespoons dark soy sauce
¼ teaspoon sugar
3 tablespoons canola, corn, or peanut oil
1½ tablespoons cornstarch, dissolved in ¼ cup water
1 egg, beaten

1. Rinse the lobster in cold water and dry with paper towels or plunge it into a pot of boiling water for a few seconds. Cut and chop the lobster through the shell into 14 pieces as shown. Make the first cut down the middle, splitting the lobster in two. Collect the tomalley, place it in a bowl, and break it into small pieces. Discard the legs, intestine, sacks in the tip of the head, and spongy gills.

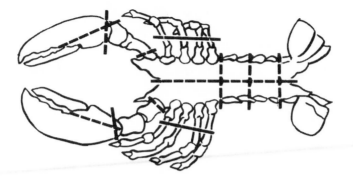

2. Combine the pork, gingerroot, garlic, black beans, and sherry in a small dish. Set aside. Mix together salt, soy sauce, sugar, and ¾ cup water in another dish. Set aside.

3. Heat the oil in a wok or stir-fry pan over medium-high heat. When the oil is hot but not smoking, add the pork mixture and the tomalley; they should sizzle. Stir for 2 to 3 minutes, or until the pork is no longer pink.

4. Add the lobster pieces and give a couple of big turns with a spatula. Add the soy sauce mixture. Cover and bring to a boil. Reduce the heat to a simmer and cook for 3 to 4 minutes, or until the lobster shell turns bright coral and the meat turns white and pink.

5. Uncover the pan and transfer the lobster pieces with a slotted spoon to a serving plate. Increase the heat to medium-high. When the liquid begins to boil, stir in the cornstarch slurry. When the liquid thickens, add the egg, stirring a few times to create ribbons. Return the lobster to the pan and give a couple of big turns with a spatula to mix well. Serve hot.

Stir-fried Squid
with Mixed Vegetables

Serves 3 to 4, or 5 to 6 as part of a multicourse meal

S quid, naturally low in fat, is an excellent choice for stir-frying, but it becomes tough and rubbery if overcooked. The squid body should be scored and blanched before stir-frying so it will cook quickly. Most markets now offer squid already cleaned. If you need to clean it yourself, see the directions below.

The Chinese also use dried squid, which is golden in color; it must be softened and reconstituted in water before using. Sometimes a combination of fresh and dried squid is used. I prefer fresh squid because it's more tender than the dried kind.

健康

1 pound fresh squid, cleaned
3 tablespoons canola, corn, or peanut oil
2 garlic cloves, crushed and peeled
2 slices unpeeled gingerroot, 1 × ⅛ inch each
1 carrot, peeled and thinly sliced on the diagonal
½ green bell pepper, cut into 1-inch chunks
1 cup broccoli florets
2 cups bok choy chunks
1 small onion, quartered
½ cup Chinese Chicken Broth (page 64) or canned chicken broth
2 tablespoons fermented black beans, chopped
1 cup snow peas, ends snapped off and strings removed
½ teaspoon salt, or to taste
2 teaspoons cornstarch, dissolved in 2 tablespoons water

1. Rinse the squid thoroughly, inside and out, with cold water and drain. Cut down 1 side of the body tube and spread out flat with the inside facing up. Lightly score the flesh in a fine crisscross pattern and cut into pieces about 2 to 3 inches square. If the head with the tentacles is large, cut it in half. Bring water to a boil in a saucepan, remove from the heat, and plunge the squid in the water for 15 seconds. The squid will turn opaque and it will curl.

Immediately drain in a colander and rinse in cold water to stop further cooking. Shake out excess water and drain thoroughly. Set aside.

2. Heat 1 tablespoon of the oil with the garlic and gingerroot in a wok or stir-fry pan over high heat, stirring until the oil is hot but not smoking; the garlic and gingerroot will sizzle and become fragrant. Add all the vegetables except the snow peas. Stir for about 30 seconds. Add the broth, reduce the heat to medium, and cover the pan. Cook, covered, for 1 to 2 minutes, or until the vegetables are tender.

3. Return the heat to high and add the blanched squid, black beans, and snow peas. Stir for 30 seconds to 1 minute. Taste and add salt, if necessary. Add the cornstarch slurry. Stir until sauce is thickened. Serve immediately.

禧

Note To clean squid, peel off and discard the spotted skin from the body. Rinse the body and tentacles thoroughly. Pull off the head and tentacles together. The intestines will follow. Cut the tentacles from the head and reserve. Discard the remainder. Be sure to remove and discard the small hard beak at the center of the tentacles if it is still attached. Pull out the long, clear cartilagelike quill from the center of the body and discard. Rinse the cleaned body and tentacles in cold water and drain thoroughly.

Clams in Black Bean Sauce

Serves 2, or 4 as part of a multicourse meal

*T*he Chinese serve clams cooked in their shells on special occasions like the lunar New Year. They are considered symbolic of prosperity and wealth because when the clam shells open they resemble the shape of the silver ingots used in old China.

祿

12 littleneck or cherrystone clams (about 2 pounds)

2 garlic cloves, lightly crushed and peeled

2 slices unpeeled gingerroot, 1 × ⅛ inch each

1 scallion, green and white parts, cut into 1-inch lengths, bulb split

3 tablespoons fermented black beans, coarsely chopped

2 tablespoons dark soy sauce

1 tablespoon dry sherry

2 teaspoons sugar

2 tablespoons canola, corn, or peanut oil

2 teaspoons cornstarch, dissolved in 1 tablespoon water

Cilantro sprigs, for garnish

1. Cover the clams with fresh cold water and soak for about 30 minutes. Scrub the shells with a stiff brush and rinse thoroughly to remove all sand and grit. Remember shells and all will cook in the sauce and you don't want it to become gritty. Drain. Set aside. If not cooking right away, place in the refrigerator.

2. Combine the garlic, gingerroot, scallion, and black beans in a small dish. Set aside. Combine the soy sauce, sherry, sugar, and ½ cup water in another dish. Stir until the sugar is dissolved. Set aside.

3. Pour the oil into a wok or stir-fry pan and place over high heat. Add the black bean mixture to the pan and stir until fragrant. Add the clams and stir for about 30 seconds. Add the soy sauce mixture, stir to mix, and cover the pan. Cook over medium heat for about 5 minutes, or until the clams just open. Stir occasionally for even cooking.

4. Remove the lid and thicken the sauce with the cornstarch slurry. When the sauce has thickened, transfer the clams to a serving platter and garnish with cilantro. Serve immediately.

Poultry

Poultry, especially chicken, is almost as ubiquitous as pork in China. Chickens, like pigs, are simple to care for, mature quickly, and can be raised by almost anyone with a little plot of land.

As with seafood, the Chinese like their chicken freshly killed for the best flavor. A walk through the open markets in the Far East reveals stalls with live chickens in bamboo cages and shoppers walking home with a live chicken strung up by its feet.

It is very convenient that Western supermarkets have available an array of whole chickens and chicken parts all neatly packaged and ready to cook. In China, chickens are only available whole, so it is up to the cook to prepare it and decide which portions should be used in which dishes. In general, the drier breast meat is used for stir-frying or deep-frying; the dark meat (legs, wings, thighs) is used for braising and stewing.

Since Chinese dishes use a lot of chicken breast meat, you can save substantially on food costs by deboning the chicken breasts yourself instead of buying fillets. Not only will you have the satisfaction of learning a new skill, you'll also be able to make a tasty chicken broth with the bones. (Directions for deboning chicken breasts are on pages 168–169.) We always remove and discard the skin and fat before cooking chicken breasts. This reduces the fat content substantially since most of the fat in poultry lies right under the skin.

When it comes to serving whole chicken, the Chinese do not carve it Western style, but chop it up, bones and all, into bite-size pieces. These pieces are then reassembled on a platter.

The Chinese prefer the dark meat near the bone. We feel it is tastier. My mother liked to eat the bone marrow too and would break the larger bones open to suck it out. Traditionally, the Chinese like to have whole chicken cooked on the rare side with a little blood still apparent near the bones. This is especially true for such dishes as White Cooked Chicken, Drunken Chicken, and Soy Sauce Chicken. However, for health reasons it is not advisable to eat rare chicken.

Duck is popular with the Chinese as well. There are many regional duck specialties, of which Peking Duck is the most well known outside of China. There are restaurants in Peking that feature only Peking Duck and side dishes prepared with duck parts (tongues, feet, etc.). The Chinese rarely prepare Peking Duck at home since they do not have ovens. It was really a specialty left to the realm of a restaurant chef. The one duck recipe featured in this book, Shanghai Duck, is an easy, family-style whole duck that we regularly prepared at home; it's a real favorite for Shanghai people. At other times, we would buy Cantonese-style roasted ducks in Chinatown or have Peking Duck at our own restaurant.

Sliced Chicken with Broccoli

Serves 3 to 4, or 5 to 6 as part of a multicourse meal

*F*resh vegetables always give the best results. After one cooking class I taught, a student remarked how much crisper the broccoli was in my dish than in hers when she prepared the same recipe at home. It turned out she had used frozen broccoli. If you are rushed, you can get all kinds of cut-up raw vegetables at a supermarket salad bar. They may cost more than starting from scratch, but it's better than going to the freezer.

1 pound broccoli

1 pound skinless boneless chicken breasts, sliced (page 43)

2 teaspoons dry sherry

3 teaspoons cornstarch

1 teaspoon salt

3 tablespoons canola, corn, or peanut oil

¼ cup water

1 slice unpeeled gingerroot, 1 × ⅛ inch

1 garlic clove, crushed and peeled

1 (8-ounce) can sliced bamboo shoots, drained (about 1 cup)

1. Trim the broccoli stalks and peel them with a small paring knife. Slice the flower head off the stalks and cut it into bite-size florets. Roll-cut the peeled stalks into 1½-inch pieces as described on page 46. You should have about 4 cups. Set aside.

2. Place the chicken in a bowl, add the sherry, 1 teaspoon of the cornstarch, and ½ teaspoon of the salt, and stir. Set aside. Mix the remaining 2 teaspoons cornstarch and ½ teaspoon salt with ½ cup of cold water. Set aside.

3. Pour 1 tablespoon of the oil into a wok or stir-fry pan and place over high heat. When the oil is hot but not smoking add the broccoli and stir for about 30 seconds. Stir in the ¼ cup water, reduce heat to medium, and cover the pan. Continue cooking, stirring occasionally, for about 2 to 3 minutes, or until broccoli turns a darker green and is tender-crisp. Pour onto a shallow platter and set aside.

4. Heat the remaining 2 tablespoons of oil in the same pan over high heat until hot but not smoking and add the gingerroot and garlic, stirring until they are fragrant and release their flavor, about 30 seconds. With a spoon, stir up the chicken again and turn it all into the pan. Stir briskly for about 3 minutes, or until the chicken turns white. Add the bamboo shoots and return the broccoli to the pan, stirring constantly. Pour in the cornstarch mixture and continue stirring until the gravy is slightly thickened. Remove and discard the gingerroot and garlic, if desired. Serve hot.

Stir-fried Chicken with Cucumbers

Serves 3 to 4, or 5 to 6 as part of a multicourse meal

Y ou've probably noticed how important cutting is to Chinese cooking. The ingredients are usually cut in a uniform shape for a pleasant presentation. In this unusual, refreshing dish, the chicken is sliced to the same flat shape as the cucumbers. It takes a little practice to get the technique just right. You can cut the chicken into cubes instead, but the slices make a lovelier dish.

1 long seedless cucumber or 1 pound regular cucumbers

1 pound skinless boneless chicken breasts, sliced (page 43)

3 teaspoons cornstarch

2 teaspoons dry sherry

1 teaspoon salt, or to taste

3 tablespoons canola, corn, or peanut oil

2 garlic cloves, crushed and peeled

1 tablespoon fermented black beans, coarsely chopped

1. Wash the cucumber. European cucumber can be left unpeeled. If using regular cucumbers, partially peel by removing alternating ½-inch strips of skin down the long side. Trim away ¾ inch from each end and split the cucumbers lengthwise. Scrape and discard the seeds from regular cucumbers with a teaspoon. Slice the cucumbers on the diagonal ½ inch thick. You should have about 3½ to 4 cups. Set aside.

2. Place the chicken in a small bowl, stir in the cornstarch, sherry, and salt, and mix well. Set aside.

3. Pour the oil into a wok or stir-fry pan and place the pan over high heat. Add the garlic and stir around the pan until the oil is hot but not smoking; the garlic will sizzle. Stir up the chicken again and add it all to the pan. Stir briskly for 2 to 3 minutes, or until the chicken is opaque.

4. Add the cucumber slices and stir another 2 minutes. Toss in the black beans and stir for another 30 seconds, or until the ingredients and flavors are evenly mixed. Taste and add another ½ teaspoon of salt if you wish. Discard the garlic, if desired. Serve hot.

Chicken with Mushrooms

Serves 3 to 4, or 5 to 6 as part of a multicourse meal

*I*f you want to make this recipe more exotic, use half fresh and half dried black mushrooms. Soften the dried mushrooms in hot water, trim the stems, and cut the caps into pieces similar to the fresh mushrooms. You may also wish to try other kinds of fresh mushrooms, such as porcini or shiitake.

禄

1 pound skinless boneless chicken breast, cut into ¾-inch cubes (about 2 cups)
1 teaspoon dry sherry
2 teaspoons cornstarch
1½ teaspoons salt
3 tablespoons canola, corn, or peanut oil
2 slices unpeeled gingerroot, 1 × ⅛ inch each
1 garlic clove, crushed and peeled
¾ pound fresh button mushrooms, cleaned and quartered (2 cups)
¾ pound fresh snow peas, ends snapped off and strings removed (2 cups)
1 (8-ounce) can sliced bamboo shoots, drained (1 cup)

1.   Place the chicken in a bowl. Add the sherry, 1 teaspoon of the cornstarch, and salt and stir together until the chicken is well coated. Set aside. Dissolve the remaining teaspoon of cornstarch in 1 tablespoon water. Set aside.

2.   Pour the oil into a wok or stir-fry pan and place over high heat. Add the gingerroot and garlic and stir around the pan until the oil is hot but not smoking; the gingerroot and garlic will begin to sizzle.

3.   Stir the chicken again and pour it into the pan. Stir constantly until the chicken turns white, about 2 minutes. Add the mushrooms, snow peas, and bamboo shoots. Continue stirring until the snow peas turn a darker green.

4.   Give the cornstarch mixture a quick stir to be sure it is completely dissolved and pour it into the pan. Continue stirring until the liquid thickens. Remove and discard the gingerroot and garlic. Serve immediately.

Chicken with
Mixed Vegetables

Serves 3 to 4, or 5 to 6 as part of a
multicourse meal

*Y*ou can use many kinds of vegetables for this dish, but I like this particular mix because the colors are bright and the flavors combine well with the chicken. Since there is
no soy sauce in this dish, the colors of the vegetables and the chicken shine right
through.

1 pound skinless boneless chicken breast, cut into ¾-inch dice (about 2 cups)

1 tablespoon cornstarch

2 teaspoons dry sherry

3 tablespoons canola, corn, or peanut oil

1 carrot, peeled and roll-cut (page 46)

2 celery stalks, sliced on the diagonal ¼ inch thick

1 medium red bell pepper, seeded, cored, and cut into 1½-inch dice

2 cups bok choy, washed, drained, and cut into 2-inch pieces

½ cup Chinese Chicken Broth (page 64) or water

2 slices unpeeled gingerroot, 1 × ⅛ inch each

1 teaspoon salt, or to taste

1.   Place the chicken in a bowl and add the cornstarch and sherry. Stir
until well mixed. Set aside.

2.   Heat 1 tablespoon of the oil in a wok or stir-fry pan over high heat
until the oil is hot but not smoking. Test by dipping the end of one of the
vegetables in the oil; it should sizzle. Add the vegetables to the pan and stir
for about 2 minutes. Add the broth, stir, and cover. Reduce the heat to medium and steam for 2 minutes, or until the vegetables are tender-crisp. Transfer
the vegetables and their juices to a platter.

3.   Add the remaining 2 tablespoons of oil to the same pan. Place over
high heat and stir in the gingerroot and salt. Stir for about 30 seconds or until
the gingerroot sizzles; do not let it burn. Stir up the chicken again and add it
to the pan. Stir for 2 to 3 minutes, or until the chicken is almost done.

4. Return the vegetables and any juice from the platter to the pan, mix thoroughly, and cook until vegetables are heated and chicken is done. Taste and add salt, if necessary. Remove and discard the gingerroot. Transfer the chicken and vegetables to a platter. Serve immediately.

Chicken Chop Suey

Serves 4

C hop Suey, which loosely translates as "mixed up," is not authentically Chinese. Like Chow Mein, it was conceived in the United States and was extremely popular with Americans who thought it was a Chinese dish.

When our restaurant opened in 1958, my mother did not want to serve either Chop Suey or Chow Mein, but she quickly found that customers were unhappy not to find them on the menu. She reluctantly added sections to the back of the menu for these two categories. As our customers came to appreciate real Chinese food, they stopped ordering Chow Mein and Chop Suey and did not miss them when they eventually disappeared from the menu.

Yet, old favorites die hard for some people. Our close friend and business associate, Mel Novatt, himself a world traveler and gourmet, surprised, even shocked, me one day when he admitted that one of his favorite Chinese dishes was Chicken Chop Suey and that he was disappointed that it had become almost impossible to get. In one Cantonese restaurant in Boston, he implored me to order it for him. The waiter was taken aback and asked two times if American Chop Suey was really what I wanted. Mel was a happy man that evening.

I am including a simple Chop Suey recipe here because although it is not authentic, it is nutritious and tasty when it is made well. Always use fresh vegetables and be sure not to overcook the bean sprouts. They are best when they are tender but still crisp. Serve the dish with steamed rice or crisp chow mein noodles.

(continued)

3 tablespoons canola, corn, or peanut oil

2 slices unpeeled gingerroot, 1 × ⅛ inch each

½ pound skinless boneless chicken breast, cut into ¾-inch cubes (about 1 cup)

1 medium onion, shredded (about 1 cup)

2 celery stalks, shredded (1 cup)

1 (8-ounce) can bamboo shoots, drained and sliced or shredded (1 cup)

2 cups shredded napa cabbage (about ½ pound)

2 chicken bouillon cubes, dissolved in ½ cup hot water

3 cups bean sprouts (about 6 ounces)

1 tablespoon cornstarch, dissolved in 2 tablespoons water

1.   Pour the oil into a wok or stir-fry pan and place over high heat. Add the gingerroot and stir around the pan for about 15 seconds or until the oil is hot but not smoking; the gingerroot will sizzle.

2.   Add the chicken and stir constantly for about 1 minute. Stir in the onion, celery, bamboo shoots, cabbage, and chicken bouillon solution. Stir around a few times and cover the pan. Cook, covered, for about 3 minutes, stirring occasionally, until the vegetables lose their raw look. Add the bean sprouts and stir another minute, or until the sprouts are lightly wilted but still crisp.

3.   Stir in the cornstarch slurry and cook, stirring constantly, until the sauce thickens. Serve hot.

健康

Note   See directions for shredding vegetables on page 45.

Mandarin Orange Chicken

Serves 3 to 4, or 5 to 6 as part of a multicourse meal

My version of the classic Orange Chicken requires no deep-frying, so there's a saving of time, effort, and calories. I use frozen orange juice concentrate, which blends exceptionally well with the spicy hotness of chilies. If you don't like chilies, you can omit them.

Stir-frying the snow peas separately and using them to ring the chicken makes a very nice presentation for dinner parties. For a family meal, you can return the peas to the pan just after the oranges and mix them in.

福

1 pound skinless boneless chicken breasts, cut into ¾-inch dice (about 2 cups)

2 teaspoons dry sherry

3 teaspoons cornstarch

2 teaspoons sugar

1 tablespoon cider vinegar

3 tablespoons light soy sauce

3 tablespoons frozen orange juice concentrate

4 tablespoons canola, corn, or peanut oil

¼ pound snow peas, ends snapped off and strings removed, cut on the diagonal into ½-inch pieces

2 to 4 dried chilies, seeds removed (see page 12)

1 garlic clove, crushed and peeled

2 slices unpeeled gingerroot, 1 × ⅛ inch each

1 (11-ounce) can mandarin oranges, drained

1.   Place the chicken in a bowl, stir in the sherry and cornstarch and mix well. Set aside. In another bowl, combine the sugar, vinegar, soy sauce, and orange juice concentrate and mix well. Set aside.

2.   Heat 1 tablespoon of the oil in a wok or stir-fry pan over medium heat until hot but not smoking. Test by dipping the end of a piece of snow pea in the oil; it should sizzle. Add the snow peas and stir just until they turn a darker green, about 30 seconds. Transfer the snow peas to a large serving platter and spread them out. Do not pile up the snow peas, but spread them out so they will not overcook in their own heat.

3.   In the same pan, heat the remaining 3 tablespoons of oil with the chili peppers over medium heat. As the oil heats up, the peppers will turn dark brown and become very fragrant. Discard the chilies when they are almost black but not burned. Add the garlic and gingerroot and stir around the pan a few times until they begin to sizzle.

4.   Increase the heat to high, stir up the chicken again, and add it. Stir for about 1 minute, add the orange sauce, and continue stirring another minute or two. When the chicken is almost done, discard the garlic and gingerroot. Add the mandarin oranges and stir gently to heat the oranges and finish cooking the chicken — not more than 1 minute or the oranges will fall apart.

5.   Arrange the snow peas in a ring around the edge of the platter and spoon the chicken and oranges into the center. Serve hot.

Cutting up a Whole Cooked Chicken, Chinese Style

切

When the Chinese cook a whole chicken, they like to chop it all up into bite-size pieces for serving. The pieces are reassembled on a platter to look like a whole chicken with the wings and legs positioned properly. Here's how to do it.

Allow the chicken to cool for a few minutes to firm up the meat and reduce splattering. Be sure to wear a large apron.

- Cut off the wings and then cut them apart at the joints. Leave the wingtip whole but chop the other two pieces in half. Place the pieces on either side of an oval platter, reassembled to look whole.
- Cut off the legs at the hip joint, close to the body. To do this, pull the legs away from the body and bend at the hip to expose the joint for easier cutting. Cut the legs apart. With a Chinese knife, chop the thigh and drumstick into 3 pieces about 1 inch wide. Reassemble the pieces on either side of the platter below the wings.
- With the chicken breast side up, cut through the breast with a knife or a pair of scissors. Take your time and place the knife down into the bird and cut-chop firmly. Pull open the cavity to expose the backbone. Chop (or cut with scissors) along the side of the backbone, then along the other side, separating the neck and backbone from the carcass. If desired, chop the backbone crosswise into 1-inch pieces and reserve it to enrich and flavor soup noodles.
- Place a body half, skin side up, on the cutting board. Chop into 2 pieces lengthwise and then crosswise into 1 × 2 inch pieces, being careful to keep the pieces together so they can be easily reassembled on the serving platter. Repeat for the other half.
- Assemble the body pieces, skin side up, in the middle of the serving platter. Always have the most attractive and meaty breast pieces on top, over the bonier rib pieces, for a beautiful and rich presentation. Garnish the platter with sprigs of parsley or cilantro.

Note When you get Cantonese duck or chicken in Chinatown, they chop up the whole carcass without removing the backbone. The Chinese usually serve the neck and backbone along with the other meat, hidden under the breast pieces. I save those pieces to use in another meal.

Almond Chicken

**Serves 3 to 4, or 5 to 6 as part of a
multicourse meal**

Nuts appear frequently in Chinese cooking in desserts, fillings, sweet soups, and stir-fry dishes. The almonds offer a crunchy contrast to the chicken and vegetables. In this dish, all the ingredients should be diced to about the size of whole almonds.

禄

1 pound skinless boneless chicken breast, cut into ½-inch dice (about 2 cups)

2 teaspoons cornstarch

1 teaspoon dry sherry

1 teaspoon salt, or to taste

3 tablespoons canola, corn, or peanut oil

1 slice unpeeled gingerroot, 1 × ⅛ inch

½ cup canned bamboo shoots, drained and diced

½ cup canned whole water chestnuts, drained and quartered

1 medium green bell pepper, seeded, cored, and diced

1 medium red bell pepper, seeded, cored, and diced

½ cup whole almonds, blanched or natural, toasted

1. Place the chicken in a bowl. Add the cornstarch, sherry, and salt and stir to coat the chicken thoroughly. Set aside.

2. Pour the oil into a wok or stir-fry pan and place over high heat. Add the gingerroot and stir it around until the oil is hot; the gingerroot will sizzle. Stir the chicken up again and pour into the pan. Stir constantly for 1 to 2 minutes, or until the chicken pieces are separated and almost cooked.

3. Add the bamboo shoots, water chestnuts, and peppers. Stir well for 1 minute, or until the peppers are tender-crisp. Add the almonds and mix thoroughly. Remove and discard the gingerroot, if desired. Serve immediately.

壽

Variation   To give the dish a slightly sweet taste, add 1 to 1½ tablespoons hoisin sauce when adding the vegetables and reduce the salt to ½ teaspoon.

Chicken with Cashew Nuts

Serves 3 to 4, or 5 to 6 as part of a
multicourse meal

This chicken recipe has been an outstanding favorite at our family's Cambridge restaurant for as long as I can remember. There, the cashews are deep-fried, but at home I prefer to toast the nuts instead. This reduces the amount of oil without reducing the flavor.

禧

1 pound skinless boneless chicken breast, cut into ¾-inch cubes (about 2 cups)

2 teaspoons cornstarch

2 teaspoons dry sherry

½ teaspoon grated peeled gingerroot

2 tablespoons dark soy sauce

2 tablespoons hoisin sauce

1 teaspoon sugar

4 tablespoons canola, corn, or peanut oil

1 garlic clove, crushed and peeled

1 cup whole blanched cashews, toasted

1 teaspoon sesame seed oil

1.   Place the chicken in a bowl. Add the cornstarch, sherry, and gingerroot and stir together until well mixed. Set aside.

2.   Combine the soy sauce, hoisin sauce, sugar, and 2 tablespoons water in a small bowl and stir until smooth. Set aside.

3.   Pour the oil into a wok or stir-fry pan and place the pan over high heat. Add the garlic and stir it around the pan until the oil is hot and the garlic sizzles, about 30 seconds. Do not let it burn. Stir up the chicken mixture again and add it all to the hot oil. Continue stirring until the chicken is almost done, 1 to 2 minutes. Remove and discard the garlic.

4.   Reduce the heat to medium and stir in the soy sauce mixture. Continue stirring until the ingredients are well blended. Add the cashew nuts and stir another 30 seconds. Drizzle with sesame seed oil and give a couple of big turns with a spatula. Serve immediately.

How to Debone a
Whole Chicken Breast

Deboning a chicken breast is done easily with just a few strokes of a good sharp knife.

- Tear off and discard the skin and fat. Cut or tear away and discard any loose membrane or excess fat from the cavity. Rinse the breast in water and pat dry with paper towels.
- Lay the breast, bone side up, on a cutting board and with the tip of your knife or with kitchen scissors cut into and through the center bone, splitting the breast in two.

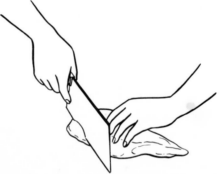

- Lay the breast half, bone side down, on the cutting board. Make a slash through the meat at its thinnest part over the rib cage. Do not cut through the rib bones.

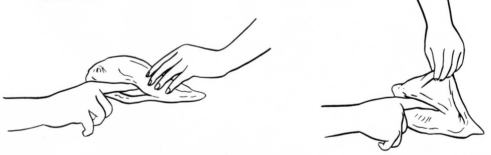

- Insert your index finger into the slash and run it up to the center bone, keeping it close to the bone and loosening the flap of meat from the bones underneath.

- If necessary, use the tip of the knife to loosen the meat from the bones. Lift the meat from the bone and set it back down on the cutting board. Pull the tenderloin free from the larger fillet. (If it is still attached to the breast bone,

  cut around the membrane that holds it in place.) Repeat with the other piece.
- You should now have four pieces of meat, two fillets and two tenderloin strips. Save the bones to make Chinese Chicken Broth (page 64) or place in a bag and freeze for later use.
- Cut and trim away any peripheral fat and membrane. I do this by using my hand to spread the membrane to the sides and then trimming it with the tip of my knife.
- Place the tenderloin on the cutting board and grasp between your fingers the end of the tendon that runs from one end of the meat, where it is clearly visible, into the meat. If it is slippery, use a piece of paper towel for a better grip. Using the edge of the knife blade, lightly scrape the tendon to expose enough for a good grip. Hold the knife down on the meat and pull the tendon out toward you. The knife will hold the meat in place while the tendon is neatly extracted.

Kung Pao Chicken

Serves 3 to 4, or 5 to 6 as part of a
multicourse meal

This is a famous Szechuan dish known as *Kung Pao Chi Ting*. At the time of the *Qin* (pronounced ch'in) dynasty, the person in charge of protecting the heir apparent to the throne held the title of Kung Pao, Kung meaning castle and Pao, to protect. During one period, the Kung Pao was a man from Szechuan Province whose favorite dish was spicy diced chicken with peanuts. It came to be named after him.

福

1 pound skinless boneless chicken breasts, cut into ¾-inch cubes (about 2 cups)
3 tablespoons dark soy sauce
1 teaspoon salt
1 tablespoon cornstarch
1 teaspoon dry sherry
1 tablespoon sugar
1 tablespoon cider vinegar
1 teaspoon sesame seed oil
2 to 4 dried chilies, seeds removed
3 tablespoons canola, corn, or peanut oil
½ teaspoon Szechuan peppercorns, toasted and ground
1 garlic clove, peeled and sliced
1 scallion, green and white parts, cut into 1½-inch lengths, bulb split, plus
    2 tablespoons thinly sliced scallions
2 slices unpeeled gingerroot, 1 × ⅛ inch each
½ cup unsalted blanched peanuts, toasted, or unsalted dry-roasted peanuts

1.   Place the chicken in a bowl. Add 1 tablespoon of the soy sauce, salt, and cornstarch and mix well. Set aside. Mix the remaining 2 tablespoons of soy sauce together in a small bowl with the sherry, sugar, vinegar, and sesame seed oil. Set aside.

2.   Pour the cooking oil into a cold wok or stir-fry pan and add the chilies. Heat the pan over medium-high heat and stir the peppers until they turn dark brown. Add the peppercorns, garlic, scallion pieces, and gingerroot and stir a moment or two. Mix up the chicken again and pour it into the pan. Stir briskly.

3. After stirring for about 1 minute, add the soy sauce mixture, the peanuts, and the thinly sliced scallions. Turn the heat up to high and stir for about 30 seconds until well mixed. Remove the chilies and gingerroot, if desired. Serve hot.

禄

Note You may substitute 1 to 3 teaspoons crushed red pepper for the dried chilies. Add with the peppercorns, garlic, and scallions.

壽

Chicken Livers
and Snow Peas

**Serves 3 to 4, or 5 to 6 as part of a
multicourse meal**

*T*he Chinese appreciate organ meats, but I find that many Americans — even my own
husband — do not. Those who do like liver (and I know there are many of you out
there) will find stir-fried liver dishes different and easy to prepare.

½ pound chicken livers (about 1½ cups)

1 teaspoon dry sherry

3 tablespoons dark soy sauce

3 teaspoons cornstarch

3 tablespoons canola, corn, or peanut oil

¼ pound snow peas, ends snapped off and strings removed

1 slice unpeeled gingerroot, 1 × ⅛ inch

1 (8-ounce) can sliced bamboo shoots, drained (1 cup)

¼ teaspoon salt, or to taste

1.   Peel the membrane off the chicken livers with your fingers. Cut into
½-inch pieces and place in a bowl. Stir in the sherry, 1 tablespoon of the soy
sauce, and 1 teaspoon of the cornstarch and mix well. Set aside.

2.   Dissolve the remaining cornstarch in the remaining soy sauce and ¼
cup cold water. Set aside.

3.   Heat 1 tablespoon of the oil in a wok or stir-fry pan over medium-
high heat until the oil is hot. Test by dipping an end of a snow pea into the
oil; it should sizzle. Add the snow peas to the hot oil and stir for about 1
minute, or until the peas turn a darker green. Do not overcook. Remove and
spread out on a platter.

4.   Heat the remaining oil in the same pan over high heat. Add the
gingerroot and stir around the pan until it is fragrant and sizzles. Stir up the
chicken livers again and pour into the pan. Stir constantly for about 3 minutes
or until blood no longer seeps out.

5.   Add the bamboo shoots and stir for 30 seconds. Stir up the cornstarch
mixture again and add it. Return the snow peas to the pan and continue stirring
until the sauce thickens. Serve immediately.

Curry Chicken

Serves 3 to 4, or 5 to 6 as part of a multicourse meal

For this dish, I use Indian curry powder. My mother preferred curry paste, which is available in specialty stores or Asian markets. She would then omit the chili powder.

The traditional Chinese recipe calls for small pieces of chicken with the bones left in, but I have changed it to boneless chicken to make it easier to eat. Serve the dish with steamed white rice or brown Basmati rice, steamed vegetables, and Spicy Mango Chutney (page 330) on the side.

健康

2 tablespoons curry powder

1 tablespoon chili powder

2 cups chicken broth or water

2 tablespoons all-purpose flour

3 tablespoons canola, corn, or peanut oil

1 large onion, sliced (about 2 cups)

1 to 1¼ pounds skinless boneless chicken breast, cut into 1½-inch chunks

1 teaspoon salt

⅓ to 1 cup chopped cilantro leaves (optional)

1 to 2 cups Spicy Mango Chutney (page 330) (optional)

1.   Stir the curry and chili powders together with ½ cup water or broth in a small bowl until thoroughly mixed. Set aside. Combine the flour and ½ cup water or broth in another small bowl. Stir until smooth, with no lumps. Set aside.

2.   Heat the oil in a stir-fry pan or heavy pot over medium-high to high heat. When the oil is hot, add the onion and stir until translucent and just beginning to brown around the edges. This will take about 5 minutes.

3.   Add the curry mixture and stir a few times. Add the chicken and stir for 2 to 3 minutes, or until all the chicken is coated with the curry. Pour in the remaining 1 cup water or broth and bring to a boil. Cover the pan and simmer over low heat for 10 to 15 minutes, or until the chicken is fully cooked.

4.   Stir in the salt. Remove the chicken and onions with a slotted spoon to a serving dish. Quickly bring the curry sauce to a boil over medium-high

(continued)

heat and pour in the flour slurry, stirring constantly until the sauce thickens, about 3 minutes. Pour the gravy over the chicken. (The curry may be made ahead and reheated. Warm over low heat, stirring constantly.) Serve hot with small dishes of chopped cilantro and chutney for individual garnish, if desired.

Lemon Chicken

Serves 2 to 3, or 4 to 5 as part of a multicourse meal

*A*t our restaurant the chicken is dredged in water-chestnut starch, which is available in Chinese grocery stores, instead of cornstarch, for a crisper crust.

2 skinless boneless chicken breasts, with small fillet removed (about ¾ pound)
1 egg
½ teaspoon salt
Juice of 1 lemon, strained (about ¼ cup)
5 tablespoons (firmly packed) light brown sugar
1 slice unpeeled gingerroot, 1 × ⅛ inch
2 tablespoons cornstarch plus additional for dredging chicken
1 cup canola, corn, or peanut oil
1 teaspoon sesame seed oil
Lemon slices and parsley, for garnish

1.   Place the chicken breasts on a cutting board and remove any visible fat. With the broad side of a Chinese knife or a heavy object such as a rolling pin, pound the chicken breasts to flatten slightly.

2.   Lightly beat the egg and salt in a shallow bowl. Place the breasts in the egg mixture and turn a few times to coat evenly. Set aside for 10 minutes.

3.   Combine the lemon juice, sugar, gingerroot, and 1 cup water in a small saucepan on an unlit burner. Remove a third of the mixture and combine with the 2 tablespoons of cornstarch, stirring until the cornstarch is dissolved.

4.   Heat the oil over medium heat in a stir-fry pan or skillet large enough to hold the breasts. Place cornstarch in a pie pan. Remove the breasts from the egg and press into the cornstarch, coating both sides well and shaking off excess. When the oil is hot, fry the breasts for 8 to 10 minutes, turning until both sides are lightly browned and chicken is cooked through. Remove to a plate lined with paper towels to absorb the excess oil. Cut each chicken breast into ¾-inch-wide slices. Arrange on a shallow platter and keep warm as you cook the sauce.

5. Heat the lemon mixture in the saucepan over medium heat. When it comes to a boil, stir up the cornstarch slurry and pour it in. Stir until the sauce is thickened. Taste for tartness and add more sugar if desired. Discard the gingerroot. Stir in the sesame seed oil. Pour the sauce over the chicken and garnish with lemon slices and parsley. Serve hot.

禄

Note Chicken breasts cook more evenly and remain flatter when the small fillet underneath is removed. You can leave it on, but you should at least remove the tendon. Once I've removed the tendon, I separate the fillets and freeze the smaller ones for stir-fry dishes.

Empress Chicken

Serves 4, or 6 to 8 as part of a multicourse meal

*T*his is a lofty name for a convenient family dish when you don't have the time or appetite for a whole chicken. Not only does this dish take under an hour to prepare and cook, it holds very well in a warm oven. It can also be made a day ahead and reheated without any loss of texture or flavor. Serve it with hot white rice.

4 chicken wings
4 whole chicken legs
1 cup dried black mushrooms, soaked in hot water for 15 minutes
1 scallion, folded to 3 inches and tied with a cotton string or thread
1½ cups canned whole bamboo shoots, drained and cut into chunks
½ cup dark soy sauce
2 cups Chinese Chicken Broth (page 64) or water
3 whole star anise
2 slices unpeeled gingerroot, 1 × ⅛ inch each
1 tablespoon dry sherry
1 teaspoon salt, or to taste

1.   Cut the chicken wings into three through the joints. Discard the wing tips or save them for making broth. Cut the chicken legs in two through the joints. Chop the leg and thigh into 2 pieces each.

2.   Bring water to a boil in a large pot and scald the chicken by dropping the pieces into the boiling water. When the water returns to a boil, drain the chicken in a colander, rinse with cold water, and drain again.

3.   Squeeze out the water from the mushrooms and cut off the woody stems with scissors and discard. Leave the caps whole.

4.   Put the blanched chicken with the rest of the ingredients into a large saucepan or Dutch oven. Cover and bring to a boil. Reduce the heat and simmer, covered, for 30 minutes, or until the chicken is tender. Stir occasionally to prevent sticking and for even color.

5.   Uncover, increase the heat to medium, and bring the liquid to a boil. Baste the chicken for even color and flavor and continue cooking for 10 minutes, reducing the liquid. Remove the scallion and discard. Serve hot or warm.

Yunnan Steam Pot Chicken

Serves 3 to 4, or 6 as part of a
multicourse meal

Y ou will need a Chinese steam pot (page 38) with at least a two-quart capacity to
prepare this dish in the traditional manner. The steam enters the closed container
through an inner spout. The slow cooking results in a rich, flavorful broth.

禧

2 to 2¼ pounds chicken, cut through the bones into 2-inch pieces
3 slices unpeeled gingerroot, 1 × ⅛ inch each
2 scallions, green and white parts, cut into 2-inch lengths, bulb split in half
8 dried black mushrooms, soaked in hot water for 15 minutes, woody stems
    discarded and caps quartered
½ cup sliced bamboo shoots, drained
¼ pound Smithfield ham, fat removed, cut into 2-inch slices
2 cups Chinese Chicken Broth (page 64) plus ½ teaspoon salt or
    1 (13¾-ounce) can chicken broth and enough water to make 2 cups
1 tablespoon dry sherry
½ teaspoon salt

1. Arrange the chicken with the gingerroot, scallions, black mushrooms, bamboo shoots and ham in a steam pot. Combine the chicken broth
and sherry and salt and pour over the chicken.

2. Cover the steam pot and place in a water bath in a large stockpot,
wok, or covered roaster. The water should come up just to the handles of the
steam pot. Cover the stockpot or wok and steam for about 1½ hours, or until
the chicken is cooked through. Replenish the water in the outside pot as
needed.

3. Remove steam pot from the pan, discard
the gingerroot and scallions and skim off any
surface fat. Serve the chicken and
broth directly from the
steam pot at the table.

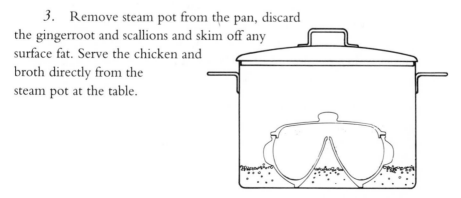

Poultry

White-cooked Chicken

**Serves 6 to 8 as part of a
multicourse meal**

*T*his Chinese method of poaching chicken uses the passive heat of boiled water to cook. It is slow, but the result is well worth the wait.

The quality of the chicken is very important here. My mother always insisted on using fresh-killed chickens. When I was a child, every week we would make the trek to a shop in the back of Harvard University where my mother could pick out a live chicken. It would disappear through an open doorway to a back room to be butchered. The butchering took place in full view of the shop entrance. The butcher would leave on the head and feet and put all the innards back into the cleaned and dressed bird.

My mother always brought along a jar partially filled with a water-and-salt solution. She would give it to the butcher to collect the blood, which she made into a delicious blood pudding for soups. Nothing was wasted.

健康

1 whole chicken, freshly killed if possible (3 to 5 pounds)
1 tablespoon dry sherry
3 slices unpeeled gingerroot, 1 × ⅛ inch each
1 scallion
Soy Sauce Dip (page 324), for serving

1. Carefully lower the chicken into a large pot of boiling water and let sit for 2 to 3 minutes to clean and sear. Drain and pull out any pinfeathers with tweezers. Set aside.

2. Choose a large pot that will hold the whole chicken comfortably and fill it with enough water to submerge the chicken. (If you are unsure of how much water is enough, put the chicken in the pot, cover with water, and remove the bird.) Bring to a boil over high heat. Carefully slip the chicken into the water. Be sure it is totally submerged. Add the sherry, gingerroot, and scallion. When the water starts to boil again, turn off the heat, cover the pan tightly, and leave the chicken in the hot water for 1 hour.

3. After 1 hour, remove the cover and turn the heat to high. Watch the pot carefully and as soon as the water returns to a boil, immediately turn off the heat, cover tightly, and let sit for another hour.

4. Check for doneness by piercing the thigh with a chopstick or testing with an instant-read thermometer. The juices should be clear and the temperature 165°F. If the juices are bloody, repeat the boiling and soaking procedure a third time, letting the chicken stand in the water for 30 minutes before draining. Discard the liquid, it doesn't have much taste.

5. Let the bird cool. Serve at room temperature. (Or refrigerate the chicken, covered, overnight.) Serve the chicken chopped up, Chinese style (pages 164–165), or carved Western style with a soy sauce dip.

福

Drunken Chicken

Serves 6 to 8 as part of a multicourse meal

*T*his traditional Shanghai-style cold appetizer is a great dish for a hot summer's day when served with a salad or steamed garden vegetables. The chicken is poached whole and then marinated in wine for at least twelve hours. The Chinese marinate it in different kinds of rice wine, but excellent results can be had with the more readily available pale dry sherry.

I have offered two poaching techniques. The first, which my mother taught me, takes longer but gives better texture and flavor. The second is faster, and I find it is still good. Marinating the bird in sherry brings back its moisture and flavor. This dish is best served as part of a multicourse meal.

禄

1 whole chicken, freshly killed if possible (3 to 4 pounds)
4 slices unpeeled gingerroot, 1 × ⅛ inch each
1 tablespoon salt
3 cups dry sherry
Cilantro sprigs, for garnish

1. Rinse the chicken and remove the neck and giblets. Discard excess fat from the cavity opening. If there are still pinfeathers, pluck them out with tweezers.

2. Cook the chicken as described on page 178 or bring water to a boil in a pot large enough to hold the chicken and enough water to cover it. When the water boils, add the gingerroot and submerge the bird. When the water returns to a boil, turn the heat to low. Cook, covered, at a very slow simmer for 40 minutes. Turn off heat and let stand for 30 minutes. Test for doneness by piercing the thigh with a chopstick; the juices should be clear with no tinge of pink. Or, test the thickest part of the thigh with an instant-read thermometer; the temperature should be 165°F. If the bird is not done, turn heat back on to medium and bring just to a boil. Turn heat off and let stand for 15 minutes. Test for doneness again.

3. When the chicken is done, drain thoroughly and let cool until you can handle it. Place it in a plastic bag large enough to hold the whole bird and still be tightly secured. Place the bag in a large bowl or baking pan to catch any drips or leaks. Mix the salt with the sherry and stir until all the salt has dissolved. Pour mixture into the plastic bag with the bird, squeeze out air from bag, and secure tightly. Refrigerate for at least 12 hours, turning occasionally for even marinating.

4.   When ready to serve, chop the chicken up, Chinese style (pages 164–165), or place it on a platter and carve at the table. Garnish platter with sprigs of cilantro.

Drunken Chicken Breasts

Serves 4, or 6 to 8 as part of a multicourse meal

This nontraditional version of Drunken Chicken (page 180) uses only the breast meat. The sliced chicken makes a lovely light summer lunch when served with freshly tossed mixed greens and crusty French bread. Or you can cut the pieces smaller and serve them as a cold appetizer.

壽

2 whole chicken breasts (about 2 to 3 pounds)
4 slices unpeeled gingerroot, 1 × ⅛ inch each
1 tablespoon salt
3 cups dry sherry
Cilantro sprigs, for garnish

1.   Bring water to a boil in a pot large enough to hold the chicken comfortably. Rinse the breasts and trim away excess fat. Add the chicken and the gingerroot to the water. When the water returns to a boil, reduce the heat to low. Cover and simmer for 15 to 20 minutes. Turn off the heat and let stand for 20 minutes. Test for doneness by piercing the thickest part of the breast with a chopstick. The juices should be clear without any tinge of pink.

2.   Remove the chicken from the water, cool and place in a plastic bag. Dissolve the salt in the sherry and pour over the chicken in the bag. Squeeze the air from the bag and secure tightly. Set the bag in a roasting pan or dish to catch any drips or leaks and marinate in the refrigerator for at least 12 hours. Turn occasionally for even marinating.

3.   Remove the meat from the breast bone and slice into ¾-inch-thick pieces. Arrange in an overlapping design on a platter, pour about ¼ cup of the marinating liquid over the chicken and garnish with cilantro sprigs.

Soy Sauce Chicken

Serves 3 to 4, or 6 to 8 as part of a multicourse meal

For the Chinese, Cantonese-style soy sauce chicken, duck, and pork are as poplar and versatile as cold cuts are to Americans. They aren't used in sandwiches but as appetizers, side dishes, or as part of a multicourse meal, usually served at room temperature. Leftover pieces, especially the bony backs, are saved to add to soup noodles to make the broth even tastier. You can see the prepared meats hanging in the windows of grocery stores in Chinatown. You can buy a whole or half chicken and have it chopped up — bones and all — into bite-size pieces. It's quite a show to watch the chefs chop. They often work behind a clear plexiglas wall, both for sanitary reasons and to keep the juices from splattering everywhere and making a mess.

You can prepare your own Soy Sauce Chicken with this recipe. I often drop a few shelled hard-boiled eggs into the cooking liquid at the point when the chicken is turned over. They should be basted and turned occasionally for even color. The giblets may also be cooked along with the chicken. Be sure to allow them to simmer for at least twenty-five minutes to ensure that they are cooked through. Serve the chicken with Chinese Steamed Bread (page 122) to dip in the delicious gravy.

1 chicken (3 to 4 pounds)
3 slices unpeeled gingerroot, 1 × ⅛ inch each
2 whole star anise
1 (3-inch) stick cinnamon
1 (3-inch) piece dried or fresh orange peel
½ cup dark soy sauce
3 tablespoons dry sherry
½ cup sugar
1 tablespoon sesame seed oil (optional)

1.   Rinse and drain the chicken. Remove any excess fat from the cavity and discard.

2.   Place the gingerroot, star anise, cinnamon, orange peel, soy sauce, sherry, sugar, and 1 cup water in a Dutch oven or roaster large enough to hold the whole chicken. Stir to dissolve the sugar and bring to a boil.

3. Add the chicken, breast side down, and with a large spoon or bulb baster, baste a few times. Turn the heat to low, cover, and simmer for 25 minutes. Baste frequently and check that the liquid remains at just the barest simmer.

4. Turn the chicken over and continue to simmer, covered, for 20 to 25 minutes. Uncover the pan, bring the liquid to a boil over medium heat, and baste frequently for about 10 minutes, or until the skin is brown. Turn off the heat and let stand, covered, for 1 hour. Test for doneness by sticking a chopstick into the thigh; if the juices run clear the chicken is done. If not, turn the heat on to medium and bring to a boil again. Turn off the heat and let stand for 15 minutes. Check for doneness again and repeat if necessary.

5. Carve the chicken, place on a platter, and sparingly pour some of the cooking juices over it. Mix sesame seed oil, if using, into the cooking liquid and serve the remaining juices on the side. (To serve Chinese style, see pages 164–165, cut up the chicken and reassemble all the pieces on the platter. Mix the sesame seed oil, if using, into the cooking liquid and lightly drizzle the juices over the chicken pieces.) Serve cold.

Chinese Chicken Salad

Serves 4 to 6

*I*t wasn't until I was an adult and visited Los Angeles that I ever tried a Chinese chicken salad. Our Los Angeles sales representative and friend, Gus Dallas, introduced me to it, and I came back to Boston determined to develop a chicken salad of my own. This one is much lighter and lower in fat than Western chicken salads. Serve it with Pan-fried Scallion Cakes (page 303) or Minute Scallion Pancakes (page 305) and fill a bowl with extra noodles to let guests add more if they like. Add the noodles to the salad just before serving or they will become soft and soggy.

健康

½ cup rice vinegar

1 tablespoon cider vinegar

4 teaspoons sugar

2 teaspoons sesame seed oil

½ teaspoon grated peeled gingerroot

1 pound skinless boneless chicken breast, poached, or about 2 cups shredded
   cooked chicken

4 cups shredded iceberg lettuce (½ medium head)

2 cups grated carrots (about 2 medium)

¼ cup chopped chives or scallions

1½ cups chow mein noodles

½ cup sliced almonds, toasted

1. Combine the vinegars, sugar, sesame seed oil, and gingerroot in a small bowl or lidded jar and stir or shake until the sugar is dissolved. Set aside.

2. Tear the chicken with your hands into tiny shredded pieces. Combine the pieces in a large salad bowl with the lettuce, carrots, and chives. Just before serving, pour the dressing over the salad and toss until thoroughly mixed. Sprinkle with chow mein noodles and almonds. Serve immediately.

Note See page 45 for directions for shredding vegetables.

The Best Part of the Chicken Breast

The tender meat of the chicken tenderloin is considered the best part of the chicken. In Chinese families where the elderly are revered, this special part is often saved for the grandparents. But nothing is wasted in China — even the tendon that is removed from the tenderloin has its place. It is saved by placing it in an out-of-the-way place like the kitchen window to dry. Then it is deep-fried in hot oil until it puffs up, much like pork rind, and used to garnish dishes.

Cold Cucumber Salad with Chicken Shreds

Serves 4 to 6 as part of a multicourse meal

*T*his dish was often served at our dinner table, especially during the summer, and it was one of my first potluck contributions when I was in school. If you have any left-over roast chicken or turkey, use it here.

1 long seedless cucumber or 1 pound regular cucumbers
¼ cup smooth peanut butter
½ teaspoon salt, or to taste
1 tablespoon sesame seed oil
½ cup shredded cooked chicken or turkey

1.   Wash the seedless cucumber, split in half lengthwise, and slice on the diagonal, ¼ inch thick. If using regular cucumbers, partially peel, leaving strips of green skin, split in half lengthwise, and with a teaspoon scoop out the seeds and discard. Slice on the diagonal, ¼ inch thick.

2.   In a small bowl, gradually stir ¼ cup cold water into the peanut butter and mix with a rubber spatula to make a smooth paste. Add the salt and sesame seed oil. Set aside.

3.   When ready to serve, mix the cucumber slices with the shredded chicken and peanut dressing.

Shanghai Red-cooked Duck

Serves 4 to 5, or 6 to 8 as part of a
multicourse meal

M y late father loved to have this dish in the traditional manner with Red-mouthed Green Parrot (page 271) and Chinese Steamed Bread (page 122) to soak up the delicious soy sauce gravy. When he moved to Hawaii for health reasons and would return to Boston for visits, I often prepared this for him.

I also like to make this dish for dinner parties since it can be prepared in advance and kept warm or made a day ahead and warmed up. The Chinese do not use knives at the table, even when a whole duckling is served; they pull off pieces with chopsticks. For company, I cut pieces off the duck so everyone can pick up tasty morsels of duck without a struggle.

1 duckling, thawed if frozen (4 to 5 pounds)
½ cup sugar
1 tablespoon dry sherry
¾ cup dark soy sauce
8 scallions, green and white parts, cut into 3 pieces
2 slices unpeeled gingerroot, 1 × ⅛ inch each
3 whole star anise

1. Remove and discard any large pieces of fat from the cavity. Carefully lower the duckling and the giblets into a large pot of boiling water and let soak 2 to 3 minutes until the skin shrinks and is covered with goose bumps. This will clean the duck and open the pores. Drain and pull out any pinfeathers with tweezers. Rinse and drain the bird thoroughly.

2. Combine the sugar, sherry, soy sauce, and ½ cup water in a small bowl. Stir to dissolve the sugar.

3. Put the scallions, gingerroot, star anise, and giblets in the bottom of a heavy oval pot or Dutch oven that will just hold the whole bird comfortably. Place the duckling, breast side down, in the pot and pour the soy sauce mixture over. Cover the pot and bring to a boil.

(continued)

4. Reduce the heat to low and simmer for 1½ to 2 hours, or until the duckling is tender. Halfway through cooking, turn the duckling over so the breast is facing up. If much of the liquid has evaporated, add another ½ cup of water. Test if the duckling is done by piercing the thigh with a chopstick. If it goes in easily, the bird is done.

5. When the duck is ready, remove the cover and skim off the fat with a spoon or bulb baster. Turn the heat to medium and baste the duck frequently for 15 minutes, or until the skin becomes dark brown and about ½ to 1 cup of liquid remains. Transfer the duckling and the liquid to a large oval platter with enough depth to hold the liquid. Or serve directly from the cooking pot. Remove and discard the gingerroot and star anise if desired. Serve hot.

Pork 豬肉

P ork is the national meat of China. When we say *rou,* which means meat, we mean pork; the words are synonymous. Other meats are described as beef meat or sheep meat, but pork is so universal it doesn't need a modifier.

The reason for pork's popularity is a practical one. Land in China is scarce and valuable but pigs are easy to raise on small plots. Every household can raise its own pigs in the backyard.

Pork works well in Chinese dishes. It has a mild taste that does not interfere with milder sauces and light soups. It also has a smooth texture that is not fibrous, so it is a good choice for quick cooking such as stir-frying.

My mother's name is a good example of how ubiquitous pork is to the Chinese. Her name in Chinese is *Liao Jia Ai* 廖家艾. Chinese women retain their maiden name throughout their life, even after marriage. Married women may be called Mrs. So-and-So, but when they are called by their own name, it's always their maiden name. My mother's middle name, which is part of her given name, is the character *Jia* 家, which means house or home. If the character is taken apart and examined, the radical or top portion of the ideogram looks like the roof of a house with a chimney 宀. The character that is under the roof is the literary word for pig 豕. I find it significant that the word for home uses the ideogram of a pig under a roof. Doesn't "A pig in every home" sound a little like the Chinese version of "A chicken in every pot"?

This way I can take out only as much as I need. Pork tenderloin is another lean cut I like to use. It has very little fat and is easy to cut into slices, cubes, or medallions.

The Chinese like to eat pork fat. The thick fat under the skin in the pork shoulder, which is used for Shanghai Ham, has always been considered a delicacy. Much of that tradition comes from the need for extra calories in a land where famine was chronic. Of course, we know now that animal fat is very high in cholesterol and is not healthy to eat. For health reasons everyone, even in China, is now well aware that excess consumption of animal fat is not good for you. Choose lean meat and trim it well before cooking.

Pork Shreds with Green Beans

猪肉

Serves 3 to 4, or 5 to 6 as part of a multicourse meal

My husband and I are partial to green beans in season. In this dish, they are practically a meal-in-one.

健康

1 pound green beans

1 cup shredded lean pork (about ½ pound)

1 teaspoon dry sherry

2 teaspoons cornstarch

2 tablespoons dark soy sauce

3 tablespoons canola, corn, or peanut oil

1 cup thinly sliced onion

1 slice unpeeled gingerroot, 1 × ⅛ inch

½ cup water

Salt to taste

1. Snap the ends from the green beans and break them into 2-inch pieces. Wash and drain thoroughly.

2. Place the pork in a bowl, stir in the sherry, cornstarch, and soy sauce, and mix well. Set aside.

3. Heat 2 tablespoons of the oil in a wok or stir-fry pan over high heat. Add the gingerroot and stir a few times until the oil is hot and the gingerroot sizzles. Add the onion to the pan and stir-fry for 1 minute. Stir up the pork again and pour it into the pan. Stir-fry for about 3 minutes, or until pork is cooked through. Transfer the meat and onions to a platter.

4. Add the remaining tablespoon of oil to the same pan and stir in the green beans. Stir-fry for about 1 minute. Add the water, stir, bring to a boil, and cover. Reduce the heat to medium-low and cook, covered, for 9 to 12 minutes, depending upon how crisp you like your beans. Stir occasionally for even cooking.

5. Return the meat to the pan and stir thoroughly until the pork and gravy are well mixed into the beans. Taste and add salt, if desired. Discard the gingerroot, if desired, and transfer to a serving platter. Serve hot.

福

Note   See page 44 for directions for shredding the pork.

Moo Shi Pork

Serves 4, or enough to fill about 12 pancakes

M oo Shi refers to the fragrant yellow flowers of the sweet olive tree (Osmanthus fra-grans), which are used in China as a flavoring, because the scrambled eggs in this dish are believed to resemble the tiny flowers. In China, only wood ears and golden needles are used in the dish. Restaurants in this country add fresh mushrooms, bam-boo shoots, cabbage, and sometimes bean thread. I have given my recipe, which is enriched with bean sprouts, cabbage, and mushrooms, because that's the one I prefer.

Moo Shi Pork is served with Mandarin Pancakes (page 118), sometimes called ''doilies'' because of their delicate composition. Hoisin sauce is spread on a pancake, 3 or 4 tablespoons of Moo Shi are placed in a strip down the middle, and the pan-cake is rolled up and eaten. Don't overfill the pancake or it will be impossible to eat neatly. The pork is on the dry side so it won't drip out of the pancake. If you don't have time to make your own pancakes, you can purchase them frozen in Asian mar-kets. You can also eat Moo Shi Pork in an unconventional but equally good manner — over steamed rice. In that case, serve a small dish of hoisin sauce as a condiment.

3 tablespoons dried wood ears

¼ cup dried golden needles (about ½ ounce)

½ cup shredded lean pork (about ¼ pound)

1 teaspoon dry sherry

3 tablespoons light soy sauce

1 teaspoon cornstarch

4 tablespoons canola, corn, or peanut oil

2 eggs, beaten

2 slices unpeeled gingerroot, 1 × ⅛ inch each

1½ cups shredded green cabbage (about 5 ounces)

1 cup sliced mushrooms

2 cups bean sprouts (about 6 ounces)

2 scallions, green parts cut into 1-inch pieces, bulbs split in half

1½ teaspoons salt, or to taste

1.   Soak the wood ears and golden needles separately in hot water to cover for 15 minutes, or until soft. Squeeze out the water, clean, rinse, and drain. Remove any tough parts and chop the wood ears coarsely into pieces about ½ inch in size. Cut off the stems of the golden needles if they are tough, and cut in half. Set aside.

2.   Place the pork in a bowl, stir in the sherry, soy sauce, and cornstarch, and mix well. Set aside.

3.   Heat 2 tablespoons of the oil in a wok or stir-fry pan over medium-high heat. When oil is hot, pour in the eggs and scramble into fine pieces. Remove the eggs from the pan. Set aside.

4.   Pour the remaining 2 tablespoons of oil into the same pan and place over high heat. Add the gingerroot and stir a few times until the gingerroot begins to sizzle. Stir up the pork again and pour it into the pan. Add the cabbage and 2 tablespoons of water. Stir about 2 minutes, or until the pork turns color and the cabbage just begins to wilt. Add the mushrooms, bean sprouts, scallions, wood ears, and golden needles. Stir constantly for 1 minute, or until the fresh vegetables are tender and the pork is thoroughly cooked.

5.   Return the eggs to the pan and stir until well mixed. Taste for salt. Discard the gingerroot. Serve hot.

壽

Note   See pages 44–45 for directions for shredding the pork and cabbage.

Bean Sprouts with Shredded Pork and Chinese Chives

Serves 4, or 8 as part of a multicourse meal

*C*hinese chives are also known as garlic chives because they have a deep garlic flavor. They are easy to grow, but be sure to plant plenty of them since you need to use a whole bunch at a time.

禧

1 cup shredded lean pork (about ½ pound)
2 teaspoons dry sherry
2 teaspoons cornstarch
½ teaspoon sugar
3 tablespoons light soy sauce
¼ pound Chinese chives or scallions
3 tablespoons canola, corn, or peanut oil
2 slices unpeeled gingerroot, 1 × ⅛ inch each
¾ pound bean sprouts (4 heaping cups)

1. Place the pork in a bowl, stir in the sherry, cornstarch, sugar, and soy sauce, and mix well. Set aside.

2. If using the chives, trim off and discard the white ends. Wash the leaves thoroughly and cut into 1-inch lengths. If using scallions, trim away root ends and wash the scallions well. Split the bulb and cut the whole scallion, white and green part, into 2-inch pieces.

3. Pour the oil into a wok or stir-fry pan and place over high heat. Add the gingerroot and stir around the pan until the oil is hot; the gingerroot will sizzle. Stir up the pork again and pour into the pan. Stir constantly until the pork pieces are separated and lose their pink color, about 2 minutes.

4. Add the chives or scallions and the bean sprouts and stir until the sprouts wilt, 2 to 3 minutes. Discard the gingerroot, if desired. Serve immediately.

Note See page 44 for directions for shredding the pork.

Pork Shreds with Bean Thread and Napa Cabbage

Serves 3 to 4, or 5 to 6 as part of a multicourse meal

*B*ean thread, made from mung beans, is also known as cellophane noodles because when it is cooked it becomes transparent. Bean thread has no flavor itself, but it soaks up the flavors of the gravy and other cooking ingredients. Be careful not to overcook the bean thread and be sure to serve the dish as soon as it is ready, or the noodles will become very soft and sticky.

1 cup shredded lean pork (about ½ pound)
1 teaspoon cornstarch
3 tablespoons light soy sauce
1 teaspoon dry sherry
¼ pound bean thread (2 2-ounce packages)
½ pound napa cabbage, about 4 cups
3 tablespoons canola, corn, or peanut oil
1 slice unpeeled gingerroot, 1 × ⅛ inch
⅓ cup thinly sliced scallions
½ cup chicken broth or water

1.   Place the pork with the cornstarch, soy sauce, and sherry in a bowl and stir together well. Set aside.

2.   Soak the bean thread in hot (not boiling) water until soft. Drain carefully, keeping the strands together, and cut into 6-inch lengths with scissors. Set aside. Wash the cabbage leaves thoroughly, drain and cut into 1½-inch chunks. You should have about 4 cups. Set aside.

3.   Pour the oil into a wok or stir-fry pan and place over high heat. Add the gingerroot and stir until the oil is hot; the gingerroot will begin to sizzle. Add the scallions and stir for about 15 seconds. Stir up the pork again and pour into the pan, stirring constantly for about 1 minute. Add the cabbage and stir again for 1 minute.

(continued)

4.   Pour the broth into the pan, stir to mix, and cover. Let steam for about 4 minutes. Uncover, reduce the heat to medium, and stir in the softened bean thread. Stir for about 2 minutes, or until the bean thread becomes translucent. Serve immediately.

壽

Note   See page 44 for directions for shredding pork.

Shredded Pork with Bean Sprouts and Szechuan Vegetable

Serves 2 to 3, or 4 to 5 as part of a multicourse meal

When *Szechuan vegetable, also called Szechuan preserved vegetable, is added to a dish, it gives a distinctive pungent flavor to the other ingredients. It is a very versatile canned condiment with a long shelf life, even after opening. My mother and I keep some on hand at all times.*

禧

1 cup shredded lean pork (about ½ pound)
1 teaspoon cornstarch
1 teaspoon dry sherry
½ cup shredded Szechuan vegetable (page 28)
3 tablespoons canola, corn, or peanut oil
2 slices unpeeled gingerroot, 1 × ⅛ inch each
¾ pound bean sprouts (4 heaping cups)
2 tablespoons light soy sauce, or to taste

1.   Place the pork in a bowl, stir in the cornstarch and sherry, and mix well. Set aside.

2.   Place the Szechuan vegetable in a strainer and rinse to remove excess salt and chili. Drain well. If not shredded, cut into thin slices, and shred. Set aside.

3.   Pour the oil into a wok or stir-fry pan and place the pan over high heat. Add the gingerroot and stir until it begins to sizzle. Stir up the pork again, add to the pan, and cook for about 2 minutes, or until all the pink is gone from the meat. Break the meat up as you stir to keep shreds from sticking together.

4.   Add the Szechuan vegetable and the bean sprouts. Stir thoroughly for 1 minute. Drizzle the soy sauce over the mixture and stir until it is well mixed and the bean sprouts are tender-crisp. Discard the gingerroot, if desired. Transfer to a platter. Serve immediately.

Note   I always rinse Szechuan vegetable before I use it. If you like a spicier and more savory dish, use it as it comes from the can. Adjust the amount of soy sauce accordingly.

See pages 44–45 for directions for shredding the pork and Szechuan vegetable.

Stir-fried Pork
with Asparagus

**Serves 3 to 4, or 5 to 6 as part of a
multicourse meal**

I keep a few boneless pork chops, individually wrapped, in the freezer for easy last-minute stir-fry dishes like this one. Hoisin sauce lends a delicate sweetness to the sauce, which enhances the natural goodness of fresh asparagus.

1 pound asparagus
½ pound lean pork or boneless loin chops
2 teaspoons cornstarch
1 teaspoon sherry
1 tablespoon dark soy sauce
2 tablespoons hoisin sauce
1 teaspoon sugar
3 tablespoons canola, corn, or peanut oil
¼ cup water
1 garlic clove, peeled and sliced

1.   Break off or cut the tough ends from the asparagus, trim away the lower scales from the spears, and wash well. Cut on the diagonal into 1½- to 2-inch pieces.

2.   Cut the pork into ¼-inch-thick strips the same length as the asparagus. Place in a bowl, stir in the cornstarch and sherry, and mix well. Set aside. Combine the soy sauce, hoisin sauce, and sugar in another bowl. Set aside.

3.   Heat 1 tablespoon of the oil in a wok or stir-fry pan over high heat until hot but not smoking. Test by dipping an asparagus into the oil; it should sizzle. Add the asparagus and stir for about 30 seconds, or until they just turn a darker green. Add the water and cover the pan. Cook, covered, over medium heat until tender, 3 to 5 minutes, depending upon the thickness of the spears. Stir occasionally for even cooking. Remove the asparagus and any liquid to a platter.

4. Pour the remaining 2 tablespoons of oil into the same pan, add the garlic, and place over high heat. When the garlic sizzles, stir up the pork again and pour into the pan. Stir constantly until the meat is no longer pink, about 2 to 3 minutes. Add the soy sauce mixture and stir for about 20 seconds, return the asparagus to the pan, and stir another 30 seconds or so, until well mixed. Serve hot.

Chungking Pork

**Serves 3 to 4, or 5 to 6 as part of a
multicourse meal**

*T*his is a classic Szechuan dish named after Chungking (Chongqing), a major city in
Szechuan Province. It is also known as Twice-cooked Pork, although the literal
translation of the Chinese name is "return the meat to the pan," because the pork is
first poached and then stir-fried. I have simplified the recipe, without sacrificing flavor,
by eliminating the first cooking.

祿

¾ pound pork tenderloin

2 teaspoons dry sherry

4 teaspoons cornstarch

2 tablespoons fermented black beans, coarsely chopped

1 teaspoon crushed red pepper, or to taste

3 tablespoons hoisin sauce

2 teaspoons dark soy sauce

4 tablespoons canola, corn, or peanut oil

½ pound green cabbage, cut in 1½-inch chunks (about 3 cups)

1 medium green or red bell pepper, seeded, cored, and cut into 1½-inch chunks

3 slices unpeeled gingerroot, 1 × ⅛ inch each

2 garlic cloves, crushed and peeled

(continued)

1. Slice the tenderloin crosswise ⅛ inch thick. If necessary, freeze briefly first. Place in a bowl, stir in the sherry and 2 teaspoons of the cornstarch, and mix well. Set aside. Dissolve the remaining cornstarch in ¼ cup of water. Set aside.

2. Stir the black beans and crushed red pepper together in a small bowl. Set aside. Combine the hoisin sauce and soy sauce in another small bowl. Set aside.

3. Heat 2 tablespoons of the oil in a wok or stir-fry pan over high heat. When the oil is hot but not smoking, add the cabbage; it should sizzle. Stir-fry for about 3 minutes. Add the peppers and cook for 2 minutes. The cabbage may slightly brown. Remove the vegetables to a plate.

4. Pour the remaining 2 tablespoons of oil into the same pan and place over high heat. Add the gingerroot and garlic and stir around the pan until they become fragrant and begin to sizzle. Do not brown. Stir the pork up again and add to the pan, stirring briskly, until the meat is no longer pink, about 2 to 3 minutes.

5. Stir in the black bean mixture, mix around a few times, add the sauce mixture, and stir a few times to mix. Return the vegetables to the pan, stir, then add the cornstarch slurry, and stir for 30 seconds. Discard the gingerroot and garlic, if desired. Serve hot.

Kan Shao Green Beans
with Pork

Serves 4, or 6 as part of a
multicourse meal

*K*an shao, *which means "dry cook," is a Szechuan style of cooking in which the ingredients are stir-fried over high heat until the liquid has completely reduced. The result is a truly rich and savory dish since the ingredients absorb all the flavors. For a meatless version of this dish, see Kan Shao Green Beans (page 270). The kan shao technique can also be used with eggplant or shrimp.*

1 pound green or wax beans

½ cup ground pork or beef (4 ounces)

1 tablespoon dry sherry

1 teaspoon cornstarch

3 tablespoons fermented black beans, coarsely chopped

1 tablespoon minced peeled gingerroot

2 garlic cloves, minced

1 teaspoon crushed red pepper, to taste

3 tablespoons dark soy sauce

1 teaspoon sugar

3 tablespoons canola, corn, or peanut oil

1. Snap the ends and string the beans. Break them into 2-inch lengths. Rinse and set aside to drain in a colander.

2. Mix the meat with the sherry and cornstarch. Set aside.

3. Mix the black beans, gingerroot, garlic, and red pepper in a small dish. Set aside. Combine the soy sauce, sugar, and ½ cup water in another small bowl. Set aside.

4. Heat the oil in a wok or stir-fry pan over medium-high heat. Add the black bean mixture and stir a few times until aromatic. Stir up the meat mixture and pour it into the pan. Turn the heat to high and stir-fry until the meat turns color and separates, about 2 minutes.

5. Add the green beans and the soy sauce mixture. Stir a few times and then reduce the heat to medium. Cook, covered, for 5 minutes. Remove the lid and stir constantly over high heat for about 5 minutes, or until the liquid is almost gone. Serve hot.

Szechuan Stir-fried
Eggplant with Pork

Serves 3 to 4, or 5 to 6 as part of a
multicourse meal

lthough this dish contains no fish, the eggplant is cooked in the same type of flavorings that are used in the highly savory "fragrant fish sauce" of Szechuan (Sichuan)
Province. This dish contains very little meat, and you can make it without any meat
at all, if you like. If your eggplant is garden fresh, leave the skin on for added texture, otherwise peel it entirely or peel it in strips. Omit the crushed pepper for a less
spicy version.

禧

1 to 1¼ pounds eggplant, regular or Asian

1 teaspoon salt

3 tablespoons thinly sliced scallions plus additional for garnish, green and white
    parts

1 tablespoon minced peeled gingerroot

1 teaspoon minced garlic (about 1 clove)

1 to 3 teaspoons crushed red pepper, or to taste

1 tablespoon Szechuan hot bean sauce

1 tablespoon cider vinegar

1 teaspoon sugar

1 tablespoon dark soy sauce

⅓ cup ground lean pork (3 ounces)

1 tablespoon sherry

1 teaspoon cornstarch for the pork plus 2 teaspoons, dissolved in 1 tablespoon
    water for sauce

3 tablespoons canola, corn, or peanut oil

1 cup water

    1.   Wash the eggplant and trim off the stem. Leave the skin on if egg-
plant is very fresh and the skin tender. Otherwise peel or peel in strips. Quarter
the eggplant lengthwise and cut each quarter into 1-inch long pieces. If the
eggplant is large, cut it into eighths first; the pieces should be bite size. Place

in a colander, sprinkle with salt, toss, and let stand for 20 minutes. Rinse, drain, and pat dry. Set aside.

2. In a small dish, mix together the 3 tablespoons of scallions, ginger-root, garlic, and red pepper. Set aside. In another small dish, combine the hot bean sauce, vinegar, sugar, and soy sauce. Set aside. In a third bowl, stir together the pork, sherry, and 1 teaspoon cornstarch. Set aside.

3. Pour the oil into a wok or stir-fry pan and place over high heat. Heat the oil to hot but not smoking. Test by dipping a piece of eggplant into the oil; it should sizzle. Stir the eggplant into the hot oil. The eggplant will initially absorb all the oil but will release it as it cooks. Do not add more oil. Cook, stirring and pressing the eggplant against the bottom of the pan with the back of a spatula, for about 6 minutes, or until it is soft and turns dark. Add the pork and stir-fry until the meat changes color and becomes crumbly. Add the scallion mixture and stir for 1 minute.

4. Add the bean sauce mixture and water and stir to mix. Cover the pan, reduce the heat to medium, and simmer, stirring occasionally, for 2 to 3 minutes, or until tender. Remove the cover and thicken the sauce with the cornstarch slurry. Transfer to a shallow platter and sprinkle with thinly sliced scallions. Serve hot.

Meat-stuffed Cucumbers

**Serves 4 to 5, or 6 to 8 as part of a
multicourse meal**

M*y mother often prepared this dish for us when we were young, perhaps because the
ingredients are easy to obtain and the finished dish can be kept warm while waiting
for stragglers to come to the dinner table. It's a typical family-style recipe that's not
served in restaurants. Any leftover ground meat should be formed into small meatballs
and cooked alongside the cucumbers.*

健康

4 medium cucumbers

¾ pound ground lean pork or beef

½ cup corn flakes or bread crumbs

2 teaspoons dry sherry

3 tablespoons plus 2 teaspoons dark soy sauce

3 tablespoons cornstarch

About ¼ cup all-purpose flour, for dredging

3 tablespoons canola, corn, or peanut oil

½ teaspoon salt, or to taste

1 teaspoon sugar

1. Peel the cucumbers, leaving alternating ½-inch-wide strips of skin
behind for color. Trim off about ½ inch from each end and then cut the
cucumber into 2-inch pieces. Carefully hollow out the inside by removing
the seeds with a teaspoon. Discard the seeds and set the cucumber pieces aside.

2. Place the meat in a bowl. Add the corn flakes, sherry, the 3 tablespoons soy sauce, 2 tablespoons of the cornstarch, and 3 tablespoons water.
Stir the mixture together well. Mix the remaining 1 tablespoon cornstarch
with ¼ cup of water. Set aside.

3. Tightly fill each cucumber piece with the meat mixture. Spread the
meat out at both ends to form a plug to prevent the meat from shrinking back
into the cucumber as it cooks. Dip the ends in flour.

4. Pour the oil into a deep skillet and place over high heat. When the
oil is hot, place the stuffed cucumbers, meat end down, in the pan and brown
well. Turn to brown the other end. Place cucumbers on their side and add 1
cup water, the 2 teaspoons soy sauce, salt, and sugar. Cover and simmer on

low heat for 20 to 30 minutes, or until the cucumbers are tender and translucent. Turn occasionally for even cooking.

5. Remove the cover and baste for 5 minutes. With a slotted spoon, transfer the cucumbers to a heated platter. Skim the fat off the sauce. Turn the heat up to medium and when the gravy boils stir in the cornstarch mixture. Stir until the gravy thickens, then pour it over the cucumbers. Serve hot.

Note If you are not serving the cucumbers right away, cover the pan and keep hot in a low oven. There are no crisp vegetables that will overcook. The dish also heats up well in the microwave.

Lion's Head

Serves 6 to 8, or 10 as part of a multicourse meal

This famous dish from Yangchow (Yangzhou), near Nanking (Nanjing), is another of my mother's favorites. She used to say that a good Lion's Head should be so tender that it cannot be picked up with chopsticks; you have to use a spoon. Her comments from her book describe the dish well:

"New customers of our restaurant are always surprised about this dish and ask if it is really made from a lion's head. Of course it is not. Chinese people like to put words like dragon, phoenix, or lion into names of dishes, because in Imperial China, dragon and phoenix symbolized emperors and their dishes. So, to use these names indicates the high quality of the food. As for lion, it is the king of the jungle. To use its name means high quality and large size. In the menu, Lion's Head is actually large meatballs, the size of a baseball or tennis ball."

2 pounds ground pork (4 cups)
⅓ cup dark soy sauce plus 1½ tablespoons for the gravy
2 teaspoons dry sherry
2 teaspoons light brown sugar
½ teaspoon salt, or to taste
4 tablespoons cornstarch
2 pounds Chinese cabbage, preferably napa, washed and cut into 2-inch pieces
2 tablespoons canola, corn, or peanut oil

Pork

(continued)

1. Place the meat in a bowl. Add the ⅓ cup of soy sauce, the sherry, 1 teaspoon of the brown sugar, salt, 1 tablespoon of the cornstarch, and ½ cup cold water to the meat. Use your hands to mix together well. Let stand for at least 15 minutes.

2. In a deep plate, mix the remaining 3 tablespoons of cornstarch with 2 tablespoons of cold water into a thin paste. Divide the meat into 8 portions and form each into a ball with your hands.

3. Heat the oil in a stir-fry pan, preferably nonstick, over medium heat. Coat the meatballs with the cornstarch paste, tossing gently between your hands for even coating. They will be sticky and the cornstarch paste watery.

4. Brown the lightly coated meatballs in the hot oil for about 5 minutes, or until evenly browned. Do not crowd the pan; cook in batches, if necessary. Handle the meatballs gently as they will be soft. I find it easiest to use 2 spatulas to turn the meat, carefully loosening the bottom before turning. Transfer each browned piece gently with a slotted spoon to a flameproof casserole. Reserve the oil that is left in the pan for later use.

5. Combine the remaining 1½ tablespoons soy sauce and 1 teaspoon sugar with ½ cup water and add it to the pot with the meatballs. Cover and simmer over low heat for 1½ to 2 hours, or until the meatballs are cooked through.

6. Meanwhile stir the cabbage into the same pan used to brown the meatballs. If necessary add the cabbage in stages, waiting for the first to wilt and make room for the next batch. Cook over medium-high heat for about 5 minutes, or until all the cabbage has wilted.

7. Remove the cover from the casserole and lift the meatballs out with a slotted spoon and place on a dish. Skim the fat from the liquid. Spread the cabbage around the casserole and arrange the meatballs over the cabbage. Simmer, covered, for about 10 minutes to heat through. Serve hot from the casserole.

Note This is a good dish for entertaining, especially if your meal includes a number of stir-fry dishes. Cook the meatballs the day before. Early on the day you will serve the dish, cook the cabbage with the meatballs and set aside until ready for its last 10 minutes of reheating.

Steamed Meat Cake

**Serves 3 to 4, or 5 to 6 as part of a
multicourse meal**

Steamed Meat Cake and rice are a real Chinese home favorite. I introduced this dish to our New York sales representative, Tom Scafati, one day as we had dinner in New York's Chinatown. In Chinese restaurants the meat cake is sometimes enriched with preserved duck eggs or dried and salted fish, and he was a little leery at first. But it was love at first bite!

1 pound ground pork (2 cups)

½ cup canned water chestnuts, drained and minced

1 tablespoon fermented black beans, minced

1½ tablespoons thinly sliced scallions

2 teaspoons grated peeled gingerroot

1 teaspoon dry sherry

½ teaspoon light brown sugar

1 tablespoon cornstarch

1 egg

1.   Use you hands to mix all the ingredients together in a mixing bowl. Press the meat evenly into a 9-inch pie pan or similar heatproof dish with a rim.

2.   Place a steamer filled with water over high heat and bring it to a boil as described on page 36. Be sure your steamer is large enough to hold the pan or dish with room for the steam to circulate freely and for you to be able to get the pan out. Place it in the steamer, reduce the heat to medium, and maintain a steady boil. Cover the steamer and cook the meat cake for 10 to 15 minutes, or until the meat is cooked through and has liquid all around it. The time depends on how thick the meat cake is. Test for doneness by using a fork or knife to cut into the center of the cake to see if the meat is cooked. If it is still pink, steam a few minutes more and test again.

3.   When the meat cake is done, turn off the heat and remove the plate from the steamer. Serve the meat cake hot, directly from the pan or dish.

Pork

Sweet and Sour Pork, Cantonese Style

Serves 2, or 4 as part of a
multicourse meal

*T*he traditional southern Chinese sweet and sour dish is made with much less batter than in this recipe, but this is the one Americans know best. For best results use lean pork that is free of gristle. The batter must be prepared exactly as described and the pork fried twice at a temperature no less than 375°F. to ensure crispness. A deep-fry basket makes it easy to remove the cooked pork from the oil.

The same ingredients and technique can be used with chicken, shrimp, or beef. Cooking times need to be adjusted accordingly.

健康

½ cup peeled and roll-cut carrots (page 46)

1 small green bell pepper, seeded, cored, and cut into 1-inch cubes (½ cup)

½ cup canned pineapple chunks, well drained

½ cup all-purpose flour

¼ cup cornstarch plus 3½ tablespoons dissolved in ⅓ cup water

½ teaspoon baking powder

1 tablespoon beaten egg plus enough water to make ½ cup

1 teaspoon canola, corn, or peanut oil

About ½ pound lean boneless pork chops, cut into 1-inch or smaller cubes
  (about 1 cup)

1 teaspoon dry sherry

¼ teaspoon salt

Dash black pepper

Canola, corn, or peanut oil, for frying

¾ cup sugar

⅓ cup ketchup

1 tablespoon light soy sauce

¼ teaspoon salt

⅔ cup water

½ cup cider vinegar

1.   In a small saucepan of boiling water, parboil the carrots for 1 minute. Add the green pepper to the same water. As soon as it comes back to a boil, drain the vegetables and rinse in cold water to stop cooking. Add the pineapple to the vegetables and set aside.

2.   Combine the flour, ¼ cup cornstarch, baking powder, egg mixture, and oil in a mixing bowl and beat with a wooden spoon until the mixture is a smooth paste. Set aside.

3.   In another bowl, stir the pork, sherry, salt, and pepper together. Set aside.

4.   In a wok or stir-fry pan, heat 2 inches of oil to a temperature of 375°F. to 400°F. Dip the marinated cubes of pork into the batter to coat completely. Carefully drop the pork into the hot oil, 1 piece at a time. Deep-fry until light golden brown. Remove with a wire skimmer, spread out on paper towels, and let cool. Reserve the oil in the pan. (You may deep-fry the pork to this point in advance and keep it in the refrigerator for a few days or in the freezer. The oil may be strained and kept for a day or two; otherwise use fresh oil for the second frying.)

5.   Make the sweet and sour sauce only when ready to proceed with the second frying. Combine the sugar, ketchup, soy sauce, salt, and water in a 2-quart saucepan. Bring to a boil and add the vinegar. When the liquid comes back to a boil, stir in the cornstarch solution. Cook until the sauce thickens. Add the parboiled vegetables and the pineapple to the sauce, then add 1 tablespoon of hot oil from the deep-fry pan to give the sauce a shine.

6.   While preparing the sauce, reheat the deep-fry oil to 400°F. for a second frying. Add all the pork to the oil and fry until the pieces are heated and crisped. (Frozen or refrigerated pork should be brought to room temperature before being cooked.) Remove with a wire skimmer and drain on paper towels. (If not ready to serve the dish immediately, you can keep the sauce warm on the stove and the pork warm in a 325°F. oven for 10 minutes, no longer. Put together just before serving.)

7.   Put the pork in a deep plate and pour the sweet and sour sauce over. Serve immediately.

Sweet and Sour Pork, Northern Style

**Serves 3 to 4, or 5 to 6 as part of a
multicourse meal**

福

This traditional northern Chinese version of sweet and sour pork does not require the batter or double deep-frying of the Americanized Cantonese style. Here I've given a recipe for the familiar sweet and sour sauce made with ketchup and, as a variation, a dark sauce made with black Chinkiang vinegar.

福

1 pound lean pork loin

1/4 teaspoon pepper

1 egg

1 tablespoon light soy sauce

3 tablespoons cornstarch

1/3 cup white or cider vinegar

1/3 cup sugar

1/3 cup water

2 1/2 tablespoons ketchup

1/4 teaspoon salt

1 cup canola, corn, or peanut oil, for frying

1 tablespoon and 2 teaspoons cornstarch dissolved in 3 tablespoons water

1 tablespoon canola, corn, or peanut oil (optional)

1 cup canned pineapple chunks, drained

1. Cut the pork into 3/4-inch cubes and toss with the pepper. Stir the egg, soy sauce, and 3 tablespoons cornstarch together in a bowl. Add the pork and stir to coat well. Let stand for 10 minutes.

2. For the sweet and sour sauce, combine the vinegar, sugar, water, ketchup, and salt in a saucepan. Stir together and set on an unlit burner while cooking the pork.

3. Heat the cup of oil in a wok or stir-fry pan to 350°F. Gently drop half of the pork, 1 piece at a time, into the hot oil and fry until light brown and crisp, about 6 minutes. Stir gently with a wire skimmer so all sides brown

and the pieces don't stick together. Remove the pork from the oil with the skimmer and spread out on paper towels. Keep warm in a low oven. Bring the oil back to 350°F. and fry the remaining pieces the same way.

4. Turn on the burner under the sauce to medium. Bring the mixture to a boil and stir in the cornstarch slurry. Continue stirring until the sauce thickens and turns translucent. If desired, add the tablespoon of oil to give the sauce a glaze. Stir thoroughly. Add the pineapple and heat just until warm. Transfer the pork to a serving platter and pour on the hot sauce. Serve immediately.

禄

Variation   Omit the vinegar, ketchup, and pineapple from the sweet and sour sauce and add ¼ cup plus 1 tablespoon Chinkiang vinegar. Prepare as in steps 2 and 4. Sprinkle the finished dish with 2 tablespoons toasted sesame seeds. To toast seeds, spread them on an ungreased baking pan and toast in a 350°F. oven for about 10 minutes, or in a dry skillet over low heat, stirring occasionally, until golden.

Sweet and Sour Spareribs, Shanghai Style

Serves 2, or 4 as part of a
multicourse meal

W hen my husband and I visited my mother's ninety-three-year-old sister in Szechuan (Sichuan) Province, she made these ribs for us. So we would feel welcome and at home, she instructed her family to prepare the Liao family's home-style dishes from Jiading, a suburb of Shanghai. These and other wonderful dishes were lovingly and swiftly readied in a tiny six- by six-foot outdoor kitchen with a two-burner bottled gas stove. No oven. The sink, with only cold water, was outside on the other side of the wall. I carefully watched the housekeeper, Er-jie (second sister), prepare the ribs and was able to re-create the dish at home — so well that my husband declared it just as tasty as what we ate in China.

A very important ingredient in this recipe is the black rice vinegar called Chinkiang vinegar. It is named after the city in which it is brewed. That city, spelled Zhenjiang in pinyin, is located in the Jiangsu Province, in which my mother's home town, called Jiading, is located. So you see this dish was very specially chosen for our visit. There really is no substitute for this rich, flavorful vinegar. Ask for it in Asian markets.

1 large egg

1 tablespoon dark soy sauce plus 1 teaspoon for the sauce

2 tablespoons cornstarch plus 2 teaspoons cornstarch, dissolved in 3 tablespoons water

1 pound pork spareribs or baby back ribs, cut across the bone into 1-inch-wide strips (ask your butcher to do this)

1 cup canola, corn, or peanut oil

5 tablespoons Chinkiang vinegar

3 tablespoons sugar

1 teaspoon dry sherry

1 teaspoon sesame seed oil

1.   In a large mixing bowl, lightly beat the egg with 1 tablespoon soy sauce and the 2 tablespoons of cornstarch until it makes a thin paste. Cut between the bones of the ribs to separate. Add to the paste and stir to coat. Let stand for about 15 minutes.

2.   Pour the oil into a wok or stir-fry pan and place over medium-high heat. When the temperature reaches 300°F., carefully add the ribs, a batch at a time, and fry for about 6 minutes, or until they are browned and crisp. Stir gently to keep the ribs from sticking together. Remove with a wire skimmer and place on paper towels. Repeat with remaining ribs.

3.   In a small bowl mix together the vinegar, sugar, sherry, sesame seed oil, the remaining teaspoon of soy sauce, and 3 tablespoons water. Stir until sugar is dissolved. Pour into a clean wok, stir-fry pan, or deep skillet and heat over medium-high heat. When the sauce comes to a boil, add the fried ribs and stir a few times. Add the cornstarch slurry and stir until sauce has thickened and all the ribs are evenly coated. Transfer to a platter. Serve hot.

禄

Spareribs in
Black Bean Sauce

Serves 3 to 4, or 5 to 6 as part of a
multicourse meal

Most people think of spareribs as a long affair calling for a two-fisted eating technique, but the Chinese don't usually serve such large pieces of meat. They cut the meat into small portions that can be handled with chopsticks. Ask your butcher to cut across the bones into 1-inch strips. You can then cut them apart through the meat into separate little pieces at home.

3 tablespoons fermented black beans, coarsely chopped

1 tablespoon dry sherry

2 teaspoons sugar

2 tablespoons light soy sauce

2 teaspoons minced garlic

1 teaspoon crushed red pepper (optional)

1 tablespoon canola, corn, or peanut oil

1½ pounds pork spareribs, trimmed, cut into 1-inch lengths, and ribs
  separated

1½ teaspoons cornstarch, dissolved in 1 tablespoon water

1. Combine the black beans with the sherry, sugar, soy sauce, garlic, red pepper, and ¾ cup water in a small bowl and mix well. Set aside.

2. Heat the oil in a wok or stir-fry pan over high heat until hot but not smoking. Test by dipping a sparerib into the oil; it should sizzle. Add the spareribs to the hot oil and brown for 4 to 5 minutes. Stir in the black bean mixture, cover, and cook over medium-low heat for 20 to 25 minutes, stirring occasionally, until ribs are cooked. Test by taking out a thick piece of rib and cutting through the meat. If meat is very pink, continue cooking until it tests done.

3. Remove the cover and turn the heat up to medium-high. When the sauce boils, add the cornstarch slurry and stir until the sauce thickens. Serve immediately or set aside and reheat later.

Shanghai-style Pork Chops

Serves 4

*E*ating a whole pork chop with chopsticks is simple — provided you are adept with them and have no qualms about taking bites out of a piece of meat and then putting it down on your plate while you eat some rice. This dish is clearly not one to serve at banquets, where casual home-style eating habits are deemed inappropriate.

健康

3 tablespoons dark soy sauce
1 tablespoon light brown sugar
½ cup water plus 2 tablespoons
1 tablespoon canola, corn, or peanut oil
4 pork chops, on the bone or boneless, about ¾ inch thick
½ cup thinly sliced onion

1. In a small bowl, mix together the soy sauce, sugar, and water. Set aside.

2. Pour the oil into a stir-fry pan with a wide flat bottom or into a 10-inch nonstick skillet and place over medium-high heat. When the oil is hot enough for the meat to sizzle, add the pork chops. Brown on both sides, about 3 minutes per side. Transfer to a plate, leaving the oil and meat juices in the pan.

3. Stir the onion into the same pan and cook until the edges are lightly browned, 2 to 3 minutes. Return the chops to the pan and pour in the soy sauce mixture. Cover and cook over medium-low heat for 5 minutes. Turn once halfway through cooking for even cooking and flavor.

4. Remove the cover and baste for 30 seconds. Transfer to a serving platter. Serve hot.

White-cooked Pork with Garlic Dressing

**Serves 4 to 5, or 6 to 8 as part of a
multicourse meal**

*T*he term white-cooked refers to cooking in water or broth without any heavy seasoning
so that the meat remains light in color. Since such dishes are served cold, they can be
prepared a day or two ahead, making them convenient for parties. White-cooked Pork
is usually served as an appetizer, but it is a refreshing change on a hot summer's
night with a fresh salad of mixed greens.

福

1¼ to 1½ pounds pork tenderloin or boneless pork loin roast

4 slices unpeeled gingerroot, 1 × ⅛ inch each

2 tablespoons dry sherry

2 scallions, white and green parts, cut into 3-inch pieces

2 garlic cloves, minced

3 tablespoons light soy sauce

1 teaspoon rice vinegar

2 teaspoons light brown sugar

1 teaspoon sesame seed oil

½ teaspoon hot chili oil, or to taste (optional)

2 tablespoons water or reserved cooking juices

Cilantro sprigs, for garnish

1. Trim away the fat from the pork. Place the meat, gingerroot, sherry,
and scallions in a 2½-quart saucepan. Cover with 6 cups of water, or enough
to completely cover the meat. Bring to a boil over medium-high heat. Reduce
the heat to low and simmer gently, uncovered, for 45 minutes to 1 hour, or
until the temperature on an instant-read thermometer registers 150°F. to
160°F. or meat is just evenly pink at center.

2. Drain the meat, reserving 2 tablespoons of the cooking liquid for
the dressing, if desired, and discard the gingerroot and scallions. Cool the meat
to room temperature and refrigerate for at least 2 hours or overnight so the
meat firms up for easier slicing.

3. When ready to serve, mix together the garlic, soy sauce, vinegar,
sugar, sesame seed oil, hot chili oil, if using, and water or reserved cooking

juices. Slice the chilled meat ⅛ inch thick. Arrange the slices in an overlapping pattern on a platter. Garnish the center of the platter with cilantro sprigs. Just before serving, pour the dressing over the meat or serve it in a small bowl as a dip.

Shanghai Red-cooked Ham

Serves 5 to 6, or 8 to 10 as part of a multicourse meal

How my father loved this dish! Like many Chinese he liked to eat the rind and underlying fat of the braised pork. This same red-cooked technique is used for pig's feet — a popular dish served with drinks, always at home with close friends. Pig's feet can't really be enjoyed unless you pick them up with your fingers.

禄

4 pounds fresh ham, pork butt, or shoulder
1 cup dark soy sauce
½ cup sugar
1 tablespoon dry sherry
2 slices unpeeled gingerroot, 1 × ⅛ inch each
4 whole star anise
1 cup water

1. Bring a large pot of water to a boil and carefully lower the pork into the boiling water. Let soak for 2 to 3 minutes. Drain and rinse in cold water.

2. Place the ham in a Dutch oven or large pot and add all the rest of the ingredients. Bring to a boil over medium-high heat, cover, and reduce the heat to low. Maintain a simmer for about 2 hours or more, until the meat is cooked and tender. Turn the ham over occasionally to encourage even cooking, flavor, and color and replenish water as necessary.

3. Uncover and increase the heat to medium. Boil gently, basting, until the gravy is reduced to about 1 cup. This will take 15 to 20 minutes. Skim off the fat. Serve hot or cold.

Note The leftover gravy, called "lu," can be saved and used to cook hard-boiled eggs or to flavor Half Moon Eggs in Soy Sauce (page 253).

Pork

Chinese Cabbage with Sweet Sausage

Serves 3 to 4, or 5 to 6 as part of a
multicourse meal

I always keep Chinese sausages and napa cabbage on hand. The sausages, which are air dried, have a pleasantly sweet taste and are available in Asian markets. They keep in the refrigerator for a month or more and in the freezer for much longer. Since napa cabbage keeps a long time in the vegetable crisper, I always have the makings of this emergency dish at my fingertips.

禧

1½ pounds napa cabbage

3 Chinese sausages (about 5 ounces)

3 tablespoons canola, corn, or peanut oil

1 slice unpeeled gingerroot, 1 × ⅛ inch

½ cup Chinese Chicken Broth (page 64) or water

½ teaspoon salt

½ teaspoon sugar

2 teaspoons cornstarch, dissolved in 1 tablespoon water

1.   Rinse the outside of the cabbage and remove any yellow or discolored leaves. Split the cabbage in half through the root and then cut each half into quarters. Each quarter should be 3½ to 4 inches wide. If the cabbage is very large, cut each quarter in half again. Trim away the thick root end from the cabbage heart, and then cut the quarters across into 2-inch sections. Set aside.

2.   Slice the sausages on the diagonal ¼ inch thick. Set aside.

3.   Heat the oil in a wok or stir-fry pan over high heat until hot but not smoking. Test by dipping a piece of sausage into the oil; it should sizzle. Add the sausage and gingerroot to the hot oil and stir a few times. Add the cabbage and stir for about 1 minute. Add the broth, cover the pan, and reduce the heat to medium-high. Simmer for 5 to 8 minutes, or until the cabbage is wilted and tender. Stir occasionally for even cooking.

4.   Add the salt, sugar, and cornstarch slurry and stir until the liquid is thickened. Discard the gingerroot, if desired. Serve hot.

Beef and Lamb

牛肉羊肉

Neither beef nor lamb is as popular in China as is pork. China, with a land mass larger than that of the United States, has only ten percent arable land. The rest is mountains or desert. With a fifth of the world's population residing in China, how to feed everyone has always been a pressing issue. Cattle and sheep need land to graze, but with so little flat land available for growing crops, the Chinese could not afford to use it for grazing animals. Pound for pound, soy beans provide more protein than beef. The land had to be used to grow food for people, not for animals.

If beef is not easily available, why then are there so many beef recipes? Most of the dishes that use beef originally called for pork and were adapted in America, where beef is king. Beef is rarely used, however, in white-cooked or soup dishes. This is because beef has a stronger and more pronounced flavor than pork. It tastes better in heavier, soy sauce–based sauces and gravies.

Because meat is easily available in this country and as a concession to Western tastes, larger and larger amounts of meat found their way into recipes. In general, the Chinese like to have more vegetables than meat, but here in America many people want the opposite. We learned in our restaurant business that some Westerners would be upset and feel they weren't getting their money's worth unless the dish had a good portion of meat in it. This attitude is changing as more and more nutritional studies show that a diet high in animal protein is not healthy. Although larger portions of meat are used here than in China, each serving is still only about four ounces of beef for each person. And because stir-frying is so flexible, you can further reduce the amount of beef in a recipe and increase the vegetables, if you wish. You will, of course, need to adjust the seasoning and cooking time accordingly.

The cut of beef I prefer for stir-frying is flank steak, although you can use other cuts such as blade, sirloin, or top round. (When I do use blade steak, I trim away the large gristle running through the center of the meat before slicing.) Flank steak is very easy to slice. I usually buy a whole flank steak and slice it all up, using only what I need and freezing the rest in 1- or 2-cup portions for future use. I don't recommend buying meat that is already sliced and packaged for stir-frying. It's often more expensive and usually improperly cut.

Lamb is not a popular meat in China as a whole, mainly because of its strong aroma and flavor. Northern China, however, has many lamb dishes, having been introduced to that meat in the thirteenth century by the invading Mongols and Tartars. Since many of these nomadic invaders were Moslem, their influence is still felt in some of the very fine Moslem restaurants in and around Beijing that feature lamb.

Beef and Scallions
in Oyster Sauce

**Serves 3 to 4, or 5 to 6 as part of a
multicourse meal**

Consider this a master recipe for a beef stir-fry. In place of the scallions, you could use asparagus or zucchini slices. Harder vegetables, such as broccoli and carrots, should be parboiled for about a minute before being added.

健康

1 pound flank steak, sliced (page 42)

2 teaspoons cornstarch

1 tablespoon dry sherry

1 teaspoon sugar

2 tablespoons dark soy sauce

3 tablespoons oyster sauce

3 tablespoons canola, corn, or peanut oil

1 slice unpeeled gingerroot, 1 × ⅛ inch

1 garlic clove, crushed and peeled

About 10 scallions, white and green parts, cut into 2-inch lengths, bulb split
    (3 cups)

1 medium red bell pepper, seeded, cored, and sliced into ½-inch strips

1. Place the beef in a bowl, stir in the cornstarch, sherry, sugar, soy sauce, and oyster sauce, and mix well. Set aside.

2. Pour the oil into a wok or stir-fry pan and set over high heat. Add the gingerroot and garlic and push them around the pan until they sizzle and the oil is hot. Be careful not to burn the garlic. Stir the meat up again and pour it into the pan. Stir briskly for about 1 minute, or until the beef loses its pink color.

3. Add 2 tablespoons of water to the pan and stir in the scallions and pepper. Stir over high heat for 2 minutes more, or until the beef is cooked and the vegetables are tender-crisp. Discard the gingerroot and garlic, if desired. Serve hot.

Beef with Mixed Vegetables

牛肉羊肉

**Serves 4 to 5, or 6 to 8 as part of a
multicourse meal**

*T*his is a good dish to make when your vegetable drawer holds small amounts of many
different vegetables. You should have about six to eight cups in all. I've given specific
proportions in this recipe, but you can vary them according to what you have on
hand. Keep the vegetables in separate bowls to add them one at a time, starting with
the vegetables that take longer to cook. Bean sprouts and such leafy vegetables as
spinach or watercress don't work well together with chunky vegetables since the ingredients in a Chinese dish should be uniform in shape. I like the heightened flavor
fermented black beans give to this dish, but if you have difficulty finding them, just
do without.

福

1 pound flank steak, sliced (page 42)
4 tablespoons dark soy sauce
1 tablespoon cornstarch
1 tablespoon dry sherry
1 teaspoon sugar
3 tablespoons canola, corn, or peanut oil
2 cups broccoli florets
1 cup cauliflower florets
½ cup sliced carrots
½ cup water
1 cup red bell pepper chunks
1 cup sliced celery
1 (8-ounce) can sliced water chestnuts, drained (1 cup)
2 slices unpeeled gingerroot, 1 × ⅛ inch each
1 garlic clove, crushed and peeled
1 tablespoon fermented black beans, coarsely chopped (optional)
Salt

1. Place the meat in a bowl, stir in the soy sauce, cornstarch, sherry,
and sugar, and mix well. Set aside.

2.   Heat 1 tablespoon of the oil in a wok or stir-fry pan over high heat until hot but not smoking. Test by dipping a vegetable into the oil; it should sizzle. Add the broccoli, cauliflower, and carrots to the hot oil and stir-fry for 1 minute. Add ¼ cup of the water. Reduce the heat to medium, stir a few times, and cover the pan. Cook for 2 minutes. Add the pepper, celery, and water chestnuts and stir-fry for another 2 minutes, or until tender-crisp. Transfer the vegetables to a shallow platter.

3.   Add the remaining 2 tablespoons of oil to the same pan. Add the gingerroot and garlic and stir around the pan until the oil is hot but not smoking; the gingerroot and garlic will begin to sizzle. Stir up the beef again and pour it into the pan. Stir constantly until the beef is almost cooked, about 2 minutes. Add the remaining ¼ cup water and the black beans, if using. Stir to mix and return the vegetables to the pan. Taste and add salt, if desired. Stir thoroughly. Serve hot.

禧

Note   If the sauce seems thinner than you'd like (some vegetables release more liquid than others), thicken with 1 teaspoon cornstarch dissolved in 1 tablespoon water.

See pages 42–43 for directions for slicing the beef.

Beef with Asparagus

牛肉羊肉

Serves 3 to 4, or 5 to 6 as part of a
multicourse meal

M y mother taught me to remove the small lower leaves that look like scales on the asparagus spear for a neater appearance and to get rid of any lingering sand or grit. The very first time I saw an asparagus plant was at the Greenough farm in Massachusetts. We used to have annual picnics there with the Greenough family and their guests. I remember meeting a relative of theirs, Beverly Sills, who had not yet been discovered by the general public, and the composer Dan Pinkham. My mother was particularly thrilled with the fresh vegetables. We would go into the fields and pick our own vegetables for lunch.

1 pound flank steak, sliced (page 42)
2 teaspoons cornstarch
1 tablespoon dry sherry
2 tablespoons dark soy sauce
½ teaspoon sugar
1 pound asparagus
3 tablespoons canola, corn, or peanut oil
¼ cup water
1 slice unpeeled gingerroot, 1 × ⅛ inch
1 large onion, sliced ½ inch thick (1 cup)

1.   Place the beef in a bowl, stir in the cornstarch, sherry, soy sauce, and sugar, and mix well so the meat is well coated. Set aside.

2.   Snap or cut off the tough ends of the asparagus and strip off the small leaves on the spear up to 2 inches from the tip. Wash the asparagus and cut on the diagonal into 2-inch pieces.

3.   Heat 1 tablespoon of the oil in a wok or stir-fry pan over high heat until hot but not smoking. Test by dipping a piece of asparagus in the oil; it should sizzle. Add the asparagus and stir-fry for about 30 seconds. Add the water. Stir briefly and cover. Cook, covered, for 1 to 2 minutes, just until the vegetables are tender–crisp. Pour the asparagus onto a serving platter.

4.   Put the remaining 2 tablespoons of oil into the same pan, add the gingerroot and stir around the pan until it begins to sizzle. Stir in the onion and cook for about 1 minute, stirring constantly. The onions should wilt but not brown. Stir up the beef again and turn it all into the pan. Stir constantly. When the beef is almost done, about 2 minutes, return the asparagus to the pan and stir thoroughly until reheated. Discard the gingerroot, if desired. Serve immediately.

Beef with Broccoli

Serves 3 to 4, or 5 to 6 as part of a multicourse meal

Chinese restaurants often serve this over a bed of freshly steamed rice as a one-dish meal for people who want a quick lunch or snack, or who are dining alone.

禧

1 pound flank steak, sliced (page 42)

3 tablespoons dark soy sauce

1 tablespoon cornstarch

1 tablespoon dry sherry

1 teaspoon sugar

1 pound broccoli

3 tablespoons canola, corn, or peanut oil

¼ cup water

1 slice unpeeled gingerroot, 1 × ⅛ inch

1 garlic clove, crushed and peeled

½ teaspoon salt, or to taste

(continued)

Beef and

Lamb

1. Place the beef in a bowl and add the soy sauce, cornstarch, sherry, and sugar. Stir until well mixed. Set aside.

2. Peel the stalks of the broccoli. Cut off the flower head, leaving a 2-inch or shorter stem on the florets. Roll-cut the stems as described on page 46 and cut the broccoli into bite-size florets about 2 inches long. You should have about 4 cups.

3. Heat 1 tablespoon of the oil in a wok or stir-fry pan over high heat until the oil is hot but not smoking. Test by dipping a piece of broccoli into the oil; it should sizzle. Add the broccoli and stir constantly for about 30 seconds. Stir in the ¼ cup water, reduce heat to medium, and cover the pan. Continue cooking, stirring occasionally for another minute or two until broccoli is tender-crisp. Remove from the pan and spread out on a plate. Do not pile into a bowl, as the heat generated by the broccoli will overcook the pieces on the bottom.

4. With the heat still on high, pour the remaining 2 tablespoons of oil into the same pan. Add the gingerroot and garlic and stir around the pan a few seconds until they are fragrant and begin to sizzle. Stir up the beef again and add to the pan. Stir until the meat is almost done, about 2 minutes. Return the broccoli and mix thoroughly. Taste and add salt if necessary. Remove the gingerroot and garlic, if desired. Serve hot on a platter.

Beef with Cauliflower and Tomatoes

Serves 3 to 4, or 5 to 6 as part of a multicourse meal

Y *ou may never have thought of stir-frying tomatoes, but they work very well as long as they are firm and you do not overcook them. I prefer to use cherry tomatoes in this dish because they stay neat and look so lovely with the white cauliflower.*

1 pound flank steak, sliced (page 42)

2 tablespoons dark soy sauce

1 tablespoon cornstarch

1 tablespoon dry sherry

1 teaspoon sugar

¾ pound cauliflower

8 to 10 cherry tomatoes or 2 medium tomatoes

3 tablespoons canola, corn, or peanut oil

¼ cup water

1 slice unpeeled gingerroot, 1 × ⅛ inch

2 tablespoons fermented black beans, chopped

1. Place the beef in a bowl. Add the soy sauce, cornstarch, sherry, and sugar and stir together. Set aside.

2. Separate the florets from the stem of the cauliflower and cut them into bite-size pieces. Set aside. Cut the cherry tomatoes in half or cut regular tomatoes into eighths. Set aside.

3. Heat 1 tablespoon of the oil in a wok or stir-fry pan over high heat until the oil is hot. Add the cauliflower and stir 1 minute. Pour in the water, reduce the heat to medium, and cook, covered, until the cauliflower is tender-crisp, 3 to 5 minutes. Stir occasionally for even cooking. Remove the cauliflower from the pan and spread out on a plate.

4. Add the remaining 2 tablespoons of oil to the same pan. Place the pan over high heat and add the gingerroot. Stir the gingerroot around the pan until the oil is hot but not smoking and the gingerroot is sizzling. Stir up the beef mixture again and pour it into the pan. Stir until the meat changes color and is almost cooked, about 2 minutes.

5. Add the black beans and stir to combine. Add the tomatoes, stir about 1 minute, and return the cauliflower to the pan. Mix thoroughly with a couple of big stirs. Transfer to a serving platter and discard the gingerroot, if desired. Serve immediately.

Beef with Green Beans

Serves 3 to 4, or 5 to 6 as part of a multicourse meal

M y mother was very skilled at choosing the perfect combination of entrees for a meal. She believed that at least one dish should have a sauce that would go with white rice. With its rich, savory sauce, this dish is certainly one of them. Fermented black beans make it especially flavorful.

福

1 pound green beans
¾ pound flank steak, sliced (page 42)
2 tablespoons dark soy sauce
1 tablespoon cornstarch
1 tablespoon dry sherry
1 teaspoon sugar
3 tablespoons canola, corn, or peanut oil
¼ cup water
1 slice unpeeled gingerroot, 1 × ⅛ inch
3 tablespoons fermented black beans, coarsely chopped

1. Break off and discard the ends of the beans. Snap the beans in half or thirds to make pieces about 2½ inches long. Rinse and set aside.

2. Place the beef in a bowl, add the soy sauce, cornstarch, sherry, and sugar and mix well. Set aside.

3. Heat 1 tablespoon of the oil in a wok or stir-fry pan over high heat until the oil is hot but not smoking. Test by dipping the tip of a spatula into the beef mixture and then into the oil; it should sizzle. Add the green beans and stir for about 1 minute. Add the water and reduce the heat to medium. Cover the pan and cook the beans for 6 to 9 minutes, or until tender-crisp. Pour the beans and any liquid onto a platter.

4. Add the remaining 2 tablespoons of oil to the same pan and raise the heat to high. Add the gingerroot and black beans and stir them around the pan until they sizzle and become fragrant. Stir the beef mixture up again and pour it to the pan. Stir for about 2 minutes, or until the beef is no longer pink.

5.   Return the beans with any liquid on the platter to the pan and stir for 30 seconds, or until thoroughly mixed and heated. Discard the gingerroot, if desired. Serve immediately.

Beef in Oyster Sauce

Serves 3 to 4, or 5 to 6 as part of a multicourse meal

O yster sauce, a rich, savory condiment made with oyster extract, is widely used in southern Chinese cooking. It makes a wonderful gravy for even the simplest of ingredients, and does wonders for the beef and onions in this recipe. For a very special treat, use a Vidalia onion if available, in place of the yellow onion.

1 pound beef flank steak, sliced (page 42)
1 tablespoon cornstarch
1 tablespoon dry sherry
1 tablespoon dark soy sauce
2 teaspoons sugar
3 tablespoons canola, corn, or peanut oil
1 large onion, peeled and quartered
2 slices unpeeled gingerroot, 1 × 1/8 inch each
2 garlic cloves, crushed and peeled
1/4 cup water
4 tablespoons oyster sauce

1.   Place the beef in a bowl, stir in the cornstarch, sherry, soy sauce, and sugar, and mix well. Set aside.

2.   Heat the oil in a wok or stir-fry pan over high heat until hot but not smoking. Test by dipping the tip of a spatula in the beef mixture and then into the oil; it should sizzle. Add the onion, gingerroot, and garlic. Stir constantly for 1 minute. Do not brown.

3.   Stir up the beef mixture again and pour it into the pan. Stir briskly for about 2 minutes, or until the beef is almost done. Add the water and oyster sauce and stir over high heat for 1 minute or less, or until the beef is cooked and the ingredients are well mixed and heated through. Discard the gingerroot and garlic, if desired. Serve immediately.

Beef and

Lamb

Beef with Red Onions

Serves 3 to 4, or 5 to 6 as part of a multicourse meal

My mother, my brother Stephen, and I had this dish many times as we went by train from Quangzhou (Canton) to Shanghai. As we traveled north, away from the areas of abundant produce, the train's cooks would turn more and more to root vegetables, which keep well without refrigeration. You may substitute Spanish or Vidalia onions.

1 pound flank steak, sliced (page 42)
1 tablespoon cornstarch
1 tablespoon dry sherry
3 tablespoons dark soy sauce
1 teaspoon sugar
4 tablespoons canola, corn, or peanut oil
1 slice unpeeled gingerroot, 1 × 1/8 inch
2 medium red onions, peeled and cut into 1-inch chunks (about 2 cups)
1 small red bell pepper, seeded, cored, and cut into 1-inch chunks
1/4 cup water or broth (optional)

1.   Place the beef in a bowl, stir in the cornstarch, sherry, soy sauce, and sugar, and mix well. Set aside.

2.   Pour 2 tablespoons of the oil in a wok or stir-fry pan and set over high heat. Add the gingerroot and stir around the pan until the oil is hot; the gingerroot will sizzle. Add the onions and stir for about 30 seconds. Add the pepper and cook, stirring constantly, for another 30 seconds, or until the vegetables are tender-crisp. Remove from the pan and spread out on a plate.

3.   Add the remaining 2 tablespoons of oil to the same pan. When it is hot, stir up the beef mixture again and add it. Stir constantly for about 2 minutes, adding 1/4 cup water, if desired, for more gravy and to keep the meat from sticking to the pan. Stir until the meat is almost done. Return the vegetables to the pan and stir for about 30 seconds to mix. Serve hot.

Beef with Mixed Sweet Peppers

Serves 3 to 4, or 5 to 6 as part of a multicourse meal

I like the colorful contrast that green, red, and yellow bell peppers give to this dish, but if you are unable to get red or yellow peppers, substitute all green ones.

禧

1 pound beef flank steak, sliced (page 42)

3 tablespoons dark soy sauce

1 tablespoon cornstarch

1 tablespoon dry sherry

1 teaspoon sugar

4 tablespoons canola, corn, or peanut oil

1 green pepper, seeded, cored, and cut into 1-inch chunks

1 red bell pepper, seeded, cored, and cut into 1-inch chunks

1 yellow bell pepper, seeded, cored, and cut into 1-inch chunks

1 slice unpeeled gingerroot, 1 × ⅛ inch

1 (8-ounce) can sliced bamboo shoots, drained (about 1 cup)

½ teaspoon salt, or to taste

1. Place the beef in a bowl, stir in the soy sauce, cornstarch, dry sherry, and sugar, and mix well. Set aside.

2. Heat 2 tablespoons of the oil in a wok or stir-fry pan over high heat until hot. Test by dipping a spatula into the beef mixture and then into the oil; it should sizzle. Add the peppers and stir for 1 minute. Transfer to a platter.

3. Heat the remaining oil in the same pan and add the gingerroot. Stir a few times until it is fragrant and begins to sizzle. Stir up the beef mixture again and pour into the pan. Stir constantly for about 2 minutes, or until beef is almost done. Add the bamboo shoots and return the peppers to the pan. Stir well for 30 seconds or more to reheat the vegetables. Taste and add salt, if desired. Serve hot.

Beef with Snow Peas

*H*ere's an old favorite that everyone seems to love.

健康

1 pound beef flank steak, sliced (page 42)

2 tablespoons dark soy sauce

1 tablespoon dry sherry

1 tablespoon cornstarch

1 teaspoon sugar

3 tablespoons canola, corn, or peanut oil

2 slices unpeeled gingerroot, 1 × ⅛ inch each

¼ cup broth or water (optional)

¼ pound snow peas, ends snapped off and strings removed

1 (8-ounce) can sliced water chestnuts, drained (1 scant cup)

1. Place the beef in a bowl, stir in the soy sauce, sherry, cornstarch, and sugar, and mix well. Set aside.

2. Pour the oil into a wok or stir-fry pan and place over high heat. Add the gingerroot and stir around the pan until the oil is hot; the gingerroot will sizzle. Stir up the beef again and pour it into the hot oil. Stir constantly for about 2 minutes. If the meat sticks to the pan, add a few tablespoons of broth or water, a little at a time. Do not add more than ¼ cup.

3. Add the snow peas and water chestnuts and continue stirring for about 1 minute, or until the snow peas are tender-crisp. Transfer to a platter and remove and discard the gingerroot, if desired. Serve immediately.

Beef with Zucchini

*A*t the end of the summer, when all the gardeners you know are trying to give away
their surplus zucchini, this stir-fried dish is not only delicious but economical. Small
zucchini are better than large.

福

1 pound flank steak, sliced (page 42)

3 tablespoons dark soy sauce

1 tablespoon cornstarch

1 tablespoon dry sherry

1 teaspoon sugar

2 to 3 tablespoons water

3 tablespoons canola, corn, or peanut oil

1 slice unpeeled gingerroot, 1 × ⅛ inch

1 garlic clove, crushed and peeled

1 medium red onion, peeled and cut into wedges (about 2 cups)

3 small zucchini, sliced ¼ inch thick (about 3 cups)

½ teaspoon salt (optional)

1.   Place the beef in a bowl, stir in the soy sauce, cornstarch, sherry,
and sugar, and mix well. Set aside.

2.   Place the oil in a wok or stir-fry pan and place over high heat. Add
the gingerroot and garlic and stir around the pan with a spatula until they
begin to sizzle. Do not brown. Add the onion and stir constantly for 1 minute.
Stir the beef mixture up again and add to the pan. Cook another minute,
adding water, a tablespoon at a time, to keep the meat from sticking to pan.

3.   Add the zucchini and cook for about 2 minutes, stirring constantly.
Taste and add salt, if desired. Serve hot.

Curried Beef

C urry is not native to China, but the Chinese do like curried meat dishes. If I am serving a curry dish as a single entree, I make a vegetable side dish and serve plenty of hot white or brown rice with an array of condiments, such as chopped roasted peanuts, cilantro, and a generous bowl of Spicy Mango Chutney (page 330).

1 pound flank steak, sliced (page 42)

4 tablespoons cornstarch

2 tablespoons curry powder

2 teaspoons sugar

1 tablespoon chili powder

2 cups water

3 tablespoons canola, corn, or peanut oil

2 cups sliced onion

2 carrots, peeled and roll-cut (page 46)

1½ teaspoons salt, or to taste

1. Place the meat in a bowl, stir in 1 tablespoon of the cornstarch, and mix well. Set aside.

2. Stir together the curry powder, sugar, and chili powder with ½ cup of the water in a small bowl. Set aside. Mix the remaining 3 tablespoons of cornstarch with another ½ cup of the water. Set aside.

3. Pour the oil into a wok or stir-fry pan and place the pan over high heat. When the oil is hot but not smoking, add the onion and carrots; they should sizzle. Stir for about 2 minutes, add the meat, and stir constantly for about 2 minutes, or until the beef has turned color but is not completely cooked. It should be pink in the center.

4. Add the curry mixture, stir a few times, and add the remaining 1 cup of water. Bring the mixture to a boil, reduce the heat to very low, cover, and simmer gently for 10 minutes. Add salt to taste. Mix the cornstarch solution again, pour it in, and stir until the sauce is thickened. Serve hot.

Spiced Soy Sauce Beef

**Serves 8 to 10 as part of a
multicourse meal or 12 to 16 as an appetizer**

*M*y mother used to prepare this dish for picnics because it is so good cold. In China, the meat is sliced very thin and arranged in an overlapping design on a cold platter for banquets. The meat is delicious alone or even between slices of bread spread with mayonnaise. It runs the gamut from picnic to banquet!

壽

3 to 3½ pounds pot roast or boneless chuck
1 tablespoon dry sherry
⅓ cup dark soy sauce
2 tablespoons sugar
1 cup water
3 slices unpeeled gingerroot, 1 × ⅛ inch each
2 whole star anise

1. Trim off the excess fat from the meat. Keep the meat in one piece. Combine the sherry, soy sauce, sugar, and water in a small bowl or measuring cup. Stir until sugar is dissolved.

2. Place the meat, gingerroot, and star anise in a large heavy pot. Pour the soy sauce mixture over the meat and bring to a boil. Reduce the heat and simmer, covered, for 3 hours or more, until meat is tender but still firm. Turn the meat occasionally for even cooking and to prevent it from sticking to the pan. If the liquid dries out before the beef is tender, add ¼ to ½ cup of water, as needed.

3. Remove the meat from the pot, reserving the cooking juices. Cool the meat at room temperature until thoroughly cool and firm. Cut the meat into thin slices no longer than 3½ inches; cut in half if longer. Sparingly drizzle the sauce over the meat and serve.

Spicy Beef with Carrots and Celery

**Serves 3 to 4, or 5 to 6 as part of a
multicourse meal**

*T*he traditional method of preparing this Szechuan dish is to deep-fry the shredded beef
in oil first. Shredding the meat with the grain gives it a chewy texture and frying
makes it dry and crispy. I have adapted the recipe to use a stir-fry method, which is
faster and lower in fat — and every bit as delicious.

1 pound flank steak, shredded (see page 42)

2 tablespoons dark soy sauce

1 teaspoon dry sherry

2 teaspoons grated peeled gingerroot

4 tablespoons canola, corn, or peanut oil

1½ cups shredded carrots (about 3 medium)

2 cups shredded celery (about 4 stalks)

1 to 3 teaspoons crushed red pepper, or to taste

½ teaspoon salt, or to taste

1 teaspoon cornstarch, dissolved in 1 tablespoon water

1. Place the beef in a bowl, stir in the soy sauce, sherry, and gingerroot, and mix well. Set aside.

2. Heat the oil in a wok or stir-fry pan over high heat until hot but not smoking. Test by dipping the end of a spatula into the beef mixture and then into the oil; it should sizzle. Stir the beef up again and add it all. Stir briskly for about 2 minutes, or until the shreds separate and are no longer pink. Remove the beef with a slotted spoon to a plate, leaving the liquid in the pan.

3. Return the pan to high heat, add the carrots, and cook for 30 seconds. Add the celery and red pepper and stir for 1 minute. Return the beef to the pan and stir a few times. Taste the gravy and add salt, if desired. Add the cornstarch mixture and stir until the gravy is thickened. Serve immediately.

禄

Note If you like, substitute ½ to 1 fresh chili, chopped, for the crushed red pepper.

See pages 44–45 for directions for shredding the flank steak and vegetables.

Tangy Stir-fried Beef Salad

Serves 4 to 6

A lthough this salad is not traditional, it fits right in with our contemporary, health-conscious lifestyle. Serve the salad with chow mein noodles, pita bread, or French bread.

健康

1 pound flank steak, shredded (page 44)

3 tablespoons dark soy sauce

1 tablespoon dry sherry

1½ teaspoons grated peeled gingerroot

2 teaspoons sugar

1 tablespoon cornstarch

3 tablespoons canola, corn, or peanut oil

½ teaspoon crushed red pepper, or more to taste (optional)

4 cups shredded iceberg lettuce

2 cups grated carrots (about 2 medium)

¼ cup chopped chives or scallion, white and green parts

3 tablespoons chopped cilantro or parsley

½ cup rice vinegar

3 tablespoons sugar

2 teaspoons sesame seed oil

1 tablespoon balsamic or red wine vinegar

(continued)

1.   Place the beef in a bowl, stir in the soy sauce, sherry, ½ teaspoon of the gingerroot, sugar, and cornstarch, and mix well. Set aside.

2.   Heat the oil in a wok or stir-fry pan over high heat. When the oil is hot, add the beef mixture and stir briskly for about 1 minute. Add the red pepper, if using. If the cornstarch begins to stick to the pan, add 2 to 3 table-spoons water and continue stirring until the meat is cooked. Transfer the meat to a colander set over a bowl and allow the meat to drain and cool while preparing the vegetables and dressing. Lightly press meat against the colander to help drain excess moisture.

3.   Toss the lettuce, carrots, chives, and cilantro together in a large salad bowl. Set aside.

4.   Combine the rice vinegar, sugar, remaining 1 teaspoon of ginger-root, sesame seed oil, and vinegar together in a small bowl or lidded jar. Mix or shake well until the sugar is dissolved.

5.   With a slotted spoon, add the beef mixture to the salad greens. Dis-card excess gravy. Pour on the dressing and toss to mix thoroughly. Serve immediately.

Note   See pages 44–45 for directions for shredding the flank steak and lettuce.

Chinese-style Beef Stew

Serves 6 to 8

*T*his stew with lots of root vegetables actually improves with age. After a day in the refrigerator, the flavors meld together and the overall taste is much better than when it was just made. Serve with white or brown rice, noodles, or steamed or crusty bread, the way my husband likes it.

2 tablespoons canola, corn, or peanut oil

2 pounds stewing beef, such as chuck or top round, cut into 2-inch cubes

3 cups beef stock or 2 bouillon cubes dissolved in 3 cups hot water

3 tablespoons ketchup

1 tablespoon dry sherry

2 tablespoons dark soy sauce

2 slices unpeeled gingerroot, 1 × ⅛ inch each

2 whole star anise

2 tablespoons light brown sugar

1 garlic clove, crushed and peeled

½ teaspoon ground dried orange peel or a 2-inch square of dried or fresh orange
    peel with no white pith

12 to 14 small white boiling onions (about ½ pound), trimmed and peeled

3 carrots, peeled and roll-cut into 1½-inch lengths (about 2 cups)

2 sweet potatoes, 1 to 1¼ pounds, peeled and cubed into 1½-inch pieces

Salt to taste

3 tablespoons cornstarch, dissolved in ¼ cup water

1.   Pour the oil in a large heavy saucepan or Dutch oven and place over high heat. Pat the meat dry, and when the oil is hot, brown in a single layer. Don't put all the meat in at one time, or the temperature in the pan will drop and the meat will steam instead of sear. Brown all sides. Transfer the browned meat to a bowl as you add new pieces. Continue until all the meat is browned.

2.   Return the meat to the pan. Add the stock, ketchup, sherry, soy sauce, gingerroot, star anise, brown sugar, garlic, and orange peel. The meat should be just covered. If not, add more stock or water. Bring to a boil. Cover the pan, reduce the heat, and simmer for 1½ to 2 hours or until the meat is easily pierced with a fork. If you like the meat fork tender, cook for the longer time.

3.   Add the onions, carrots, and sweet potatoes and simmer covered for about 40 minutes or until the vegetables are tender. Remove and discard the orange peel, if using a whole piece, garlic, gingerroot, and star anise. Taste and add salt if necessary.

4.   Bring the stew back to a boil. Stir in the cornstarch slurry and stir gently until the liquid is lightly thickened. Serve hot.

壽

Note   For easy removal, tie the gingerroot, star anise, garlic, and square of orange peel in a piece of cheesecloth.

Jellied Lamb Loaf

牛肉羊肉

**Serves 6 as a main course or
10 as an appetizer**

*H*ere's another recipe from my mother's Joyce Chen Cook Book. *My mother liked
to prepare this unusual dish as a cold appetizer for dinner parties. You can make it
days ahead and unmold it the day of the party. Here's what my mother had to say
about this dish: "In ancient China, Jellied Lamb with fine wine was among the most
enjoyable things for poets, philosophers, and scholars. Even now it is still the favorite
dish of many people. My father was fond of it. Lamb is supposed to be 'warm' so it
is widely relished in winter. The refrigerator, however, has not yet become common in
China, so we make jellied lamb only in the winter to have it set firm. We used pig
rind for the jelly, added during the cooking. Here, plain gelatin is more convenient."*

禧

2 to 2½ pounds lamb shoulder chops, shanks, or other stew cuts, well trimmed
½ cup light soy sauce
2 tablespoons sugar
1 tablespoon dry sherry
1 medium carrot, washed and cut into 4 pieces
2½ cups water
2 tablespoons unflavored gelatin, softened in 1 cup cold water
½ teaspoon salt, or to taste
1 thinly sliced scallion, white and green parts, or parsley sprigs, for garnish

1.   Put the lamb, soy sauce, sugar, sherry, carrot, and water in a heavy
pot or Dutch oven. Stir a few times and bring to a boil. Cover and simmer
for 1½ to 2 hours or until the meat is very tender and easily pulled from the
bone. Stir occasionally to prevent burning. Remove the pan from the heat
and let cool with the cover off.

2.   When the mixture is cool enough to handle, drain the liquid into a
measuring cup and skim off the fat. (Or refrigerate the juices until the fat
solidifies.) You should have about 2 cups of meat juices. If there is not enough,
add water to make 2 cups and return the liquid to the pan.

3.   Pick the meat from the bones and discard the carrot pieces, bones, gristle, cartilage, and large pieces of fat. Break the meat with your hands into small pieces, about ½ inch. Return the meat to the pan and bring to a boil.

4.   Remove from heat and add the softened gelatin and salt. Pour everything into a 9-inch loaf pan to cool. Refrigerate until firm.

5.   Serve cold, cut in slices or squares. Or unmold the loaf for a dramatic presentation by dipping the loaf pan for a second or two in hot water, running a knife around the edges and turning it upside down on an oblong or oval platter. Garnish with scallions or sprigs of parsley.

健康

Lamb with Scallions and Bamboo Shoots

Serves 3 to 4, or 5 to 6 as part of a
multicourse meal

福

A lthough lamb is not very popular in China, it is sometimes eaten during the winter months because it is believed to help keep the body warm.

1 pound boneless lamb loin, sliced (page 42)

2 tablespoons hoisin sauce

2 tablespoons dark soy sauce

1 tablespoon cornstarch

1 tablespoon dry sherry

1 teaspoon sugar

3 tablespoons canola, corn, or peanut oil

2 slices unpeeled gingerroot, 1 × ⅛ inch each

1 garlic clove, crushed

¼ cup water or broth

1 (8-ounce) can sliced bamboo shoots, drained (1 cup)

5 scallions, green and white parts, cut into 2-inch pieces, bulb split

1 teaspoon sesame seed oil

1. Combine lamb with the hoisin sauce, soy sauce, cornstarch, sherry, and sugar in a bowl and mix well. Set aside.

2. Pour the oil into a wok or stir-fry pan and place over medium-high heat. Add the gingerroot and garlic and stir around the pan until the oil is hot; they will begin to sizzle. Do not brown.

3. Stir up the lamb mixture again and pour into the pan. Stir thoroughly for about 1 minute until the lamb begins to change color and separate.

4. Stir in the water or broth, add the bamboo shoots, and cook for 1 to 2 minutes, stirring constantly, or until the lamb is almost cooked. Add the scallions and stir for 1 to 2 minutes, or until the scallions are wilted and the lamb is fully cooked. Drizzle on the sesame seed oil and give the ingredients a few quick tosses. Discard the gingerroot and garlic, if desired. Remove from the heat. Serve hot.

Bean Curd and Eggs

*I*n China, bean curd, or tofu, is widely used. It is very nutritious, low in fat, inexpensive, and easy to digest. In a country where meat is scarce and famine chronic, its value as a ready source of protein and calcium is immeasurable. The Western world is beginning to discover bean curd as a healthy substitute for meat with none of the fat and cholesterol.

Bean curd comes in many different textures, forms, and flavors. A good place to sample the extensive variety is at a restaurant that caters to vegetarians. Our Chinese nanny/housekeeper, or *amah* as she was called, is now retired and lives next to a Buddhist monastery on one of the Hong Kong harbor islands. When we visit her, she often takes us to the monastery for a meal. There, skilled vegetarian cooks (the nuns and monks themselves) make dishes look and taste like meat and seafood, all from vegetables and bean curd!

Although freshly made bean curd has a subtle sweet fragrance, generally it has no discernable flavor of its own. Many Westerners, unfamiliar with bean curd, find the bland flavor — and more often the soft texture — unpalatable. But the Chinese never eat bean curd plain; they enjoy it with the flavors it takes on from the sauces and ingredients with which it is cooked. I have seen many converts after they've tasted their first well-prepared bean curd dish!

Most stir-fry dishes use Chinese-style firm bean curd and not the soft Japanese or even softer silken bean curd. Japanese bean curd, however, can be used in some stir-fry dishes, such as Szechuan Spicy Bean Curd, that have no other vegetables. The texture will be very soft and custardlike. Japanese bean curd will *not* tolerate the heat of deep-frying.

Since chickens are popular and easily available, it stands to reason that eggs are also. We use both fresh and preserved eggs for entrees as well as to flavor other dishes. My mother would make a point of getting farm-fresh eggs whenever possible.

We all enjoy preserved duck eggs, available in Asian markets, as a side dish or as a flavoring for other dishes. The best known is the Shanghai specialty, the Hundred-Year-Old Eggs (sometimes hyperbolically called Thousand-Year-Old Eggs). Unshelled eggs are packed in soil, ash, and lime and then coated with rice husks. They are buried for one hundred days and come out looking very different from they way they did when they went in. The egg white becomes a transparent black-brown and the yolk is greenish and sometimes runny. Sounds awful, right? For those who love it, it is very tasty indeed. Shelled and quartered, these eggs are part of elaborate cold platters at banquet feasts. They are also drizzled with soy sauce and sesame seed oil and eaten with breakfast congee. My husband still cringes a bit when I crack open my Hundred-Year-Old Egg for breakfast.

Duck eggs are also preserved in brine. They are frequently added to steamed dishes such as Steamed Meat Cake or hard boiled and eaten at breakfast or as a snack with congee or steamed bread. My mother used to make her own salted eggs at home before they were readily available in stores. Although she also made many of her own pickles and preserves, those large crocks filled with eggs on the counter are what I remember best.

Mushrooms with Bean Curd

豆腐蛋

**Serves 3 to 4, or 5 to 6 as part of a
multicourse meal**

*T*he delicate texture of this easy dish pairs nicely with those that feature colorful, crisp
vegetables. I always keep bean curd on hand in the refrigerator or freezer for quick
dishes such as this.

1 pound firm tofu (bean curd)
2 cups fresh mushrooms (about ¾ pound)
2 tablespoons canola, corn, or peanut oil
1 teaspoon salt
1 tablespoon soy sauce
1½ teaspoons cornstarch, dissolved in ½ cup water
1 teaspoon sesame seed oil
2 tablespoons thinly sliced scallions

1. Drain the tofu, if necessary, and cut it into 1 × ½-inch pieces.

2. Trim the ends of the mushrooms. Clean the mushrooms with a
brush. Rinse quickly in cold water and slice ¼ inch thick. Set aside.

3. Heat the oil in a wok or stir-fry pan over high heat until hot but
not smoking. Test by adding a piece of mushroom to the oil; it should sizzle.
Add all the mushrooms and stir for about 2 minutes, or until they turn a darker
color. Add the tofu, salt, and soy sauce and cook, stirring constantly, for about
3 minutes. Add the cornstarch slurry and stir until the gravy thickens. Drizzle
with sesame seed oil, sprinkle with scallions, and give a couple of big stirs.
Serve immediately.

Szechuan Spicy
Bean Curd

**Serves 3 to 4, or 5 to 6 as part of a
multicourse meal**

*T*his classic Szechuan dish is called Ma Po Tofu *in Chinese, a rather unappetizing
name. Translated literally, it means pockmarked grandmother's tofu, named after the
woman who created it. The soft, Japanese-style tofu (bean curd) is preferred for this
dish. It has a smooth, silken consistency when cooked. For a vegetarian dish, omit the
ground meat.*

1 pound soft tofu (bean curd)
2 tablespoons hot bean paste
1 garlic clove, minced
1 teaspoon grated peeled gingerroot
2 teaspoons dry sherry
1 tablespoon soy sauce
½ teaspoon crushed red pepper, or to taste
1 teaspoon Szechuan peppercorns, toasted and ground
3 tablespoons canola, corn, or peanut oil
½ cup ground pork or beef (4 ounces)
1 cup Chinese Chicken Broth (page 64) or water
2 teaspoons cornstarch, dissolved in 2 teaspoons water
2 tablespoons thinly sliced scallions
1 teaspoon sesame seed oil.

1.   Drain the tofu and cut it into 1-inch cubes. Set aside. Stir the hot
bean paste, garlic, gingerroot, sherry, and soy sauce together in a small bowl.
Set aside. Combine the red pepper and ground peppercorns together in another small dish. Set aside.

2.   Heat the oil in a wok or stir-fry pan over medium-high heat until
hot but not smoking. Stir fry the ground meat until it separates into small
pieces. Add the hot bean sauce mixture and stir a few times. Add the broth
or water and pepper mixture and stir a few times to mix. Add the tofu. Stir
gently to combine and bring the mixture to a boil. Reduce the heat to low
and simmer, uncovered, for about 5 to 6 minutes to reduce the liquid by about
a quarter.

3.   Add the cornstarch slurry and stir until the sauce is thickened. Pour onto a serving platter and sprinkle with scallions and sesame seed oil. Serve hot.

Bean Curd with Crabmeat

豆腐蛋

Serves 3 to 4, or 5 to 6 as part of a multicourse meal

A light dish that allows the subtle flavor of crab to come through — a pleasant change from the usual bean curd dishes with dark sauces.

禄

1 pound firm tofu (bean curd)
¾ cup fresh lump or 1 (6-ounce) can crabmeat, drained (about ¾ cup)
1 teaspoon dry sherry
3 tablespoons canola, corn, or vegetable oil
2 slices unpeeled gingerroot, 1 × ⅛ inch each
1 cup canned chicken broth
2 tablespoons cornstarch, dissolved in ¼ cup water
1 egg white, lightly beaten
½ teaspoon salt, or to taste
3 tablespoons thinly sliced scallions

1.   Drain the tofu and cut it into 1-inch cubes. Set aside. Mix the crabmeat with the sherry. Set aside.

2.   Pour the oil into a wok or stir-fry pan and place over medium-high heat. Add the gingerroot and stir around the pan until the oil is hot but not smoking; the gingerroot will begin to sizzle. Add the crabmeat and broth and stir gently. Add the tofu. Simmer over medium-low heat for about 4 minutes.

3.   Raise the heat to high and when the mixture comes to a boil, slowly stir in the cornstarch slurry and stir until thickened. When the mixture just begins to boil again, stir in the egg white. Remove the pan from the heat, taste, and add salt as needed. Discard the gingerroot, if desired. Transfer to a serving dish and sprinkle the scallions over the top. Serve hot.

Bean Curd with Black Mushrooms and Bamboo Shoots

Serves 3 to 4, or 5 to 6 as part of a multicourse meal

A *flavorful vegetarian dish that provides protein without meat. The tender textures contrast well with crispy deep-fried or vegetable dishes.*

1 pound firm tofu (bean curd)

1 cup dried black mushrooms (about 1 ounce)

2 tablespoons dark soy sauce

1 tablespoon oyster sauce

1 teaspoon sugar

3 tablespoons canola, corn, or peanut oil

1 (8-ounce) can sliced bamboo shoots, drained (1 cup)

2 scallions, white and green parts, thinly sliced

1.   Drain the tofu and place on a cutting board. Slice horizontally in half. Slice each half crosswise into pieces about 1¾ inches long, ½ inch wide, 1 inch thick. Set aside.

2.   Soak the mushrooms in hot water to cover for 15 minutes, or until soft. Drain, squeeze out excess water with your hands, and cut off the stems with scissors. Cut the caps in half or if they are 2 inches or larger, into quarters. Set aside.

3.   Mix the soy sauce, oyster sauce, sugar, and 2 tablespoons of water in a small dish. Set aside.

4.   Heat the oil in a wok or stir-fry pan over medium-high heat. When the oil is hot but not smoking, add the bamboo shoots and mushrooms; they should sizzle. Stir for about 1 minute to heat. Add the tofu and the soy sauce mixture and stir gently so as not to break up the tofu. Stir for about 3 minutes, or until the ingredients are well heated. Transfer to a serving dish and garnish with scallions. Serve hot.

Bean Curd, Family Style

Serves 3 to 4, or 5 to 6 as part of a multicourse meal

*N*utritious, quick, and easy, the soft bean curd contrasts nicely with the mixed vegetables. For variation, use bok choy in place of green cabbage, and fresh mushrooms for the dried black. For a spicy version, add 1 teaspoon crushed red pepper to the hoisin sauce mixture.

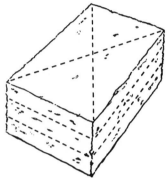

1 cup dried black mushrooms (about 8 pieces)

1 pound firm tofu (bean curd)

3 tablespoons hoisin sauce

2 tablespoons dark soy sauce

2 teaspoons cornstarch

3 tablespoons canola, corn, or peanut oil

2 garlic cloves, crushed and peeled

2 slices unpeeled gingerroot, 1 × ⅛ inch each

½ pound green cabbage, cut into 1½-inch chunks (about 3 cups)

1 medium red or green bell pepper, seeded, cored, and cut into 1½-inch chunks

1 (8-ounce) can sliced bamboo shoots, drained (1 cup)

1. Soak the mushrooms in hot water to cover for 15 minutes, or until soft. Drain, squeeze out liquid, and cut off and discard the stems. Cut the caps into quarters. Set aside.

2. Drain the tofu and place on a cutting board. Slice the tofu horizontally into three even pieces. Keeping the pieces together, cut through from corner to corner into four triangles. There should be a total of 12 triangular pieces. Set aside.

3. Mix the hoisin sauce and soy sauce with 2 tablespoons water in a small dish and set aside. Dissolve the cornstarch in ¼ cup water and set aside.

4. Heat the oil in a wok or stir-fry pan over high heat. When the oil is hot, add the garlic and gingerroot and stir until fragrant. Add the cabbage and stir-fry for 3 minutes. Add the peppers, bamboo shoots, and mushrooms, and cook for 2 minutes. It is alright if the cabbage begins to brown in spots.

(continued)

5. Add the hoisin sauce mixture and tofu to the pan and cook 2 minutes (If using crushed red pepper, add it), until the tofu is heated through. Stir gently so the tofu does not break into pieces. Stir in the cornstarch mixture and stir another 30 seconds until the ingredients are thoroughly coated. Discard the gingerroot and garlic. Serve immediately.

Fried Bean Curd
with Broccoli

豆腐蛋

Serves 3 to 4, or 5 to 6 as part of a multicourse meal

*S*erve this meatless dish as an entree alone or with white or brown rice for a well-balanced meal. Or use it as a vegetable dish in a multicourse dinner. For deep-frying the bean curd, I use a method I call shallow-frying that calls for only one cup of oil. You can substitute storebought deep-fried bean curd in this recipe.

健康

1 pound firm tofu (bean curd)

1 cup canola, corn, or peanut oil

1 pound broccoli

2 tablespoons dark soy sauce

2 teaspoons dry sherry

2 tablespoons fermented black beans, coarsely chopped

1 teaspoon sugar

2 garlic cloves, peeled and thinly sliced

1 (8-ounce) can sliced bamboo shoots, drained (1 cup)

1 tablespoon cornstarch, dissolved in 2 tablespoons water

1. Drain the tofu and place on a cutting board. Slice horizontally into three even pieces. Keeping the pieces together, cut through from corner to corner into four triangles. You should have a total of 12 triangles. Blot with paper towels. Set aside on paper towels for 15 minutes or more.

2. Cut the broccoli into 1½-inch florets. Peel the stalk with a paring knife and roll-cut the stalk into 1½-inch pieces as described on page 46.

Bean Curd

and Eggs

3.   Combine the soy sauce, sherry, black beans, sugar, and ½ cup water in a small bowl. Stir until the sugar dissolves. Set aside.

4.   Heat the oil in a wok or stir-fry pan over medium-high heat to 350°F. The oil is ready when tofu sizzles when a point is placed in the oil. Slip half the tofu into the hot oil and fry until golden brown. Turn and fry the other side. When both sides are browned (this should take about 10 to 15 minutes), remove from the oil with chopsticks, tongs, or a slotted spatula and place on a plate lined with a double layer of paper towels. Repeat with remaining tofu. Set aside.

5.   Reserve 2 tablespoons of the cooking oil and discard the rest. Place 1 tablespoon in the same pan used to cook the tofu or in a clean pan. Heat the oil over high heat until it is hot. Add the broccoli and stir for about 30 seconds. Add ¼ cup water, reduce heat to medium, cover and continue cooking, for another minute or two, or until tender-crisp. Remove and spread on a plate. Set aside.

6.   Add the second tablespoon of reserved oil to the same pan and add the garlic. Stir around the pan until fragrant and sizzling, but do not let it burn. Add the bamboo shoots, soy sauce mixture, and fried tofu to the pan and stir-fry over medium-high to high heat for 1 to 2 minutes.

7.   Return the broccoli to the pan and stir a few times. When the liquid boils add the cornstarch slurry. Stir until the sauce thickens. Serve hot.

Chilled
Bean Curd Salad

Serves 4 to 6 as a side dish

*T*his country-style dish is traditionally made with lightly mashed bean curd. If you find that unappetizing — as my husband does — cut the bean curd into very small cubes.

福

1 pound fresh soft tofu (bean curd), drained

5 teaspoons light soy sauce

1 teaspoon sesame seed oil

2 tablespoons thinly sliced scallions, green and white parts

1 tablespoon minced dried shrimp (optional)

1.   Blanch the tofu for 1 minute in enough boiling water to cover it. Drain and place in a bowl of ice water for 5 minutes to cool. When cool, drain the bean curd and pat dry with paper towels. Transfer to a shallow serving dish and coarsely crumble it with the back of a fork or cut it into ½-inch cubes.

2.   Add the soy sauce, sesame seed oil, and scallions. Toss a few times and garnish with minced dried shrimp, if desired. Serve cold.

Half Moon Eggs
in Soy Sauce

豆腐蛋

Serves 4 as part of a
multicourse meal

M y mother often made this for family meals when we needed an extra dish. The eggs are cooked just like sunny-side-up eggs, but before the whites set, the eggs are folded over. The yolks should be runny and the edges of the whites crisp. The eggs go well with rice.

禄

1½ tablespoons dark soy sauce
½ tablespoon light brown sugar
4 tablespoons canola, corn, or peanut oil
4 large eggs
1 tablespoon thinly sliced scallions or minced onion

1.   Mix the soy sauce, sugar, and 2 tablespoons of water together in a small bowl. Set aside.

2.   Pour 2 tablespoons of the oil into a nonstick 10-inch skillet and place over medium-high heat. When the oil is hot, break 2 eggs into the skillet, keeping the eggs from running into each other. When the edges of the whites are light brown and the yolks are still soft, fold the eggs over with a spatula so that it forms a half-moon shape. You may need to hold the edges down with the tip of a spatula until the whites fuse together. Transfer the eggs to a platter and fry the remaining 2 eggs in the same manner, adding another tablespoon of oil if necessary. Transfer these eggs to the platter.

3.   Add the scallions to the pan and stir around a few times. Return the fried eggs to the pan and pour the soy sauce mixture over. Shake the pan gently to heat and coat the eggs with sauce. Transfer the eggs and sauce to a serving dish. Serve immediately.

壽

Variation   Flavor the fried eggs with leftover red-cooked sauce from such dishes as Soy Sauce Chicken (page 182), Shanghai Red-cooked Duck (page 187), or Shanghai Red-cooked Ham (page 217).

Egg Foo Yung, Family Style

Serves 3 to 4, or 5 to 6 as part of a multicourse meal

E gg Foo Yung used to be very popular in Chinese restaurants. Even before I was a teenager, I helped in the family restaurant and packed many an Egg Foo Yung to go. In the restaurant, the eggs were deep-fried into small round pillows and then covered with a simple brown sauce. In my mother's family-style recipe, the eggs are pan-fried into a looser form, more akin to an omelet. It calls for less oil, and the eggs can be served with or without the brown sauce.

The ingredients for the Egg Foo Yung should all be shredded, as described on pages 44–45.

5 large eggs

1 teaspoon salt (if using canned crabmeat, reduce to ½ teaspoon)

1 teaspoon dry sherry

Dash black pepper

½ cup fresh or canned lump crabmeat or shredded cooked pork, chicken, ham, beef, or shrimp

½ cup shredded celery, no leaves

½ cup dried black mushrooms, softened in hot water for 15 minutes, squeezed dry, stems removed, and shredded

1 cup fresh bean sprouts or drained and shredded bamboo shoots

¼ cup thinly sliced onion

3 tablespoons canola, corn, or peanut oil

1. Gently beat the eggs with the salt, sherry, and pepper. Add the crabmeat, celery, black mushrooms, bean sprouts, and onion and mix well.

2. Heat the oil in a nonstick wok or stir-fry pan over medium-high heat until the oil is hot but not smoking. Test by dipping the end of a spatula into the egg mixture and then into the oil; it should sizzle. Add the egg mixture to the hot oil. Let the eggs sit without stirring until the bottom is slightly set but the top is still runny. With a spatula, turn sections of the eggs over. Con-

tinue turning the eggs until the mixture is set on both sides. Remove to a serving platter. Serve immediately.

健康

Variation   Serve the Egg Foo Yung with a restaurant-style brown sauce. Make the sauce before cooking the eggs.

Mix together 1 cup Chinese Chicken Broth (page 64) plus ½ teaspoon salt or 1 cup of canned chicken broth, ½ teaspoon ketchup, 1½ teaspoons light soy sauce, and 2 tablespoons flour, mixed with 2 tablespoons cold water into a smooth paste, in a saucepan. Cook over medium heat, stirring constantly with a wire whisk. Bring to a boil and stir until the sauce is thickened. Simmer 2 minutes to eliminate the raw taste of the flour. Pour the sauce freely over the cooked eggs.

Egg Garnish

Makes two 10-inch pancakes

W*hen I was a girl, I would make an egg pancake using this recipe and fold it up to fill a sandwich, but mostly the recipe is used to make a versatile garnish for salads and soups. It resembles very thin noodles and it works wonderfully for many dishes, such as salads and soups, where you'd like a little color.*

If you use a nonstick skillet, which I prefer, you can use less oil. Too much oil will make it difficult to form a thin pancake since the eggs will slide as you tilt the pan.

福

2 eggs
½ teaspoon salt
½ teaspoon dry sherry
2 teaspoons canola, corn, or peanut oil

1.   Beat the eggs with the salt and sherry. Heat 1 teaspoon of the oil in a 10- to 11-inch skillet over medium heat and smear it evenly over the bottom of the pan with a paper towel. Pour in half the egg mixture and tip the pan back and forth to spread out the egg into a very thin pancake. Use a spatula to help push the egg to its thinnest. Cook until the edges turn light brown and begin to curl. This will take less than 1 minute.

(continued)

2. With a spatula, transfer the egg pancake to a cutting board and cut it into 4 even strips. Pile the strips on top of one another, turn sideways, and cut across the strips to make fine shreds. Repeat with the remaining egg mixture and oil.

Mandarin Eggs

Serves 3 to 4, or 5 to 6 as part of a multicourse meal

*A*lthough this dish is traditionally made with egg yolks only, I have reworked my mother's original recipe to use whole eggs. The chicken broth thins the eggs so they remain soft and custardlike.

4 large eggs
1/3 cup finely minced canned water chestnuts
1 tablespoon thinly sliced scallion, green and white parts
1 1/2 cups Chinese Chicken Broth (page 64) plus 1/2 teaspoon salt or canned chicken broth
1/4 teaspoon salt to taste
2 tablespoons cornstarch
1/2 teaspoon dry sherry
4 tablespoons canola, corn, or peanut oil
2 tablespoons minced Smithfield ham

1. Beat together the eggs, water chestnuts, scallion, broth, salt, cornstarch, and sherry.

2. Heat the oil in a nonstick stir-fry pan or skillet over high heat until hot but not smoking. Test by dipping the end of a spatula into the egg mixture and then into the oil; it should sizzle. Add the eggs to the hot oil and stir gently but constantly in the same direction until the eggs thicken to form a soft custard, about 4 to 5 minutes. Be sure not to miss the outside edges!

3. Transfer to a serving platter and garnish with ham. Serve immediately.

Mock Crab Omelet

Serves 2, or 3 to 4 as part of a
multicourse meal

*D*uring our first trip to China after President Nixon opened relations in 1972, we had
this omelet at Number One Uncle and Aunt's house in Shanghai. (In China, we
refer to our relatives by their relationship vis-à-vis our parents.) My mother was de-
lighted with the dish and developed the recipe to feature on our public television documentary called "Joyce Chen's China."

The dish is designed to taste and look like crab. Freshwater crabs are popular in
the winter when they are in season, especially the full-bodied female with eggs. Everyone hopes for those! The carrots resemble the bright orange crab roe; the potatoes, the
white crabmeat; and the wood ears, the dark membrane that lines the top shell. And
since the Chinese eat crab with a vinegar and ginger dip, the seasonings used are
reminiscent of those flavors.

2 medium potatoes, peeled and cut in half (about 1 pound)

1 medium carrot, peeled and cut in thirds

2 tablespoons dried wood ears (about ¼ ounce)

1 teaspoon minced peeled gingerroot

1½ tablespoons cider vinegar

2 large eggs

1 teaspoon dry sherry

3 tablespoons canola, corn, or peanut oil

1 teaspoon salt

1 tablespoon thinly sliced scallions, green parts only

1.   Boil the potatoes and carrots together in a saucepan until tender.
Plunge the vegetables into cold water to cool. When cool, mash them coarsely
with the back of a fork. The texture should remain somewhat lumpy. Spread
out on paper towels to absorb the excess moisture.

2.   Soak the wood ears in 2 cups of hot water for 15 minutes, or until
soft. Drain, rinse, and squeeze out excess water. Coarsely chop.

3.   Mix the gingerroot with the vinegar. Set aside. In a separate bowl,
beat the eggs with sherry. Set aside.

(continued)

4.   Heat the oil and salt in a nonstick stir-fry pan or 10-inch skillet over high heat. When the oil is hot and fragrant, add the potatoes and carrots and stir gently. Avoid vigorous stirring as this will make the potatoes mushy. Cook for no more than 2 minutes. Stir in the wood ears and scallions, add the beaten eggs, and stir them into the vegetables gently but thoroughly until the mixture begins to become firm. Pour the vinegar and ginger mixture over the eggs and stir to mix thoroughly. The eggs should be soft, so be careful not to overcook them. Transfer the eggs to a platter. Serve immediately.

Chinese Omelet with Crabmeat

Serves 3 to 4, or 5 to 6 as part of a multicourse meal

A Chinese omelet is more like loose scrambled eggs than a formed omelet in the Western sense. If you don't like runny eggs, cook them a little longer.

禧

1 (6-ounce) can crabmeat (about ¾ cup)

6 large eggs

1 teaspoon dry sherry

1 teaspoon salt

1 tablespoon thinly sliced scallions, white and green parts

4 tablespoons canola, corn, or peanut oil

1.   Place the crabmeat with the liquid from the can in a mixing bowl. With your hands, separate the crabmeat into flakes and discard any pieces of cartilage. Set aside.

2.   Beat the eggs with the sherry, salt and scallions until well mixed but not foamy. I use a pair of chopsticks or a fork so as not to overbeat. Add the crabmeat and mix together thoroughly.

3.   Heat the oil in a wok or stir-fry pan, preferably nonstick, over high heat until hot but not smoking. Test by dipping the tip of the spatula into the egg mixture and then into the oil; it should sizzle. Add the eggs to the hot oil and with a spatula turn the eggs from the edges to the center, allowing the uncooked egg mixture to run onto the exposed pan surface. Continue until the eggs are lightly set but not dry. Remove from the heat. Serve immediately.

Bean Curd

and Eggs

Vegetables

Vegetables are perhaps the most important ingredient in Chinese cooking. They can be found in just about every dish. The Chinese are particularly fond of leafy greens such as spinach, water spinach, mustard greens, watercress, and leafy Chinese cabbages. As a child I never understood why other children hated spinach. We loved the way my mother prepared it. The first time I had spinach cooked Western-style at school — soft, mushy, and tasteless — I understood why my friends had such an abhorrence for spinach.

Any vegetable that is found in a supermarket can be used for Chinese cooking. Specialty Chinese vegetables are interesting and nice to have when available, but they are not necessary for good home cooking. Freshly picked vegetables are far superior to ones that have been out of the ground for days or even weeks; they are much preferred by the Chinese. My mother was thrilled when she could get fresh-picked vegetables and fruits; she loved to visit local farms. One of our favorites is probably the only farm left in Belmont, a suburb of Boston. The farmer, Angelo Sergi, picked his vegetables daily, and if he didn't have what my mother wanted in the stand, he let her go out into the fields and pick it herself.

It was at Sergi's farm that we would also pick wild greens. My mother's favorite is green amaranth (*Amaranthus retroflexus*), commonly known as pig weed. We called it fox tails because of its insignificant green flowers that grew in long spikes. (Do not confuse this with foxglove or *Digitalis,* a flowering garden plant that is poisonous.) My mother would stir-fry the freshly picked amaranth greens with garlic and a little oil.

Another wild green we would pick was shepherd's-purse (*Capsella Bursa-pastoris*), so called because the heart-shaped seedpods that line the flower spikes resemble the leather pouches shepherds used to carry. There was a particularly good growth of shepherd's purse in front of our local post office. My mother and I would sometimes go there to get some of the tender young greens. They would be blanched, chopped up, and added to our Peking Ravioli or wonton filling.

A selection of recipes from this chapter will make a satisfying vegetarian meal. Because vegetables are so prominent in many Chinese dishes, there are recipes in the meat chapters that can be made without the meat. I have sometimes made such suggestions.

Stir-fried Asparagus

Serves 4, or 5 to 6 as part of a
multicourse meal

蔬菜

*A*lthough the asparagus is not indigenous to China, the Chinese have added it to their repertoire and use it in many dishes. This simple stir-fry relies on the sweet freshness of springtime asparagus for flavor rather than on heavy spices. It's a dish that pairs well with Western foods like broiled or grilled fish or chicken.

健康

1 pound asparagus

2 tablespoons canola, corn, or peanut oil

½ teaspoon salt, or to taste

2 garlic cloves, thinly sliced

½ cup water

1 red bell pepper, seeded, cored, and sliced into 2-inch-long julienne strips

1¼ teaspoons cornstarch, dissolved in 1 tablespoon water

1.   Cut or snap the tough ends from the asparagus. Remove the leaf scales from the bottom of the spears. Wash thoroughly under running water and drain. Roll-cut into 1½-inch lengths as described on page 46.

2.   Pour the oil into a wok or stir-fry pan and place over high heat. Add the salt and garlic and stir around the pan until the oil is hot; the garlic will begin to sizzle. Add the asparagus and stir for about 1 minute. Pour in the water and cook, covered, over medium-high heat for about 2 minutes, or until the asparagus are tender-crisp.

3.   Stir in the red pepper and stir for 30 seconds to 1 minute, or until the pepper loses its raw look. Stir up the cornstarch slurry and pour it into the pan, stirring until the liquid thickens. Remove from the heat, taste, and add salt as desired. Serve hot.

Broccoli in  *Oyster Sauce*

**Serves 4 to 5, or 6 to 8 as part of a
multicourse meal**

*T*he rich flavors of the oyster sauce and dark soy sauce will not overpower the broccoli.
For an interesting variation, try using Chinese broccoli, available in Asian markets.

福

1½ pounds broccoli

3 tablespoons oyster sauce

1 tablespoon dark soy sauce

1 teaspoon sugar

1 teaspoon cornstarch

2 tablespoons canola, corn, or peanut oil

1 garlic clove, crushed and peeled

¼ cup Chinese Chicken Broth (page 64) or water

1.   Cut 2-inch-long florets from the top of the broccoli. Peel the tough
outer skin from the stalks and roll-cut into 2-inch lengths as described on
page 46.

2.   Blend the oyster sauce, soy sauce, sugar, cornstarch, and 3 tablespoons water together in a small bowl. Set aside.

3.   Pour the oil into a wok or stir-fry pan and place over high heat.
Add the garlic and stir around the pan until the oil is hot; the garlic will sizzle.
Turn the broccoli into the pan, stirring until the pieces turn a darker green.
Pour the broth into the pan, reduce the heat to medium, and cover. Steam
the broccoli for about 4 to 6 minutes, or until tender-crisp.

4.   Stir in the oyster sauce mixture. Stir until the sauce has thickened
and the broccoli is completely coated. Discard the garlic, if desired. Transfer
to a platter. Serve immediately.

Stir-fried Cauliflower and Broccoli

蔬菜

Serves 3 to 4, or 5 to 6 as part of a multicourse meal

*T*he contrasting colors of these two vegetables make a simple dish special. You could also use only one vegetable with, perhaps, a garnish of two tablespoons minced Smithfield ham for color and flavor.

禄

½ pound cauliflower

½ pound broccoli

2 tablespoons canola, corn, or peanut oil

1 garlic clove, crushed and peeled

½ cup Chinese Chicken Broth (page 64) or water

½ teaspoon salt

2 teaspoons cornstarch, dissolved in 2 tablespoons water

1.   Cut the cauliflower and broccoli into bite-size 2-inch-long florets. Peel the stem of the broccoli and roll-cut as described on page 46 to the same length as the florets.

2.   Pour the oil into a wok or stir-fry pan and place over high heat. Add the garlic and stir around the pan until the oil is hot but not smoking; the garlic will begin to sizzle. Add the cauliflower and stir for about 2 minutes. Add the broccoli and stir for 1 minute.

3.   Add the broth or water and cover the pan. Turn the heat to medium and simmer for 4 to 6 minutes, or until the vegetables are tender-crisp. Stir occasionally. If you like the vegetables more tender, cook them longer.

4.   Uncover the pan, sprinkle with salt, and stir to mix thoroughly. Turn the heat to high, add the cornstarch slurry, and stir until the gravy thickens. Discard the garlic clove, if desired. Serve hot.

Stir-fried Napa Cabbage

Serves 4, or 5 to 6 as part of a
multicourse meal

H ere is a simple family-style vegetable dish. You could use other kinds of Chinese cabbage, but I prefer napa cabbage, not only for its delicate flavor and texture but also because it keeps very well in the refrigerator and makes a perfect emergency ingredient.

1 pound napa cabbage

2 tablespoons canola, corn, or peanut oil

2 slices unpeeled gingerroot, 1 × ⅛ inch each

1 chicken bouillon cube, dissolved in ½ cup hot water

1½ teaspoons cornstarch, dissolved in 2 tablespoons water

1.   Remove and discard any tough, wilted, or discolored leaves from the cabbage. Cut the cabbage lengthwise into 2-inch-wide wedges. Cut out the core and cut the wedges crosswise into 3-inch lengths. Separate the leaves. Set aside.

2.   Pour the oil into a wok or stir-fry pan and place over high heat. Add the gingerroot to the oil and stir around the pan until the oil is hot; the gingerroot will sizzle. Add the cabbage and stir for about 2 minutes.

3.   Pour the chicken broth into the pan, stir a couple of times, and reduce the heat to medium. Cover and cook for another 2 minutes, stirring occasionally, or until the desired tenderness is achieved. If too much of the liquid evaporates add a few tablespoons of water. There must be liquid in the pan to bind with the cornstarch.

4.   Uncover the pan, turn the heat to high, and add the cornstarch slurry. Stir until the liquid is thickened. Discard the gingerroot, if desired. Serve hot.

Variation   Add ¼ cup dried shrimp, rinsed and drained, to the cabbage when adding the chicken bouillon in step 3.

Ginger-glazed Carrots and Parsnips

Serves 4 as a side dish

*T*he natural sweetness of these root vegetables is enhanced by the light ginger glaze.
This dish is a particularly good accompaniment for roast pork or poultry.

健康

2 tablespoons canola, corn, or peanut oil

4 medium carrots, peeled and roll-cut into 1-inch pieces (page 46)

3 medium parsnips, peeled and roll-cut into 1-inch pieces (page 46)

¼ cup water

¼ teaspoon salt

4 teaspoons light brown sugar

1 teaspoon grated peeled gingerroot

Freshly ground black pepper

1 tablespoon chopped parsley

1. Heat the oil in a wok or stir-fry pan over high heat until hot but not smoking. Add the vegetables; they should sizzle. Stir for about 2 minutes. Add the water, reduce heat to medium, cover, and cook, stirring occasionally for even cooking, for 5 to 6 minutes, or until the vegetables are tender. A fork should go in easily with just a little resistance.

2. Uncover the pan and sprinkle on the salt, sugar, gingerroot, and a dash of pepper. Turn the heat to high and stir for about 1 to 2 minutes to reduce the liquid to a glaze. Transfer to a shallow platter and sprinkle with parsley. Serve immediately.

Shanghai Bok Choy
with Black Mushrooms

**Serves 2, or 3 to 4 as part of a
multicourse meal**

Y ou'll have to make a trip to a Chinese market to find Shanghai bok choy but these tender little cabbages with their lovely jade color and delicate flavor are well worth the effort. In China, the hearts of Shanghai bok choy are considered a delicacy and are often served at banquets.

8 dried black mushrooms
1 tablespoon soy sauce
Dash black pepper
1 teaspoon sugar
$\frac{1}{2}$ teaspoon dry sherry
$\frac{1}{2}$ teaspoon salt
$\frac{1}{2}$ pound Shanghai bok choy
2 tablespoons canola, corn, or peanut oil
1 slice unpeeled gingerroot, 1 × $\frac{1}{8}$ inch
1 (8-ounce) can sliced bamboo shoots, drained (1 cup) (optional)
2 teaspoons cornstarch, dissolved in 2 tablespoons water

1.   Soak the mushrooms in 1¼ cups hot water for 15 minutes to soften. Squeeze out the excess water with your hands. With scissors, trim off and discard the woody stems. Strain the soaking liquid, reserving 1 cup. Add the soy sauce, pepper, sugar, sherry, and salt to the mushroom liquid. Set the mushrooms and the liquid aside separately.

2.   Trim away and discard any yellow or discolored leaves from the bok choy. Clean thoroughly under running water. Pull the larger outer leaves from the head one by one and cut them in half or thirds lengthwise. When you reach the very tiny center leaves, cut the whole core in half or quarters to match the size of the leaves.

3.   Bring 6 cups of water to a boil and blanch the cabbage for 2 minutes. Drain and cool immediately in cold water to refresh and stop the cooking. Gently squeeze out the excess water and set the leaves aside.

4. Pour the oil into a wok or stir-fry pan and place over medium-high heat. Add the gingerroot and stir around the pan until the oil is hot; the gingerroot will sizzle. Add the mushrooms, bamboo shoots, cabbage leaves, and the mushroom liquid. Stir until boiling. Add the cornstarch slurry. Stir until the sauce thickens. Taste and add salt, if necessary. Discard the gingerroot. Serve immediately.

禄

Note   For a banquet-style presentation, place the cabbage leaves in a sunburst shape on a platter. Pile the mushrooms and bamboo shoots in the center. Serve hot.

壽

Stir-fried Celery

*C*elery is a terrific stir-fry ingredient — crisp, low in fat, high in fiber, economical, and usually on hand in the refrigerator. Carrots add a bright color contrast to the light green celery stalks. You could also use a red bell pepper.

1 pound celery

2 tablespoons canola, corn, or peanut oil

1 garlic clove, thinly sliced

½ teaspoon salt

3 carrots, peeled and cut on the diagonal ¼ inch thick

½ cup canned chicken broth

1 teaspoon cornstarch, dissolved in 1 tablespoon water

1.　Separate the celery stalks and wash thoroughly, paying special attention to grit in the grooves on the outside of the stalks. Trim off the leaves and a little from the root end of each stalk. String the tough outer stalks. Slice each stalk on the diagonal ½ inch thick. You should have a little more than 4 cups.

2.　Pour the oil into a wok or stir-fry pan and place over medium-high heat. Add the garlic and salt and stir around the pan until the oil is hot; the garlic will begin to sizzle. Add the carrots and cook for about 1 minute.

3.　Add the celery and broth, lower the heat to medium, and simmer, covered, for 3 to 5 minutes, or until the vegetables are tender-crisp. Stir occasionally for even cooking. Uncover and add the cornstarch slurry. Stir until the liquid thickens. Taste and add salt, if desired. Serve hot.

Variation　Add ¼ cup dried shrimp, rinsed and drained, to the pan when adding the celery in step 3. Reduce the salt in step 2.

Stir-fried Green Beans

**Serves 3 to 4, or 5 to 6 as part of a
multicourse meal**

*H*ome-style Chinese cooking is surprisingly simple, often using just a few ingredients. These green beans, for example, are cooked with a minimal amount of seasonings, relying instead on the natural flavor of the vegetable. This is an excellent side dish for Western foods.

福

1 pound green or wax beans

2 tablespoons canola, corn, or peanut oil

½ cup Chinese Chicken Broth (page 64) or water

1 teaspoon salt

1 teaspoon sugar

1. Snap off the tips of the green beans and break each bean into 2 or 3 pieces about 1½ to 2 inches long.

2. Heat the oil in a wok or stir-fry pan over high heat. When the oil is hot enough to sizzle when a bean is dipped in, add all the beans and stir for 2 minutes. Add the broth or water and salt. Stir and cover the pan. Reduce the heat to medium and cook for about 6 to 9 minutes, or until the beans are tender to your liking. Stir occasionally for even cooking.

3. Add the sugar and cook, uncovered, for 1 minute, stirring frequently. Serve hot.

禄

Note   If you like a garlicky taste, add 2 minced garlic cloves with the broth in step 2.

Kan Shao Green Beans

*Y*ou can also use Chinese long beans in this recipe. Break them into pieces about one
and a half inches long. The texture will be a little softer.

壽

1 pound green beans
¼ cup fermented black beans, chopped
1 tablespoon minced peeled gingerroot
2 garlic cloves, minced
1 tablespoon crushed red pepper, or to taste
3 tablespoons canola, corn, or peanut oil
2 tablespoons light soy sauce
1 teaspoon sugar
½ cup water

1. Snap off the ends of the beans and break them into pieces about 1½
to 2 inches long. Set aside.

2. Combine the black beans, gingerroot, garlic, and red pepper in a
small dish. Set aside.

3. Heat the oil in a wok or stir-fry pan over medium-high heat until
hot but not smoking. Add the black bean mixture, it will sizzle slightly when
added. Stir until fragrant.

4. Add the green beans, soy sauce, and sugar. Stir a few times and add
the water. Stir to mix, cover, and cook over medium heat for 5 minutes.
Uncover the pan, turn the heat to high, and cook for 5 minutes, or until the
beans are tender and the liquid has evaporated. Stir frequently to ensure even
cooking and to prevent burning as the liquid evaporates. Serve hot.

Red-mouthed Green Parrot

Serves 2 to 3, or 4 to 5 as part of a multicourse meal

C hinese poets describe spinach with pink roots as a "red-mouthed green parrot." My mother often took us to a farm stand and asked if we could pick spinach ourselves; that way we could pull it up with the sweet pink roots still attached. We would leave about half an inch of the root attached, then scrape it clean with our fingernails or a small knife. Although the pink makes a prettier dish, you can use regular loose spinach. The small amount of sugar in the recipe brings back the natural sweetness of just-picked vegetables.

禧

1 pound spinach, preferably with pink roots attached
2 tablespoons canola, corn, or peanut oil
2 garlic cloves, crushed and peeled
½ teaspoon salt
1 teaspoon sugar

1.   Fill the sink with cold water and put the spinach in the water. Separate the large leaves with their stalks. Leave the smaller leaves attached to the root. Scrape the pink root with your fingernails or a paring knife. Lift the spinach from the water and place in a colander. Discard the water and repeat the washing two more times. There should be no grit in the bottom of the sink after the last washing. Drain well and leave the spinach leaves whole.

2.   Pour the oil into a wok or stir-fry pan and place over high heat. Add the garlic and salt and stir around the pan until the oil is hot; the garlic will begin to sizzle. Do not let the garlic burn or it will become bitter.

3.   Add the spinach; the oil will sizzle. Stir until the spinach begins to wilt. Sprinkle on the sugar and continue stirring until well wilted, 1 to 2 minutes. (I find chopsticks best for stirring greens.) Spread flat on a shallow platter and serve immediately.

Stir-fried Watercress with Fu Ru

**Serves 2 to 3, or 4 to 5 as part of a
multicourse meal**

*F*u ru is a kind of bean curd that is fermented in salt and wine until it develops a strong salty flavor and pungent aroma. It is often called "Chinese cheese." It is sold in jars in Chinese grocery stores.

2 bunches fresh watercress, 12 to 14 ounces
3 small cakes fu ru, about 1 inch square and ½ inch thick
2 tablespoons canola, corn, or peanut oil
1 garlic clove, crushed and peeled
2 slices unpeeled gingerroot, 1 × ⅛ inch

1.   Wash and drain the watercress, discarding any discolored leaves. Cut the sprigs in half.

2.   With a small spoon, cream the fu ru with 2 tablespoons water in a small bowl. The mixture will be a little lumpy. Set aside.

3.   Pour the oil into a wok or stir-fry pan and place the pan over high heat. Add the garlic and gingerroot and stir around the pan until the oil is hot; the garlic and gingerroot will begin to sizzle. Add the watercress and stir until wilted, about 1½ to 2 minutes. Chopsticks are helpful for stir-frying because of the stringy nature of the watercress.

4.   Add the fu ru and stir thoroughly until well mixed, about 30 seconds. Serve immediately.

Mushrooms, Bamboo Shoots, and Snow Peas

蔬菜

Serves 3 to 4 as part of a multicourse meal

*T*he Chinese like to use the number three in dishes. In Chinese this dish is known as *Three Delights. Each ingredient has a distinct texture and appearance that make the dish delightful to eat and delightful to look at.*

福

½ cup dried black mushrooms

2 tablespoons light soy sauce

1 teaspoon sugar

3 tablespoons canola, corn, or peanut oil

½ pound snow peas, ends snapped off and strings removed

½ teaspoon salt

1 (8-ounce) can sliced bamboo shoots, drained (1 cup)

1½ teaspoons cornstarch, dissolved in 1 tablespoon water

1. Soak the mushrooms in 2 cups hot water for 15 minutes, or until soft. Drain and squeeze the liquid, reserving ½ cup. Strain and mix with the soy sauce and sugar. Set aside. Trim off the mushroom stems with scissors and cut the caps in half. Cut large caps into quarters so all the pieces will be of uniform size. Set aside.

2. Heat 2 tablespoons of the oil in a wok or stir-fry pan over high heat until hot but not smoking. Test by dipping a snow pea in the oil; it should sizzle. Add the salt and then the snow peas. Stir constantly until the peas turn a darker green, about 1 minute. Transfer to a platter and spread out to stop cooking.

3. Add the remaining 1 tablespoon of oil to the same pan. Stir in the bamboo shoots and mushrooms with the mushroom liquid mixture. Stir and cook for about 2 minutes. Add the cornstarch slurry. Stir until the sauce thickens. Return the snow peas to the pan and mix thoroughly. Serve immediately.

Stir-fried Chinese Water Spinach with Fu Ru

Serves 2 to 3, or 4 to 5 as part of a multicourse meal

*T*he Chinese call water spinach hollow hearted vegetable, since the long stem is hollow like a reed. The Chinese, especially southerners, love these greens for their tender, arrow-shaped leaves and crisp stems. In Chinatown you can ask for it by its Cantonese name, *ung tsoi.* Buy a lot — it will shrink to less than half its volume when cooked.

This dish is a real down-home, country recipe that is popular in Cantonese restaurants in Chinatown but usually known only to the Chinese. It is never printed on the menu in English, and it is not always available. If you want it, you'll have to ask for it. Just ask if they have ung tsoi with fu ru *today. The waiter will surely be surprised!*

禄

1½ pounds Chinese water spinach
3 cakes fu ru, plain or chili flavored
2 tablespoons canola, corn, or peanut oil
2 garlic cloves, crushed and peeled
¼ cup water

1. Wash the water spinach thoroughly in lots of water and drain. Trim away and discard any rotting leaves. The ends tend to be tough, so cut or break off about 2 inches from the bottom of the stems. Cut or break the remaining spinach into 3-inch pieces. Water spinach is very crisp so it will break easily.

2. Remove the fu ru from the jar. Place in a small bowl and mash with the back of a spoon with 1 tablespoon of water to make a paste. It will not be completely smooth but will become so when it cooks.

3. Pour the oil into a wok or stir-fry pan and place over high heat. Add the garlic and stir until the oil is hot; the garlic will sizzle. Add the water spinach and stir until the leaves have wilted. Add the ¼ cup water and stir for about 2 minutes. Chopsticks are easier to use than a spatula here since the water spinach gets stringy as it cooks.

4. Add the fu ru paste and stir thoroughly until dissolved. Cook for 2 minutes or so, stirring. Transfer to a serving dish and serve hot.

壽

Note Even the same brand of fu ru may vary in flavor intensity. If the fu ru tastes lighter than you'd like, add another cake to the dish or flavor with some salt.

Quick Asparagus Salad

Serves 3 to 4 as a side dish

*O*ften the simplest way to prepare a vegetable is the best. Use very fresh asparagus and cook them just until tender-crisp.

禧

1 pound asparagus
3 tablespoons light soy sauce
1 teaspoon sesame seed oil or hot sesame oil

1. Cut or snap off the tough ends of the asparagus and cut off the small wedge-shaped leaves up to 2 inches from the tip. Wash well and roll-cut as described on page 46 or cut on the diagonal into 1½-inch lengths.

2. Bring 6 cups of water to a boil in a saucepan over high heat. Add the asparagus pieces. As soon as the water returns to a boil, drain and quickly cool in cold water to stop the cooking. Drain well. (The asparagus can be cooked a day ahead and refrigerated.)

3. Just before serving, place the asparagus in a serving bowl and toss with the soy sauce and sesame seed oil. Serve at room temperature.

Vegetables

Vegetarian's Delight

**Serves 6 to 8 as part of a
multicourse meal**

As with *Beef with Mixed Vegetables* (page 222), this recipe can be a flexible combination of vegetables. I don't recommend stir-frying as an excuse for cleaning out the refrigerator, but we often find ourselves with little bits and pieces of vegetables that are not enough to make anything on their own. Of course, you can prepare this any time you crave lots of colorful, crunchy vegetables as a side dish with other Chinese or Western entrees. In addition to the vegetables you may want to add some fried or dried bean curd or softened golden needles and wood ears. Adjust the amount of broth, cornstarch, and salt for larger quantities of ingredients.

I use chicken bouillon cubes dissolved in water when I don't have chicken broth on hand or need just a small amount. You can use homemade or canned broth instead. Adjust the salt accordingly.

3 tablespoons canola, corn, or peanut oil

2 slices unpeeled gingerroot, 1 × ⅛ inch each

1 garlic clove, crushed and peeled

7 to 8 cups mixed vegetables, such as broccoli, cauliflower, zucchini, summer
    squash, beans, bell pepper, carrots, bamboo shoots, and water chestnuts

1 chicken bouillon cube, dissolved in ⅓ cup hot water

½ teaspoon salt, or to taste

3 teaspoons cornstarch, dissolved in 2 tablespoons water

1. Heat the oil in a wok or stir-fry pan over high heat. When the oil is hot, add the gingerroot and garlic; they should sizzle. Stir a few times and add the vegetables, the harder root vegetables first and the more tender ones last.

2. Add the dissolved bouillon and cover the pan. Cook over medium heat for 1 to 2 minutes, or until the vegetables are tender-crisp. Stir occasionally for even cooking.

3. Uncover the pan, season with salt to taste, and mix in the cornstarch slurry. Stir until the liquid thickens. Discard the gingerroot and garlic, if desired. Serve hot.

Bean Sprout Salad
with Egg Garnish

Serves 4 to 6

W ith the exception of cucumbers and radishes, raw vegetables do not appeal to the Chinese palate. Here the bean sprouts are parboiled to remove that unappetizing raw taste. Be sure to remove the bean sprouts just as the water begins to bubble and to refresh the sprouts immediately in plenty of cold water so they will remain crisp. Add some shredded cooked chicken or diced ham to the salad before garnishing with the egg for a light luncheon dish.

2 ounces snow peas, ends snapped and strings removed (1 cup)
1 pound bean sprouts
2 tablespoons light soy sauce
1 teaspoon sesame seed oil
1 recipe Egg Garnish (page 255)

1. Bring 10 cups of water to a boil in a large saucepan over high heat. Plunge the snow peas into the water for 10 seconds. Remove with a strainer and rinse immediately with cold water to stop the cooking. Return the water to a boil and add the bean sprouts. Just as the water begins to bubble again, drain the sprouts in a colander. Rinse immediately with cold water until all the warmth is gone. Allow the vegetables to drain thoroughly.

2. Shred the snow peas on the diagonal to about the same length as the bean sprouts and toss the vegetables together in a serving bowl. Mix the soy sauce and sesame seed oil together in a small dish. Just before serving, toss the dressing with the vegetables and scatter the garnish on top. Serve immediately.

Spicy Sweet and Sour Cabbage

Serves 6 to 8

*T*his dish is often served as part of a Chinese-style cold platter; it is a great choice any time your menu calls for cole slaw or sweet and sour red cabbage. The relish may be eaten warm, but my mother always chilled it overnight to improve the flavor and texture.

禄

2 pounds napa or Chinese celery cabbage
½ tablespoon crushed red pepper, or to taste
½ cup light brown sugar
⅓ cup cider vinegar
2 tablespoons light soy sauce
1 teaspoon salt
3 tablespoons canola, corn, or peanut oil

1.   Remove and discard any tough or discolored outer leaves of the cabbage. Cut it into quarters lengthwise and cut out and discard the core. Cut each quarter across into 4-inch pieces. Shred lengthwise into ½-inch-wide strips. Toss to separate the leaves.

2.   Combine the red pepper, sugar, vinegar, soy sauce, and salt in a mixing bowl. Set aside.

3.   Pour the oil into a wok or stir-fry pan and place over medium-high heat. When the oil is hot but not smoking, add the cabbage; it should sizzle. Stir constantly until the leaves become limp and the stems loose their raw look, about 5 minutes. Remove the pan from the heat and stir in the pepper mixture.

4.   Transfer the cabbage to a large platter and spread it out to prevent overcooking. Stir occasionally to distribute the flavoring evenly. When completely cooled, lightly drain from the liquid and serve. Or refrigerate in the liquid and drain before serving.

Note   The cabbage tastes best if left to stand for at least 1 hour in the liquid. It may be kept in the refrigerator for several days.

Celery Salad

Serves 4 to 6 as a side dish

his salad is atypically Chinese in that it uses raw vegetables. Instead of blanching the vegetables, you shred and soak them in salted ice water for greater crispness. The recipe itself is quick and easy, but the shredding may take some time. A mandoline shredder makes quick work of the carrots, but I find that the celery, because of the strings, doesn't come out as well and has to be shredded by hand.

禧

2 teaspoons salt

4 cups finely shredded celery (about 8 stalks) (page 45)

1 cup finely shredded carrot, about 1 medium

1 tablespoon finely shredded peeled gingerroot (optional)

3 tablespoons light soy sauce

1 teaspoon sesame seed oil

1. Dissolve the salt in 7 cups ice water. Soak the celery, carrot, and gingerroot for at least 30 minutes but no more than 1 hour. Drain, cover, and store the vegetables in the refrigerator until ready to use.

2. Just before serving, transfer the vegetables to a serving bowl, mix in the soy sauce, and drizzle with sesame seed oil. Toss a few times to mix. Serve immediately.

健康

Note Do not add the soy sauce too early as it will stain the vegetables and spoil the presentation.

Quick Cucumber Salad

A simple-to-make salad that can be served as a side dish or an hors d'oeuvre. Children love it as a snack.

1 pound seedless or regular cucumbers
3 tablespoons light soy sauce
1 teaspoon sesame seed oil

1. Seedless cucumbers do not need to be peeled, but for a different presentation you can peel away strips of peel. Split the cucumber lengthwise and cut on the diagonal into slices ¼ inch thick. If using regular cucumbers, partially peel, split in half, and scoop out and discard the seeds. Cut as for seedless cucumber. Place in a serving bowl.

2. Just before serving, toss with the soy sauce and sesame seed oil. Serve cold.

Cucumbers in Garlic and Chili Dressing

Serves 4 to 6 as a side dish

I f you like strong flavors, you'll love this chilled salad. For a less spicy taste, reduce the red pepper to half a teaspoon.

禄

1 pound seedless or regular cucumbers
1 teaspoon salt
3 tablespoons Chinkiang black vinegar
1 tablespoon plus 2 teaspoons sugar
2 garlic cloves, peeled and minced
2 teaspoons grated peeled gingerroot
1 teaspoon crushed red pepper, or to taste
1 teaspoon light soy sauce (optional)

1.   Wash the cucumber, split in half lengthwise, and cut on the diagonal into slices ¼ inch thick. If using regular cucumbers, partially peel, split in half lengthwise, and scoop out and discard the seeds. Cut as for seedless cucumber. Place the cucumbers in a bowl and toss with the salt. Let stand for 10 to 15 minutes.

2.   Mix the vinegar, sugar, garlic, gingerroot, red pepper, and soy sauce, if using, in a small bowl. Stir until the sugar is dissolved.

3.   Rinse the cucumbers in cold water, drain thoroughly, and pat dry with paper towels. Transfer to a bowl and toss with the dressing. Serve at room temperature or chilled.

Sliced Cucumbers with Spicy Peanut Dressing

Serves 4 to 6 as a side dish

I use the very crisp long, seedless cucumber for this dish. The cucumber doesn't have to be peeled since it's not waxed but wrapped in plastic to prevent moisture loss.

1 pound seedless or regular cucumbers
¼ cup smooth peanut butter
¼ cup water, Chinese Chicken Broth (page 64), or canned chicken broth
½ teaspoon salt, or to taste
¼ teaspoon Szechuan peppercorns, toasted and ground
1 tablespoon sesame seed oil
1 teaspoon crushed red pepper

1.   Split the long cucumber in half lengthwise and cut on the diagonal into thin slices. If using regular cucumbers, peel alternating strips of the skin away, leaving some green for color, split in half lengthwise, and scoop out and discard the seeds. Cut on the diagonal into thin slices.

2.   Mix the peanut butter with the broth or water, salt, Szechuan peppercorns, sesame seed oil, and red pepper into a smooth, thin paste.

3.   Just before serving, mix the peanut dressing with the cucumber slices. Serve cold.

Minute Sweet and Sour Cucumber Salad

Serves 4 to 6 as a side dish

*T*his amazingly simple salad is very good with barbecued or grilled meats. The cucumbers make you feel refreshed the minute you start to eat them.

禧

1 pound seedless or regular cucumbers
½ teaspoon salt
2 tablespoons light brown sugar
2 tablespoons cider vinegar
½ teaspoon light soy sauce
½ teaspoon sesame seed oil

1. Split the cucumber in half lengthwise and cut on the diagonal into slices ⅛ inch thick. If using regular cucumbers, partially peel, leaving alternating strips of green skin behind, split in half lengthwise, and scoop out and discard seeds. Cut as for seedless cucumber.

2. Place the cucumber slices in a bowl, sprinkle with salt, and toss. Let stand for 15 minutes to draw out liquid. Drain and transfer to a serving bowl. (You may wish to rinse the salt off the cucumbers in cold water and pat dry with paper towels, but it is not necessary.)

3. Mix the sugar, vinegar, and soy sauce in a small dish until the sugar is dissolved. Pour the dressing and sesame seed oil over the cucumbers and toss well. Serve chilled or at room temperature.

Variation   Add ½ cup shredded or thinly sliced carrots to the cucumbers.

Steamed Eggplant Salad

**Serves 3 to 4, or 5 to 6 as part of a
multicourse meal**

*A s soon as eggplants began to ripen in my mother's garden, she would make this dish.
The skin on her just-picked eggplants was so tender she didn't even peel them. As
she was preparing the eggplant, my mother would remind us that it was one of her
father's favorite dishes. This salad can be served hot, warm, or cold. The flavor is
robust but not overwhelming.*

1 pound eggplant
3 tablespoons cider vinegar
3 tablespoons light brown sugar
2 teaspoons sesame seed oil
1 tablespoon light soy sauce
½ to 1 tablespoon minced or grated peeled gingerroot
1 teaspoon minced garlic

1.   Cut off and discard the stem. Peel the eggplant unless it is garden-fresh or very young. Cut the eggplant into 6 or 8 wedges. Spread the wedges in a steaming basket in a saucepan over water as described on page 36. The perforated steaming dish is necessary to allow any bitter juices to drain off into the boiling water. Cover the pan, bring the water to a boil, and steam for 8 to 10 minutes, or until the eggplant is very soft and easily pierced by a fork. Do not let the water boil into the eggplant. Drain. (The eggplant may be steamed in advance and stored, covered, in the refrigerator until ready to dress.)

2.   While the eggplant is steaming, combine the vinegar, sugar, sesame seed oil, soy sauce, gingerroot, and garlic in a small bowl or lidded jar and mix or shake thoroughly.

3.   Place the eggplant in a serving dish, pour the dressing over, and mix gently. Serve hot, warm, or chilled.

Note   The eggplant will be very soft and fall apart. Don't be alarmed. This salad is not particularly beautiful to look at, but it's sensational to eat!

Sweet and Sour Radish Salad

Serves 4 as a side dish

W henever we bought radishes at our local farm stand, my mother checked them carefully. They had to be crisp and not too spicy. We would buy extra and snack on them — spread with peanut butter — while watching TV. Even when I was very young, my mother let me prepare this dish seeing how much I enjoyed smashing the radishes with the cleaver.

20 radishes (2 bunches)
½ teaspoon salt
2 tablespoons light brown sugar
2 tablespoons cider vinegar
½ teaspoon sesame seed oil

1. Trim away both ends of the radishes. Wash the radishes well and drain. If the ends are discolored, scrape away the discoloration.

2. Crush each radish with the broad side of a Chinese cleaver. Cut large ones in half before crushing them. Crush just enough to crack the radish so it will absorb the dressing better.

3. Place the radishes in a bowl and sprinkle with salt. Let stand for 15 minutes. Drain and transfer to a serving bowl.

4. Mix the sugar and vinegar together in a small bowl and pour over the radishes. Drizzle with sesame seed oil, and toss to blend. Serve.

Variation   Use hot sesame seed oil in place of the regular or add about ½ teaspoon of a hot sauce like Tabasco to the dressing.

Substitute a long seedless cucumber for the radishes. Cut it in half lengthwise and into thin slices. Salt and let sit for 15 minutes. Drain and dress as in step 4.

Wilted Spinach with
Mustard Dressing

Serves 6 to 8 as a side dish

My mother remembered this cold dish from her childhood in Beijing (Peking) and developed this recipe to re-create it. She says that the Chinese like to use older spinach with long stalks for their crunchy texture. Sometimes near the end of spinach season, you can find such older spinach sold at farm stands.

2 pounds spinach
2 tablespoons dry mustard powder
½ teaspoon cider vinegar
1¼ teaspoons salt, or to taste

1. Separate the spinach and discard any yellowed or wilted leaves. Wash thoroughly in cold water, changing the water at least three times to be sure every bit of sand is rinsed away. Drain thoroughly.

2. Mix the mustard powder with 2 tablespoons cold water into a thick paste. Gradually add 2½ tablespoons more water, the vinegar, and ¼ teaspoon of the salt. Stir into a thin paste.

3. Bring 6 to 8 cups of water to a boil in a large saucepan. Add the spinach. As soon as the spinach wilts (before the water boils again), drain in a colander. Refresh immediately by plunging into a bath of cold water to cool the spinach and set the color. Drain and gently squeeze the water out with your hands.

4. Cut the spinach into small pieces and transfer to a serving bowl. Mix with the mustard dressing and remaining salt to taste. Serve cold.

Small Eats

S mall eats are the kind of snacks the Chinese enjoy at almost any time of the day or night. Instead of candy and processed foods, we eat what is sometimes called street food because it is sold on street corners or in small fast-food restaurants. Most of the appetizers and small eats in this chapter may be served Western style, as finger foods with drinks or at the table as the first course of a Chinese-style meal.

Many recipes in other chapters could actually fit in here. Noodles and fried rice, for instance, are often served as a midnight snack. Some desserts in the book, such as Steamed Egg Cake (page 347) and Sweet Red Bean Soup (page 342), could be listed here since they are often served as part of dim sum. You can see how versatile Chinese food is.

Appetizers served at formal Chinese banquets are generally cold platters with a variety of meats, seafood, and vegetables thinly sliced and arranged in elaborate auspicious designs, such as a phoenix, a dragon, or a lucky Chinese character. Many of the ingredients used in Chinese cold platters are unusual foods that are appreciated for their special appearance and texture. Some are exotic, like Hundred-Year-Old Eggs, shredded jellyfish, and sliced abalone. These may be combined with more conventional ingredients such as Pickled Carrots and Daikon, Cucumbers in Garlic and Chili Dressing (page 281), Drunken Chicken, and Red-cooked Gizzards and Livers.

Less formal meals may also start with cold appetizers, but the foods are not arranged in fanciful designs. Choose one, two, or three cold dishes from this or other chapters to serve in small dishes at the beginning of a meal for an authentic Chinese dinner. I like to serve cold appetizers at a dinner because they can be made in advance.

I have found that most Americans do not seem to like cold appetizers as much as hot appetizers — egg rolls, spring rolls, spareribs. Hot appetizers are usually served as substantial dim sum (*dian xin* in Mandarin), which means "dot the heart." The hot platters popularly known as Pu Pu Platters are not traditionally Chinese. Dim sum is served at teatime, but it can be a brunch, a whole meal, or a snack. The Cantonese have made this a tradition, and in Hong Kong at noon the many tea shops that specialize in dim sum are packed with people. The dim sum are wheeled around on carts, usually by women, and the customer picks from the myriad of items offered. At the end of the meal, the maitre d' counts the number of empty dishes and tallies up the bill.

My mother liked to tell about a famous tea shop next to a lake in China; the dining room was built on piles out over the water. As one unscrupulous gentleman ate, he would throw the dishes into the water so that his bill would be smaller!

Wontons

福 These celebrated meat dumplings can be fried or boiled to be served as hors d'oeuvres, appetizers, snacks, in soups, or as a meal in themselves. If you serve them deep-fried as hors d'oeuvres, allow four wontons per person; if boiled as a snack or light meal, ten to twelve per person. If you're putting them in a soup to be served as an appetizer, allow four to six per person; in a soup that's served as a meal, ten to twelve per person.

Filling Wontons

Wonton skins are available in the produce department of most supermarkets. A one-pound package contains about sixty skins. Any unused portion of the package will freeze well as will leftover filling. Be sure to thaw the skins thoroughly before using or they will crack and break. Since wonton skins dry out quickly, place a damp kitchen towel or moistened plain white paper towels over the skins and the formed wontons as you work.

(If you can't find wonton skins, cut egg-roll skins into four even pieces.) The simplest and fastest way to do this is to take one egg roll skin and fold it in four to mark the skin; unfold and place over the stack of wrappers, like a template, and cut carefully through the stack along the folds of the skin.

When the Chinese make wontons, they use only about half a teaspoon of filling in each. If you like more filling, you can use up to one teaspoon. Don't overstuff or the wontons won't seal securely, and you will end up with empty wonton skins and the filling at the bottom of your pot. One cup of filling (pages 293–294) will fill about a pound of wonton skins, depending on how much filling is used.

Uncooked wontons will keep for a few days in the refrigerator and longer in the freezer. To freeze, place them in the freezer on a cookie sheet. When they are frozen, hit the tray against the edge of the counter to dislodge them. Transfer to a plastic bag, seal, and place in the freezer. Frozen wontons will keep for a month or more. It is not necessary to thaw before using.

Folding Wontons

The technique for folding wontons that will be boiled is the family-style method my mother taught me. I like to use a restaurant-style fold for deep-fried wontons because they fry up puffed and important looking. You can, however, use either fold for either cooking method, just be sure to fold the wonton so that there is a little space between the filling and the sealed corners. This way the hot liquid can circulate around the wonton and cook the filling evenly. Line up the folded wontons neatly on a tray and cover with a damp cloth until ready to cook.

Family-style fold for boiled wontons

1. With a table or butter knife, place a rounded ½ teaspoonful of filling in the center of a wonton skin. Support the skin on the fingers of both hands with your thumbs on top.

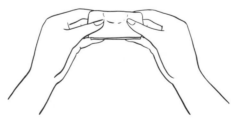

2. Fold the back edge over the filling until the back edge meets the front edge.

3. Using the thumbs, press the skin down around the filling to help center it and hold it in place. Keep the index fingers under the back of the wonton.

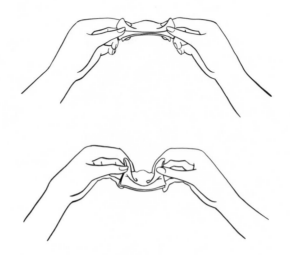

4. Now fold the back edge over again covering your thumbs.

5. Push the top corners up with your thumbs and hold them between your thumbs and your index fingers.

6. Using your finger, wet the top left corner with water or lightly beaten egg white. Bring the top right corner to the top left, and overlap the corners pressing them together to secure.

7. You now have a completed wonton that looks like a nurse's cap with the "wings" or flaps, standing up. Arrange the formed wontons on a baking tray dusted lightly with flour and cover them with a dry cloth. If the room is very dry, cover with a damp cloth. Proceed with instructions for Boiled Wontons.

Restaurant-style fold for deep-fried wontons

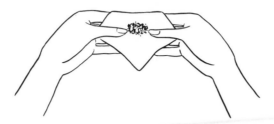

1. With a table or butter knife, place a rounded ½ teaspoonful of filling in the center of a wonton skin. Support the skin on the fingers of both hands with your thumbs on top and with one corner facing you.

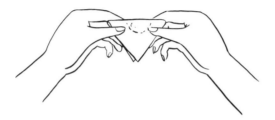

2. Fold the back corner over the filling, until the back edge meets the front edge.

3. Using the thumbs, press the skin down around the filling to help center it and hold it in place. Keep the index fingers under the back of the wonton.

4. Fold the back edge halfway toward you, covering your thumbs.

5. Push the top corners up with your thumbs, holding the corners between your thumbs and index fingers.

6.   Using your finger, wet the left corner with water or lightly beaten egg white. Bring the right corner to the left, and overlap the corners pressing them together to secure.

7.   Arrange the wontons on a baking tray lightly dusted with flour and cover them with a dry cloth. If the room is very dry, cover with a damp cloth. Proceed with instructions for Deep-fried Wontons.

Boiled Wontons

Bring 3 quarts of water to a boil in a 6-quart pot over medium high. Add as many wontons as can swim freely about. Stir gently with a wooden spoon and cover the pot. Return to a boil and immediately add 1 cup cold water. Stir again, and with the pot uncovered, let the water return to a boil, then immediately remove the pan from the heat. Let the wontons stand in the hot water with the cover on for 2 to 4 minutes. Scoop out the wontons with a wire skimmer and drain well. Serve with cider vinegar, Chinkiang vinegar, or a soy sauce dip (page 324). Be careful not to overcook the wontons or the skins will become too soft and lose their "bite."

Store leftover boiled wontons, covered, in the refrigerator. Reheat in a nonstick skillet with 1 tablespoon oil. Cook as you would home-fried potatoes — brown one side, turn, and brown the other side.

Deep-fried Wontons

Pour 2 inches of canola, corn, or peanut oil into a wok or stir-fry pan and heat to 350°F. When the oil is hot, drop in the wontons, a few at a time, stirring and turning for even browning, and fry until golden brown. Bring the oil back to temperature before frying a second batch. Remove with a wire skimmer and drain on paper towels. Transfer to a serving platter and serve as soon as possible so the wontons remain crispy. Serve hot with Chinese mustard and duck sauce or Sweet and Sour Sauce (page 327).

Store leftover deep-fried wontons in the refrigerator or freezer. Reheat on a baking sheet in a 450°F. oven for 15 minutes. It is not necessary to defrost frozen wontons before reheating.

Pork Wontons

*P*ork wontons can be boiled or deep-fried. Serve the fried wontons hot with Chinese mustard and duck sauce or Spicy Mango Chutney (page 330). Serve drained boiled wontons with a soy sauce dip (page 324) or add them to soup as on page 66.

健康

½ pound ground lean pork (about 1 cup)

1 tablespoon soy sauce

1 tablespoon sesame seed oil or vegetable oil

2 tablespoons broth or water

¼ teaspoon salt

2 teaspoons finely minced scallion

1 teaspoon cornstarch

1 teaspoon dry sherry

1 pound wonton skins

Combine all the ingredients except the wonton skins in a bowl. Stir together until well mixed. Fill, fold, and cook the wontons as described on pages 288–292.

Turkey Wontons

Makes about 60 to 90 wontons

My childhood friend Anna Ku Lau makes a wonton filling with ground turkey. She mixes in frozen chopped spinach and puts a small piece of raw shrimp into every wonton before folding. I find it easier to chop the raw shrimp and mix it right into the ground meat. Be sure to squeeze out as much water from the spinach as you can so the filling does not get too wet. These wontons may be boiled or deep-fried.

福

½ pound ground turkey
1 tablespoon plus 1 teaspoon soy sauce, light or dark
1 tablespoon canola, corn, or peanut oil
¼ teaspoon salt
⅓ cup frozen chopped spinach, thawed and water squeezed out
1 tablespoon minced scallion
1 teaspoon cornstarch
1 teaspoon dry sherry
¼ cup small shrimp, chopped fine (about 2 ounces)
1 to 1½ pounds wonton skins

Combine all the ingredients except the wonton skins in a bowl and stir together until well mixed. Fill and deep fry or boil according to the directions on pages 288–292.

Peking Ravioli

Makes 32 ravioli

*T*he Chinese term for these dumplings when they are boiled is jiao zi; when they are pan-fried, they are called guo tie, or potstickers, because they stick to the pot when cooked. My mother coined the name Peking Ravioli, because when she started serving them in our restaurant in the 1950s, no one had seen anything like them before. Borrowing from our Italian neighbors in Boston let customers know that these were dough pockets with a filling. Interestingly, although the name potsticker is common now, just about all the Chinese restaurants in the Boston area still call them Peking Ravioli because of my mother's influence. In the Chinese tradition, when our family gathered together, we would all make the ravioli, and at the end of the meal we would announce how many each of us had eaten. This is one of my mother's most treasured recipes.

I am giving you my mother's recipe as she gave it to me, including directions for boiled and fried ravioli. Plan on six to eight pieces per person as a main meal and two to three as an appetizer.

禄

2 cups all-purpose flour

⅔ cup lukewarm water

1 pound napa or Chinese celery cabbage

1½ teaspoons salt

¾ pound ground pork

1½ tablespoons dark soy sauce

1 tablespoon dry sherry

½ teaspoon sugar

1 or 2 tablespoons canola, corn, or peanut oil or bacon drippings (use 2 tablespoons if the meat is very lean)

1 tablespoon sesame seed oil

1.   Mix the flour and water together in a large mixing bowl with a wooden spoon. Remove from the bowl and knead on a lightly floured work surface for 4 minutes, or until the dough becomes smooth and elastic. If the dough seems too dry, add a few drops of water and continue kneading. Cover the dough with a damp towel and allow to rest, or as the Chinese say "wake up," for 30 minutes or more.

(continued)

2.   While the dough is resting, wash and drain the cabbage. Chop into coarse chunks, then mince very fine. Sprinkle 1 teaspoon salt over the cabbage while mincing. Place in a cloth bag or in a double layer of cheesecloth. Squeeze out enough liquid to make 1 cup. Discard the liquid. Put the remaining ingredients into a large bowl and add the cabbage. Mix well — by hand is the best way. Set aside.

3.   Using the palms of your hands, roll the "waked up" dough into two even ropes 16 inches long. Cut each rope into sixteen 1-inch pieces and shape the pieces into small balls. Flatten them with the palm of your hand and dust with flour. With a rolling pin, roll each piece into a 3-inch circle. If the dough sticks to the work surface or the rolling pin, dust with more flour. Cover the circles with a dry cloth to keep them from drying out.

4.   Place a heaping teaspoon of filling, in a log shape, in the center of a circle of dough.

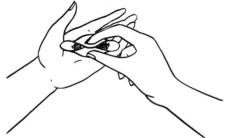

5.   Fold the dough in half and pinch the edges together just at the center of the half circle until that point is sealed.

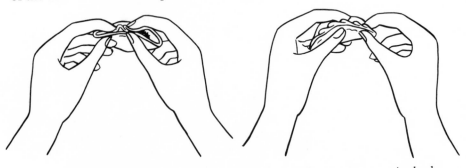

6.   Working from the pinched center toward one corner, pinch the edges together between your thumb and forefinger, pleating the dough in 3 or 4 places as you go. Repeat on other side.

7.   The pleats will create an attractive arched half moon. Be sure to seal the dumpling tightly, pinching the whole edge one more time after it has been formed.

8.   Place the ravioli on a floured surface with the pleated edges on top and cover with a dry cloth (or a damp cloth if the air is very dry) to keep them from drying out. Cook immediately according to directions for Boiled or Fried Peking Ravioli or refrigerate for several days or freeze for several weeks. To freeze, arrange the ravioli on a floured cookie sheet, and place in the freezer. When they are frozen, bang the pan on the edge of the counter to loosen them, put them in a plastic bag, seal it, and return it to the freezer. Do not drop them into a freezer bag while they are soft or they will lose their shape and stick together. Frozen Peking Ravioli do not need to be thawed before cooking.

壽

Note   Some supermarkets now sell prepared Peking Ravioli, or Potsticker, skins made from the same egg-and-flour dough used for wontons and egg-roll skins. (Don't buy wonton wrappers or egg-roll skins, because they're too thin and won't hold up.) These are often made by Japanese companies and are marketed under the Japanese name of *gyoza*. (Peking Ravioli are popular for lunch in Japan.) Chinese brands are available in Chinese grocery stores. Ready-made skins are not as soft as homemade skins so you will need to use some water or egg white to secure the seal. They are also thinner so cooking time should be reduced slightly.

Boiled Peking Ravioli

The Chinese prefer to boil their Peking Ravioli and eat them as a whole meal usually with a dip made of vinegar, light soy sauce, and Hot Chili Oil (page 329). The host sets a cruet of each on the table, and the guests mix the dip themselves. My family and I actually prefer to eat the boiled ravioli with just cider vinegar or Chinkiang vinegar. Sometimes we tease people about that because when the Chinese say "eat vinegar," it means to be jealous.

The cooking water is sometimes served as a refreshing hot beverage after the meal. I personally find it tasteless, but many Chinese are partial to it.

Bring 5 quarts of water to a boil in a stockpot. Slip the dumplings into the boiling water, one at a time, being sure there is enough room to allow them to swim about freely. Stir a few times to prevent sticking, cover, and cook over medium-high heat until the water boils again. Watch the pot; the water can foam up and boil over easily. As soon as the water returns to a boil, add 1 cup cold water, cover, and continue cooking over medium heat. When the water boils again, add another 1 cup cold water, cover, and let the water return to a boil for the third time. Remove from heat and let stand, covered, for 2 to 3 minutes. This procedure ensures that the filling cooks through.

If using ready-made skins, reduce the standing time to about 1 minute.

Remove the dumplings with a wire skimmer or slotted spoon and drain briefly in a colander. Transfer to a plate or shallow platter and serve immediately with vinegar, Hot Chili Oil (page 329), and soy sauce as table dips.

Store leftover boiled ravioli, covered, in the refrigerator. To reheat, pan-fry in a covered nonstick skillet over medium heat with about 1 tablespoon oil until heated through and lightly browned on one side.

Fried Peking Ravioli

In America, the more popular way to serve Peking Ravioli (potstickers) is not boiled, which the Chinese prefer, but pan-fried. By a clever combination of pan-frying, boiling, and steaming, the dough is browned while the meat filling is cooked through. Serve the fried dumplings with the same type of dips as for boiled dumplings.

Heat an 8- or 9-inch heavy nonstick skillet over medium-high heat until hot. Pour 1 tablespoon oil into the pan and spread it over the entire cooking surface. Starting at the outside of the pan, arrange the dumplings carefully in concentric circles, facing in the same direction and touching each other lightly. Put 2 dumplings in the center facing each other.

Add ½ cup cold water, cover, and cook over medium-high heat for 6 to 7 minutes, or until the water has evaporated. Lower the heat and cook, covered, for 2 minutes, or until the dumplings are golden brown on the bottom.

Loosen the dumplings from the bottom of the pan with a spatula without disturbing the arrangement. Select a serving plate that will fit over the skillet. Place it, upside down, on top of the skillet. Holding it in place, invert the pan and give a little shake so the loosened dumplings will fall out onto the plate. The brown bottom will now be on top. Serve immediately with vinegar, oil, and soy sauce.

Store leftover fried ravioli, covered, in the refrigerator. To reheat, pan-fry in a covered skillet over medium-heat with about 1 tablespoon oil but no water.

Joyce Chen's
Original Egg Rolls

Makes 28 egg rolls

y grade school holds an annual fund-raising event called *The Buckingham Circus*. When I was in the second grade, my mother donated her own Chinese egg rolls. She put the egg rolls on the food table, and then walked through the circus with me. When we returned to the table, the egg rolls were gone. She first thought they were not acceptable and had been put away, but one of the mothers told us that the egg rolls were an instant hit and sold out almost immediately. My mother was so happy that she went home and made more that very day. They became known as Mrs. Chen's egg rolls and were the start of my mother's reputation as a cook.

This is my mother's original recipe and here are some of her own notes:

"This is the exact filling used in the egg rolls which I made especially for the schools. This is not authentic. Chinese egg roll is called spring roll which symbolizes the coming of Spring. We serve them during the New Year holidays or as a snack in the afternoon. The spring roll is smaller-sized with thinner skin, and beef is never used for filling as the beef is not common in China.

"If you live in a city with a Chinatown or Asian market, then it is much easier to use machine-made egg-roll skins which are sold in Chinese noodle factories in five-pound packages. If they do not want to separate the package for you, then keep the unused portion in the freezer wrapped in separate smaller packages for future use in making egg rolls or wonton. Defrost the egg-roll skins thoroughly before use. The best way to fry is to wrap a few egg rolls, enough to fit in pan, and fry them while wrapping the others.

"Since there is quite a procedure to making egg rolls, I suggest making enough to please your family and your friends."

禄

(continued)

½ pound lean ground beef

1 teaspoon dry sherry

1½ teaspoons cornstarch

¼ teaspoon black pepper

1 tablespoon light brown sugar

1 tablespoon thick or dark soy sauce (If using dark soy sauce, reduce salt by
    ½ teaspoon)

2 tablespoons canola, corn, or peanut oil

3½ teaspoons salt

3 slices unpeeled gingerroot, 1 ⬚ ⅛ inch each

2 large celery stalks, shredded (page 45)

1 medium onion, thinly sliced (about 1 cup)

1½ pounds green cabbage, shredded (page 45) (about 8 cups packed)

2 tablespoons flour

1 pound bean sprouts, about 4 cups tightly packed

2 pounds egg-roll skins (about 28 sheets)

1 egg, beaten with 2 tablespoons cold water

Vegetable oil, for deep-frying

1. Mix the beef with the sherry, cornstarch, pepper, brown sugar, and soy sauce in a large bowl. Set aside.

2. Heat the oil in a wok or stir-fry pan over high heat. Add the salt and gingerroot. Add the celery and onions and cook for about 3 minutes. Add the beef mixture and stir constantly until it is cooked and separates into small pieces, about 2 minutes.

3. Transfer to a colander set over a large bowl and drain off the excess liquid. Set aside the liquid. Spread the meat on a large baking sheet to cool. Discard the gingerroot.

4. Return the reserved liquid to the wok and cook the cabbage in it over high heat until transparent and soft, about 6 minutes. If liquid is scant, add 2 tablespoons of oil to wok. Stir constantly. You may need to cook the cabbage in batches.

5. When all the cabbage is cooked, drain off any liquid, pressing the cabbage against the sides of the colander. Transfer the cabbage to a large bowl, sprinkle with the flour, and mix together thoroughly, using your hands. Keep the cabbage and beef mixtures in the refrigerator until ready to use. The filling should not be used while warm.

6. When ready to assemble the egg rolls, mix the cabbage and beef mixtures together. Mix in the bean sprouts by hand, lightly crushing them as you mix. You should have about 10 cups of filling.

7. Pour 1 inch of oil into a wok and heat to 350°F. to 375°F. while wrapping the egg rolls.

8. Place a generous ⅓ cup of filling in the center of an egg-roll skin.

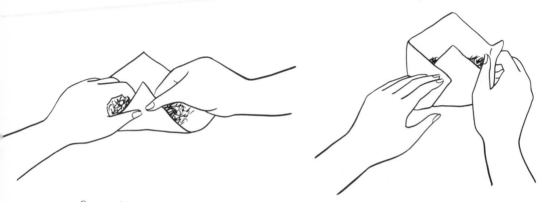

9. Fold over 1 corner of the skin to cover the filling, then fold over the right and left sides to form an envelope.

10. Brush the top with the egg mixture and finish rolling.

11. Roll neatly and tightly, making sure that all the filling is sealed securely in the wrapper. If it isn't, the egg roll may burst open in the oil.

(continued)

Small Eats

12.   Immediately deep-fry the egg rolls, 3 to 5 at a time, until golden brown. Do not let the egg rolls sit before frying, or the filling will soak through the wrapper and they will not fry up crisp and puffy. Turn the egg rolls occasionally as they cook.

13.   Remove the egg rolls and stand them on end in a colander lined with paper towels. Place the colander over a pan to catch any excess oil. If you are going to serve at a later time, line up the egg rolls on a rack to cool thoroughly. Never pile the hot egg rolls; the wrappings will turn soft and lose their crispness.

壽

Note   Fried egg rolls can be kept in the refrigerator for 4 to 5 days or frozen for about 1 month. Only the bean sprouts will lose their good texture. Reheat the rolls in a covered skillet over very low heat for 20 minutes — 40 minutes if frozen — turning once, halfway through heating. They can also be reheated in a 400°F. oven for 10 to 12 minutes (15 to 18 minutes if frozen). Place the egg rolls on a rack over a baking pan to drain off the excess oil and to help recrisp the surface.

Variation   Substitute ½ to ¾ pound ground turkey for the beef and increase the oil used in step 2 to 3 tablespoons. Add 3 tablespoons additional oil in step 4 when stir-frying the cabbage.

Pan-fried Scallion Cakes

**Makes twelve 4-inch cakes or
six 6-inch cakes**

T hese pan-fried cakes made of unleavened dough are commonly sold by street vendors in northern China. The cakes take a bit of time to make but are definitely worth the effort. I make the smaller size for passing with drinks and the larger ones for more substantial servings. For a traditional vegetarian version, omit the bacon and increase the salt to taste.

健康

3 cups all-purpose flour
1 teaspoon salt, or to taste
1 cup hot water
2 cups thinly sliced scallions, green and white parts (about 15–18)
½ cup chopped bacon (optional)
6 teaspoons sesame seed oil, for brushing
Canola, corn, or peanut oil for frying

1. To make the dough by hand, combine the flour and salt in a mixing bowl. Gradually mix in the water with a spoon until a rough dough is formed. Add more water by droplets if necessary to incorporate all the flour. Transfer the dough to a lightly floured work surface and knead until smooth. Cover with a damp cloth or damp paper towels. Let rest for 30 minutes.

2. To make the dough in a food processor, put the flour and salt in the workbowl fitted with a metal blade and pulse about 5 seconds to mix. With the machine running, pour the hot water through the feed tube and process for 20 seconds, or until a ball forms. If the dough appears dry and does not form a ball, stop the machine and take a good look. Sometimes it simply needs a few seconds to fully absorb the liquid. If after examination the dough is dry, add a few droplets of water until a rough dough is formed. Transfer the dough to a lightly floured surface, knead by hand, and cover as in step 1.

3. Roll the dough under the palms of your hands on a lightly floured surface into a rope about 12 inches long and 1¼ to 1½ inches in diameter. Cut the rope into twelve 1-inch pieces or six 2-inch pieces for larger cakes. Roll each piece into a ball. Place the balls under a damp cloth or paper towels to keep them from drying out.

(continued)   Small Eats

4.   Roll out each ball of dough into a circle about 5 or 7 inches in diameter, depending on the size the finished cake is to be, and about ¹⁄₁₆ inch thick. Brush sesame seed oil to within ½ inch of the edge, using about ½ teaspoon for the small cakes and 1 teaspoon for the large. Sprinkle the oiled part with 2 to 4 tablespoons scallions, 1 to 2 heaping teaspoons bacon, if using, and salt.

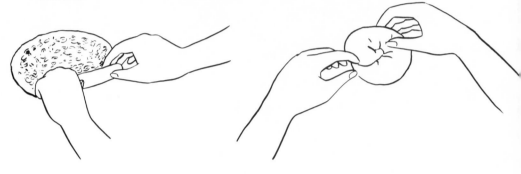

5.   Roll up the circle into a cigar shape, pinch the ends closed, and coil into a circle, tucking the ends under slightly. Press very gently with the palm of your hand to flatten.

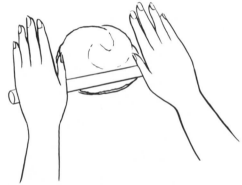

6.   With a rolling pin, gently roll into either a 4- or 6-inch circle. Be careful when rolling so that the trapped air bubbles do not burst. Some air bubbles may pop and break the surface. This is all right, but if there are too many holes, the scallions will fall out into the oil and burn. Place the cakes on a lightly floured board or baking sheet, cover with a towel, and continue until all are done. (If not frying immediately, stack the cakes, separated by lightly floured sheets of wax paper, and store them in a sealed plastic bag in the refrigerator.)

7.   When ready to cook, heat a 10- or 12-inch well-seasoned cast-iron or nonstick skillet over medium heat. When the pan is hot, add 3 tablespoons oil and wait a few seconds for it to heat. Add the cakes to the pan; they will sizzle. Add only as many cakes as will fit in a single layer without crowding. Cook about 3 minutes on each side, or until both sides are golden brown. Remove and place on paper towels. Add more oil to the pan, as necessary, and repeat until all the cakes are cooked.

8. Cut 4-inch cakes into quarters, 6-inch cakes into eighths. Serve hot. Sprinkle with additional salt, if desired.

福

Note If the cakes are not to be served right away, let them cool thoroughly, stack them, pack them in plastic bags, and refrigerate or freeze. When ready to serve, reheat on an ungreased cookie sheet in a 350°F. oven for about 15 minutes. Be careful not to overbake as the cakes will dry out and get tough. Do not reheat in a microwave oven; it is sure to make them tough.

Minute Scallion Pancakes

Makes two 10-inch pancakes

hen we were children, my mother would often make this quick version of Pan-fried Scallion Cakes (page 303) as an after-school snack — or even for breakfast. The pancakes can be made smaller and cut into wedges, then rolled and pierced with a toothpick for an appetizer or hors d'oeuvre.

禄

1 large egg
⅔ cup all-purpose flour
⅓ cup thinly sliced scallions, about 2 stalks, white and green parts
1 strip bacon, minced, or 1 heaping tablespoon dried shrimp, minced
¼ teaspoon salt, or to taste
½ cup Chinese Chicken Broth (page 64) or canned chicken broth
4 teaspoons canola, corn, or peanut oil

1. Mix all of the ingredients, except the oil, together in a mixing bowl. You will have a thin paste.

2. Heat a 10-inch well-seasoned cast-iron or heavy nonstick skillet over medium heat and pour in 2 teaspoons of the oil. Tip the pan back and forth to spread the oil evenly over the bottom and to heat it up. Pour half the batter into the skillet and spread it out to the sides of the pan with a spatula. Cook until the edges are lightly browned, then flip the pancake over to brown the other side. This should take less than 1 minute. Remove from the pan and repeat with the remaining oil and batter. Serve hot.

Chinese-style
Barbecued Spareribs

Serves 4 as main course, or 8 to 10 as an appetizer

*I*f you judge from our restaurant, everyone loves Chinese spareribs. You'll be happy to find out how easy they are to prepare at home. The cooks at the restaurant prepare the spareribs ahead of time up to the final browning step. After the first cooking, the ribs are refrigerated; they are browned only when ready to be served. You can do the browning on an outdoor grill if you like. Serve the ribs with Chinese duck sauce and Chinese mustard or with Spicy Mango Chutney (page 330). (See Note page 307 for an explanation of Chinese-style spareribs.)

2 racks spareribs, Chinese style (about 2 pounds each)
3 tablespoons dark soy sauce
4 tablespoons hoisin sauce
1 tablespoon dry sherry
1 tablespoon light brown sugar
1 tablespoon honey
½ teaspoon five-spice powder
2 garlic cloves put through a garlic press (optional)

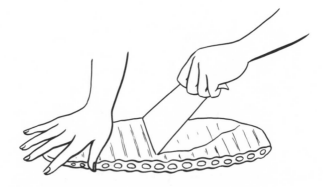

1. Trim the fat from the ribs and peel off the tough, paperlike membrane covering the inside of the ribs.

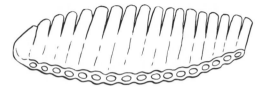

2.   Make 1½-inch-long cuts between the bones at the thicker part of the ribs. This allows the marinade to penetrate better and provides even cooking.

2.   Stir the remaining ingredients together in a small bowl. Rub the sauce all over the ribs and place them in a plastic bag or bowl. Marinate in the refrigerator for at least 1 hour or overnight.

3.   When ready to roast, preheat the oven to 350°F.

4.   Place the ribs on a rack over a roasting pan partially filled with water. Be sure that the ribs do not touch the water. Roast for 50 minutes, replenishing the hot water as necessary. Halfway through the cooking, brush the ribs with sauce, turn them over, and baste the other side.

5.   Turn the heat up to 450°F. and roast for 5 to 8 minutes on each side, or until browned and crisp. Remove from the oven and separate the ribs.

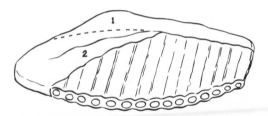

Note   Chinese-style spareribs have been trimmed of the soft, bony end called the chine bone (1) and have the brisket flap (2) removed. This makes for a more attractive uniform slab that will cook more evenly than regular spareribs. They are often available in markets and marked "Chinese style." Otherwise, buy regular spareribs and trim them. Save the brisket flap for other recipes that call for a small amount of sliced, shredded, or ground pork.

Variation   Substitute an orange-based marinade for the more familiar restaurant-style one. Combine 2 teaspoons sugar, 3 tablespoons dark soy sauce, 1 tablespoon dry sherry, 2 tablespoons ketchup, 2 tablespoons honey, 1 tablespoon hoisin sauce, ½ teaspoon five-spice powder, and 3 tablespoons frozen orange juice concentrate in a small bowl. Marinate the ribs as described in step 2 and continue with the recipe.

Pork Strips,
Chinese Restaurant Style

Serves 8 to 10 as an appetizer

*T*his Chinese-American version of Cantonese roasted pork (tsa tso) was one of the most popular appetizers on our restaurant menu. I used to put slices of this pork between pieces of French bread for lunch. Those were the days before we stopped serving French bread. I'm sure some of you remember that French bread was de rigueur at all Chinese restaurants in the 1950s. My parents learned the hard way when a disgruntled customer exclaimed as he left our restaurant when it first opened, "What kind of Chinese restaurant is this anyway? You don't even serve French bread!"

My mother's method of roasting pork over a pan of water does two things: it prevents the marinade from burning and it keeps the meat moist and juicy. I use tenderloin, a lean cut, instead of the more traditional strips of fatty pork.

禧

2 pounds pork tenderloin or boneless center cut pork loin roast
1½ tablespoons dark soy sauce
2½ tablespoons hoisin sauce
1 tablespoon dry sherry
⅛ teaspoon five-spice powder
1 tablespoon honey

1.   Trim any fat and gristle from the meat and place in a plastic bag or a dish. Set aside.

2.   Stir the remaining ingredients together in a small bowl. Pour over the meat and rub in with your fingers. Seal the bag or cover the dish and place in the refrigerator to marinate for at least 1 hour or overnight. The longer the meat marinates, the tastier and more tender it will become.

3.   When ready to roast, preheat the oven to 300°F.

4.   Place the meat on a rack set over a baking pan partially filled with water. Do not let the meat touch the water. Roast for 1½ to 2 hours, or until the meat is cooked to your liking or a meat thermometer reads 160°F. when inserted in the meat. It will still be slightly pink at the center at 1½

hours. Baste the meat 2 or 3 times with the marinade and turn the meat over halfway through the cooking. Replenish the water as necessary. Transfer to a cutting board and let rest for 15 to 20 minutes. Slice thin. Serve hot or cold.

健康

Note For parties, cut the pork into bite-size cubes and serve with toothpicks. Leftover pork can be used in other recipes calling for small amounts of cooked meat such as fried rice and salads.

福

Fried Shrimp Balls

M y mother formed the shrimp paste into balls with two moistened spoons. I find it easier to refrigerate the shrimp paste for a couple of hours to firm it up, then roll the balls between my palms, oiled to keep the paste from sticking. You may need to re-oil your hands a couple of times before all the balls are formed.

Provide Szechuan Peppercorn and Salt Dip (page 332) and dip the shrimp balls lightly before eating.

禄

1 pound shrimp, shelled and deveined
2 slices bacon
5 whole fresh (peeled) or canned water chestnuts
1 teaspoon dry sherry
½ teaspoon salt
3 tablespoons minced parsley
3 to 4 cups vegetable oil, for deep-frying
Parsley sprigs, for garnish
Lemon wedges, for garnish

1.   Rinse the shrimp and drain well. Process the shrimp, bacon, and water chestnuts in a food processor fitted with a steel blade. Process until you have a smooth paste, about 15 seconds. Transfer to a bowl and stir in the sherry, salt, and parsley. Set aside.

2.   Pour 1½ inches of oil into a wok or stir-fry pan and heat to 350°F. over medium heat. While the oil is heating, roll the shrimp paste into 1-inch balls. Oil a plate and your palms with cooking oil. Scoop up a heaping teaspoon of shrimp paste and roll it between your palms into a smooth ball. Place the ball on the oiled plate and continue until all the paste is used up.

3.   Slip the shrimp balls into the oil, about 10 at a time. Do not crowd the pan. The balls need to swim freely in the oil to brown evenly. Cook until the balls rise to the surface and are light brown, about 3 to 4 minutes. Remove the shrimp balls with a wire skimmer or slotted spoon and spread on a tray lined with paper towels. Keep the shrimp balls in a warm oven. Do not pile them in a bowl. Transfer to a platter garnished with parsley sprigs and lemon wedges. Serve hot or warm.

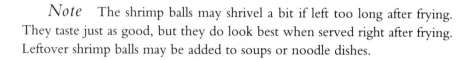

Note The shrimp balls may shrivel a bit if left too long after frying. They taste just as good, but they do look best when served right after frying. Leftover shrimp balls may be added to soups or noodle dishes.

Variation Roll or dip half of the shrimp balls in sesame seeds before deep-frying.

禧

Chinese Shrimp Chips

Makes about 130 pieces

Shrimp chips are made of shrimp, starch, and salt. They are sold dried and boxed and look like pink poker chips. When they are dropped into hot oil, they puff up to almost triple their size and become crispy like potato chips. The ones I like best are the Pigeon brand from Shanghai. Small, medium, and large sizes are available. The small ones puff to the size of a potato chip and are perfect to serve at parties. The big ones fry up to the size and shape of the sole of a shoe!

My husband sometimes complains that frying shrimp chips smells up the house. It's true; the odor of the shrimp and oil can be strong and clinging. To avoid that, especially when I am frying up a big batch for a dinner party, I set up the frying pan on the porch on a portable butane burner. I sometimes even wear a shower cap to protect my hair from the odor.

5 cups vegetable or canola oil
1 (1½-pound) package small shrimp chips

1. Pour the oil into a wok or stir-fry pan that is at least 12 inches in diameter. The oil must be at least 1 inch deep. Add more oil if it is not. Place the pan over the burner and heat to about 325°F., or until a shrimp chip slipped into the oil sizzles and puffs.

2. Fry 8 to 10 chips at a time. Stir the chips as they begin to sizzle at the bottom of the pan. In a few seconds, they will puff up and rise to the surface. Stir and push them down a couple of times, using the back of a wire skimmer. Don't let them float in the hot oil too long, or they will scorch.

3. When the chips are light pink and do not puff any more, remove them immediately with the skimmer and put them into a clean brown paper bag to drain. Give the bag a few gentle shakes to help drain all the excess oil. Transfer the fried chips to a basket or bowl lined with paper towels. The chips are best eaten immediately, but they may be set aside for later use.

Note   Humidity in the air will soften the fried chips and make them rubbery. If it is humid, cool the chips completely to avoid condensation and place in a plastic bag. Seal tight until ready to eat. The chips are best eaten the same day.

Small Eats

Cantonese-style Barbecued Chicken Wings

Serves 3 to 4 as main course, or 6 to 8 as an appetizer

*T*his sauce is the same as that for barbecued spareribs (page 306). It works just as well on chicken. The red coloring that many Americans are used to seeing in restaurant-style barbecued dishes is not traditional in Chinese home cooking, and I do not use the red dye here.

禄

2 to 2½ pounds chicken wings, about 12 to 16 pieces
3 tablespoons dark soy sauce
4 tablespoons hoisin sauce
1 tablespoon dry sherry
1 tablespoon light brown sugar
1 tablespoon honey
½ teaspoon five-spice powder
2 garlic cloves put through a garlic press (optional)

1.   Rinse the chicken wings and pat dry. Cut off the wing tips with scissors, and cut the wings into 2 sections through the joint. Discard the wing tips or save them for making broth.

2.   Stir the remaining ingredients together in a plastic bag. Add the chicken pieces, tightly seal the bag, and marinate in the refrigerator for 2 hours or overnight. Turn the bag occasionally so the chicken marinates evenly.

3.   Preheat the oven to 400°F.

4.   Remove the wings from the marinade and arrange in 1 layer in a roasting pan. Roast for 15 to 20 minutes, or until almost cooked. Turn the wings over and cook 10 minutes more until completely done. If you like, slide the wings under the broiler for the last 3 minutes for a darker finish. Serve hot or cold.

Variation   Substitute the same weight of thighs, drumsticks, or whole legs. Increase the cooking time by 15 minutes.

Small Eats

Red-cooked Chicken
Gizzards and Livers

Serves 6 to 8 as an appetizer

*I*n China, the gizzards are one of the most expensive parts of a chicken. This may seem strange, but the Chinese like the taste, texture, and flavor of the giblets and since each chicken has only one gizzard, liver, and heart, they become true delicacies. The gizzards in particular are eagerly received at Chinese banquets, where they are sliced and served as part of cold appetizer platters.

This recipe always reminds me of the time the Chinese navy came to Boston to claim an old American navy vessel that was being given to Taiwan. When my mother heard that these poor sailors were not allowed off the base, that they had only institutional Western food, and were homesick for Chinese home cooking, she made arrangements with the United States government to allow them off the base for a day of sight-seeing and a good Chinese meal. We took them to Lexington and Concord, Massachusetts — the birthplace of America — and then to our restaurant for a hearty meal.

My mother, a stickler for detail, found out that these sailors were originally from Fujian Province, an area noted for garlicky food. Among other things, she served Peking Ravioli (page 295) with a dip of fresh minced garlic. For the rest of the day, which we spent visiting a local museum, we didn't have to worry about losing anyone, we could just smell their trail!

When the ship was ready to sail back to Taiwan, my mother's parting gift was a load of frozen giblets. The sailors were thrilled with their valuable and delicious gift.

禧

1½ pounds large chicken gizzards and/or livers
½ cup dark soy sauce
¼ cup sugar
1 slice unpeeled gingerroot, 1 × ⅛ inch
1 whole star anise
2 teaspoons dry sherry
1 scallion
Cilantro sprigs, for garnish

1.   Rinse the gizzards and/or livers and remove any fat and membrane threads with your hands. Drain.

2.   Place in a heavy saucepan and add the soy sauce, sugar, gingerroot, star anise, sherry, scallion, and ¼ cup water. Cover and bring to a boil. Reduce the heat and simmer gently for 20 to 25 minutes, stirring occasionally, or until the giblets are cooked through. To test, take a gizzard out and slice it open; no blood should show.

3.   Turn the heat to high and bring the sauce to a boil. Stir the giblets for a few minutes until they develop a deep, dark color and the sauce becomes slightly syrupy. Cool the giblets in the cooking liquid.

4.   Remove the giblets from the sauce. Slice the gizzards lengthwise into thin slices and cut the liver into bite-size pieces. Serve at room temperature or chill and serve cold garnished with sprigs of cilantro.

Oven-roasted Oyster Sauce
Chicken Wings

**Serves 3 to 4 as a main course,
or 6 to 8 as an appetizer**

*T*he Chinese frequently deep-fry chicken wings, but this oven-roasting method makes a dish that is substantially lower in fat. The wings are very good with Spicy Mango Chutney (page 330).

I often pack chicken wings in the picnic basket; they taste great cold. Just bring extra napkins!

2 to 2½ pounds chicken wings, about 12 to 16 pieces
1 teaspoon grated peeled gingerroot
1 tablespoon dry sherry
3 tablespoons dark soy sauce
3 tablespoons oyster sauce
1 teaspoon sugar

1. Rinse the chicken wings and pat dry. Cut off the wing tips with scissors, and cut the wings into 2 sections through the joint. Discard the wing tips or save them to make chicken broth.

2. Combine the remaining ingredients in a plastic bag. Mix well. Add the chicken wings, seal the bag, and marinate in the refrigerator for 2 hours or overnight. Turn the bag occasionally.

3. Preheat the oven to 400°F.

4. Place the wings on an ungreased baking pan and roast for 15 to 20 minutes, or until the chicken is almost cooked. Turn the wings over and cook 10 more minutes until done. If you'd like a darker color, finish the wings under the broiler for the last 3 minutes of cooking. Serve hot, cold, or at room temperature.

Porcelain Tea Eggs

Makes 12 eggs

*T*ea eggs are popular street food in China and can be purchased from street vendors, even in such major cities as Hong Kong and Taipei. As the eggs simmer in the dark savory liquid, it seeps through cracks in the shells to form a lacy pattern similar to the crazed glaze of ancient Chinese porcelain teacups, hence the name. A long cooking is necessary for the eggs to absorb the rich flavors of the cooking liquid.

福

12 eggs
3 tablespoons black tea leaves
3 tablespoons dark soy sauce
2 tablespoons salt
3 whole star anise

1. Place the eggs in a medium saucepan and cover with cold water. Bring the water to a boil and simmer the eggs for 15 minutes. Drain the eggs and place in bowl of cold water to cool.

2. Drain the cooled eggs. Cup your hand over an egg and gently roll it on the countertop to form cracks over the entire surface of the shell. Do not peel. Repeat with the remaining eggs.

3. Place the tea leaves, soy sauce, salt, and star anise in the same saucepan. Stir to dissolve the salt. Return the eggs to the saucepan and add just enough water to cover the eggs. Bring the water to a boil, reduce the heat, and simmer for 1 hour. (The eggs may be refrigerated in the shell in the cooking liquid for several days.) Drain the eggs and cool at room temperature. Just before serving, remove the shells and cut the eggs into quarters.

Bacon-wrapped Water Chestnuts

Makes 24 pieces

*C*anned water chestnuts are fine in this dish, but do use fresh water chestnuts if they are available.

禄

24 whole water chestnuts, fresh or canned
2 tablespoons light brown sugar
8 strips bacon, cut into 3-inch-long pieces
24 round toothpicks, soaked in hot water for ½ hour

1.   Preheat the oven to 425°F.

2.   Drain the canned water chestnuts or rinse and peel the fresh water chestnuts and rinse again. Place the water chestnuts and the brown sugar in a bowl and toss together until the sugar coats the chestnuts. Set aside.

3.   Wrap a piece of the bacon around each chestnut and secure with a toothpick, piercing into the water chestnut just to the other side.

4.   Place in a single layer on an ungreased baking pan and bake for about

壽

Note   Prepare the water chestnuts through step 3 and refrigerate until ready to bake.

Black Mushroom Caps and Winter Bamboo Shoots

Makes 4 to 6 servings as an appetizer

A savory appetizer that can be put together quickly with ingredients that can always be on hand. It goes nicely with drinks and can be made ahead and refrigerated to serve cold or at room temperature.

禧

2 cups dried black mushrooms
2 (8-ounce) cans whole bamboo shoots (about 2 cups)
3 tablespoons dark soy sauce
3 teaspoons sugar
1½ teaspoons grated peeled gingerroot
3 tablespoons canola, corn, or peanut oil
Parsley sprigs, for garnish

1. Soak the mushrooms in hot water to cover for 20 minutes. When they are soft, squeeze out the water and cut off the woody stems and discard. Scissors work best. Cut the larger caps into bite-size pieces.

2. Drain the bamboo shoots and cut into bite-size pieces. Mix the soy sauce, sugar, and gingerroot together in a small bowl and set aside.

3. Pour the oil into a wok or stir-fry pan and place over medium-high heat. When the oil is hot but not smoking, add the mushrooms and bamboo shoots; they should sizzle. Stir for about 2 minutes. Lower the heat and pour in the soy sauce mixture, stirring over the heat until most of the liquid is absorbed. Transfer to a serving plate and garnish with parsley. Serve hot, warm, or cold with toothpicks.

Pickled Carrots

and Daikon

Serves 6 to 8 as a side dish

C hinese restaurants in Chinatown often serve pickles such as these to their Asian diners as a complimentary appetizer while they read the menu. I have always considered it a shame that they don't offer the same courtesy to everyone, but they seem to think that their other guests will not enjoy these more unusual dishes. If you see something on a neighboring table that you would like to try, but don't find on the menu, don't be shy — ask for it even if you have to point to another table to get the idea across.

健康

3 medium carrots (about ½ pound)
1 pound daikon (white icicle radish)
½ cup rice vinegar
½ cup sugar
¼ teaspoon salt

1. Wash and peel the carrots and radish. Cut both vegetables into matchsticks, about 2 inches long and ⅛ inch thick.

2. Plunge the carrots into a saucepan of boiling water. Remove from the heat immediately and let stand for 30 seconds. Add the daikon to the same water as the carrots and let stand for 1 minute. Drain the vegetables, rinse in cold water, and drain thoroughly in a colander, shaking off the excess water. Pack the vegetables tightly in a jar with a tight-fitting lid.

3. Combine the vinegar, sugar, and salt in a small bowl and stir until the sugar is dissolved. Pour the liquid over the vegetables and cover the jar tightly with the lid. If the liquid does not quite cover the vegetables (no more than ½ inch of vegetables should stick out), invert the jar occasionally to mix or add liquid as necessary. The pickling juices will increase somewhat in volume as moisture is drawn out of the vegetables. Refrigerate for at least 24 hours before eating.

Note   The pickles will keep in the refrigerator for 2 to 3 weeks.

Oven-roasted
Spiced Peanuts

Makes 4 cups

*T*hese roasted peanuts are sold in stores and by street vendors in China, but they are easy to make at home. Peanuts are a symbol of long life and they are always served during the lunar New Year to ensure good luck in the year to come.

壽

1½ teaspoons salt
¼ cup hot water
¼ teaspoon five-spice powder
1 pound blanched peanuts

1.   Preheat the oven to 300°F.

2.   Dissolve the salt in the hot water and stir in the five-spice powder.

3.   Place the peanuts in an ungreased roasting pan. Add the seasoned liquid and mix well. Spread out the peanuts in a single layer. Roast for about 1 hour, or until the peanuts are a very light brown. Stir every 15 minutes so the nuts brown evenly and absorb the spicy flavors.

4.   Let the nuts cool. Store in a lidded jar, a tightly sealed plastic bag, or a covered tin until ready to serve. The peanuts will keep, tightly covered, for about 3 weeks.

禧

Note   Blanched peanuts are available at health food stores.

Table Dips 調味品

ondiments and table dips are frequently served to accompany different dishes. In a Chinese home, these dips are served with specific dishes; in restaurants they are placed on the table as a matter of course. Restaurant tables are often lined with cruets of soy sauce, vinegar, and chili oil so that diners may use them singly or mix them according to taste. Many Westerners do not realize that soy sauce is meant to be used as a dip, not to be poured over rice or food.

Westerners have become so familiar with certain favorites that they expect to find them on the table regardless of what they are eating. The sweet and pungent duck sauce and Chinese mustard so popular in the East Coast of America are automatically placed at every table where Westerners are seated. They are not usually served to Chinese customers in the Far East.

Chinese restaurants on the West Coast seem to serve a more diverse selection of dipping sauces. This may be due to the influence of a larger Asian population, but even so, most Westerners are not exposed to the wide variety of sweet, salty, or spicy table sauces that the Chinese serve with different foods. Besides the simple table dips that can be made at home, there are prepared sauces, like hoisin sauce, shrimp sauce, and oyster sauce, that can be used at the table or in the kitchen.

I have made suggestions following recipes that call for dipping sauces. Some meats are white-cooked, that is, cooked without any flavoring; for these, dips are very important to give the food flavor. Steamed or poached seafood is also served with dips.

Soy Sauce Dips

調味品

Soy Sauce Dips are served with white-cooked dishes, such as White-cooked Chicken (page 178) or White-cooked Pork with Garlic Dressing (page 216), when there is very little flavor in the meat itself. The dip provides the taste. The Chinese also like these dips with dumplings, like Peking Ravioli (page 295) or Boiled Wontons (page 292). In many Chinese restaurants soy sauce, vinegar, and hot oil are placed on the table and diners mix their own dips according to their preference. Some people like to add a small amount of cider vinegar or Chinkiang vinegar and light brown sugar to the dips as well.

Soy Sauce Dip with Sesame Oil

¼ cup light soy sauce
½ teaspoon sesame seed oil

Stir the soy sauce and oil together in a small bowl when ready to serve.

Soy Sauce with Garlic Dip

¼ cup light soy sauce
½ teaspoon sesame seed oil
2 garlic cloves, peeled and minced
1 teaspoon Chinkiang vinegar

Stir the soy sauce, oil, garlic, and vinegar together in a small bowl when ready to serve.

Soy Sauce with Ginger and Scallion Dip

¼ cup light soy sauce
½ teaspoon sesame seed oil
2 teaspoons grated peeled gingerroot
2 teaspoons thinly sliced scallions

Stir the soy sauce, oil, gingerroot, and scallions together in a small bowl when ready to serve.

Chinese Mustard

This mustard, another condiment that is very popular in Chinese-American restaurants, is frequently paired with sweet and pungent duck sauce and served with such appetizers as egg rolls and spareribs. It is very easy to make at home. As with other mustard, it gets sharper if made a day ahead.

2 tablespoons mustard powder
⅛ teaspoon salt
4 tablespoons cold water
½ teaspoon cider vinegar

Mix the mustard powder and salt in 2 tablespoons of the cold water until it becomes a smooth paste. Add the remaining water and vinegar and mix thoroughly into a smooth thin paste. Cover and refrigerate for at least 1 hour or overnight before serving. The mustard will separate; stir well before serving.

Just mixed mustard sauce will taste bitter. It must rest at least an hour (overnight is better) to mellow and develop that strong, sharp, pungent taste. It is better to make it a day ahead and store it in the refrigerator for later use.

Unlike hot dog or Dijon-style mustards, Chinese mustard sauce will be thin and runny. If you like it thicker, add more mustard powder. Chinese mustard will keep a couple of weeks covered in the refrigerator; however, it is best to make small amounts each time so it will be fresh.

Hoisin Sauce Dip

調味品

*H*oisin sauce may be used right from the bottle, but thinning it with a little soy sauce and garnishing it with sesame seed oil makes it easier to spread. They also add fragrance. Use this to spread on Mandarin Pancakes (page 118) for Moo Shi Pork (page 192) or Peking Duck.

福

¼ cup hoisin sauce
2 tablespoons light soy sauce
½ teaspoon sesame seed oil

Mix the hoisin sauce with the soy sauce in a small bowl until smooth. Transfer to a small dish and drizzle with sesame seed oil. Leftover hoisin sauce can be stored in the refrigerator, tightly covered, almost indefinitely.

Sweet and Sour Sauce

Makes about 1³/₄ cups

S weet and Sour Sauce can be used in place of duck sauce as a dip or condiment with fried finger foods of any sort. It should be served hot, warm, or at room temperature. If it has been refrigerated, reheat over low heat, stirring constantly, until warm.

禄

1 tablespoon canola, corn, or peanut oil

1 garlic clove, crushed and peeled

²/₃ cup sugar

¹/₄ cup ketchup

¹/₂ cup cider vinegar

2 tablespoons light soy sauce

¹/₃ cup water

2 tablespoons cornstarch, dissolved in ¹/₃ cup water

Heat the oil in a saucepan over medium heat. Brown the garlic and discard. Combine the sugar, ketchup, vinegar, soy sauce, and ¹/₃ cup water. Pour into the pan with the oil and stir constantly with a spoon or wire whisk until the mixture is smooth and comes to a boil. Add the cornstarch slurry and stir until the sauce thickens and takes on a sheen. Keep warm over very low heat, stirring occasionally to prevent scorching, until ready to serve, or serve at room temperature.

Table Dips

Hot Chili Sauce

*T*his easy-to-make, versatile sauce can be freshly made in small quantities for dipping or for garnishing noodles. It can also be used like chili oil (page 329) to spice up stir-fry dishes by adding a little at the end of the cooking. The Chinese say that hot food "opens one's appetite," and the aroma of freshly infused peppers is indeed very appetizing.

1 tablespoon crushed red pepper
¼ teaspoon chili powder
⅛ teaspoon ground black pepper
2 tablespoons canola, corn, or peanut oil

1.   Mix the red pepper, chili powder, and black pepper together in a heatproof bowl. Heat the oil in a small saucepan over medium heat until a flake of red pepper foams immediately when dropped into the oil. If the pepper flake burns remove the oil from the heat and let it cool slightly. Test again. When the oil is ready, remove from the heat and pour over the dry spices. The oil should foam in the bowl and sizzle as it is poured. Avoid looking in the bowl or breathing in the steam to avoid irritation.

2.   Stir the sauce and transfer to a small condiment dish to cool. Serve for individual dipping.

Hot Chili Oil

Makes about 1 cup

A clear orange-red oil, this is meant not for cooking but to use as a dip or garnish for salads or to add spiciness to stir-fry and noodle dishes. Hot oil can be purchased at Asian markets, but it is really very simple to make your own.

禧

2 tablespoons crushed red pepper
1 tablespoon Szechuan peppercorns
5 slices unpeeled gingerroot, 1 × ⅛ inch each
1 cup canola, corn, or peanut oil
3 tablespoons sesame seed oil

1. Mix the red pepper, Szechuan peppercorns, and gingerroot together in a 1-quart heatproof bowl. Heat both oils in a small saucepan over medium heat to 250°F. to 275°F., or until a flake of red pepper immediately foams when dropped into the oil. Remove from the heat and immediately pour over the pepper mixture. The oil should foam and sizzle as it is poured. Do not put your face over the bowl or breathe in the steam.

2. Cover the bowl and allow the oil to cool. Let stand overnight to thoroughly infuse. Strain through a fine sieve or cheesecloth. Discard the solids.

3. Store in a tightly lidded jar away from heat and sunlight. It should keep for 6 months. Refrigerate for longer periods.

Note Instead of using sesame seed oil, my mother sometimes infused sesame seeds along with the spices.

Spicy Mango Chutney

Makes about 9 cups chutney

*T*his recipe comes from Deli Bloembergen, a close family friend and former neighbor who was born in Indonesia and lived there until she was a teenager. As a child, she spent many hours watching the family cook who was Indonesian. The chutney goes especially well with Asian dishes, curries in particular. It's also delicious with such fried foods as egg rolls and fried wontons.

5 firm mangoes, about 3 inches in diameter

2 cups (packed) light brown sugar

1½ cups wine or cider vinegar

1 cup golden raisins

1 red bell pepper, seeded, cored, quartered, and cut crosswise into slivers

3 large onions, peeled and chopped (about 4 cups)

1 teaspoon ground cardamom

4 teaspoons chili powder

2 teaspoons ground cinnamon

4 teaspoons ground coriander

2 teaspoons garlic powder

4 teaspoons grated peeled gingerroot or 4 teaspoons ground ginger

2 teaspoons grated lemon peel or dried lemon peel

2 teaspoons salt

½ teaspoon Tabasco (optional)

1. Rinse and peel the mangoes. Hold the mango in one hand and with a small knife in the other, cut the flesh off from around the pit in big hunks. Cut the pieces into ½- to 1-inch chunks. Discard the pit. Do this over the pot you will cook in to catch the mango juices.

2. Place all the ingredients in a large heavy-bottomed nonreactive saucepan, such as stainless steel or enamel-coated steel, and bring the mixture to a boil. Turn the heat to low and simmer gently, uncovered, for 30 minutes, or until tender. Stir often as the chutney burns easily.

3. Pour the hot mixture into clean jars with tight-fitting lids. Cover the jars while the chutney is hot or allow it to cool slightly first. Store in the refrigerator for about 6 months. For longer storage, pour the hot mixture into hot sterilized canning jars and seal with sterilized two-part lids.

Note To make half a recipe, use 3 mangoes and 1 cup of vinegar. Halve the rest of the ingredients and proceed as directed. If you double the recipe, you must cook it in two batches. For best results, do not make more than one batch at a time.

Variation Substitute two 8-ounce boxes of dried apricots for the mangoes. Cut each apricot in half with scissors.

Ginger and Vinegar Seafood Dip

M y mother always made this traditional seafood dip to go with steamed crabs. It is also served with other seafood, like fried shrimp or steamed fish, as well as savory dumplings, such as Peking Ravioli (page 295) and Boiled Wontons (page 292).

In China the most famous crabs are the Shanghai freshwater hairy crabs, so called because of the hairs that grow over the large claws. They are in season very briefly in late fall. Live crabs travel from Shanghai to Hong Kong tightly tied with bamboo string and packed in bamboo baskets. Garishly colored posters and neon signs herald their arrival throughout the city. The taste is exceptional — the best part is the body with lots of roe — with prices to match!

¼ cup cider vinegar
1 tablespoon minced or shredded peeled gingerroot
2 tablespoons light brown sugar, or to taste
2 teaspoons light soy sauce, or to taste (optional)

Mix together the vinegar, gingerroot, sugar, and soy sauce, if using, in a small bowl when ready to serve.

禧

Variation For a less seasoned dip, omit the sugar and soy sauce.

Szechuan Peppercorn and Salt Dip

 dry dip, this is most often served with deep-fried foods such as *Fried Shrimp Balls* (*page 310*), but can be used to flavor such diverse foods as fried chicken and salads. It makes an excellent salt substitute in stir-fry dishes. Serve at the table in a small dipping dish. Use it with a light touch; a little goes a long way. It can be stored, tightly covered, in the cupboard.

健康

2 teaspoons Szechuan peppercorns
4 tablespoons salt

1.   Put the peppercorns and salt in a dry heavy skillet and heat over medium. Shake the pan constantly until the peppercorns smoke lightly and you hear a light cracking sound and smell a fragrant aroma. Do not let the peppercorns burn. Shake the pan for another 30 seconds. Remove from heat and continuing shaking the pan for another 30 seconds.

2.   Pour the salt and peppercorns into a mortar and grind with a pestle to a fine consistency. Or process in a small food processor until fine. Or place between sheets of heavy paper and roll with a rolling pin. Strain through a sieve, discarding the particles that do not fall through.

Desserts

Daily desserts are not part of Chinese cuisine, and you'll find that the dessert chapter in a Chinese cookbook is usually rather thin. Since few people had ice boxes or refrigerators, chilled desserts were not popular; dairy products — ice cream and the like — simply weren't available. And since no one had ovens, there was no tradition of baking. When dessert was served at home, it was simple fare, like fruit or easy-to-prepare sweet soups made from beans or pureed nuts. Elaborate sweets were reserved for festivals and special occasions and tended to be rich and heavy.

It's been said that the people of Shanghai have a sweet tooth, so it's no wonder that my mother, my cousins, and I (all from Shanghai) love sweets. Many of the recipes in this chapter are a result of that. I find that hot fruit desserts, light chiffon or angel food cake, custard, sherbet, or ginger– or green tea–flavored ice cream make an excellent ending to a Chinese meal.

Fruit Desserts

The Chinese enjoy fruits after a meal — a tradition that is carried on, in a way, at Chinese-American restaurants that serve orange quarters or pineapple chunks with fortune cookies. Many tropical fruits are popular in the Far East. Most are difficult to obtain fresh, but the canned variety is still refreshing and light. With all of the last-minute stir-fry preparation, it is nice to be able to sit down and relax with a cool bowl of fruit.

Canned Fruit

These canned fruit, available in Asian markets and sometimes in larger supermarkets, make a perfect ending to a Chinese meal.

Longans The Chinese name for this small, translucent, white round fruit is dragon's eye. Chill the can and serve the longans with their syrup.

Loquats A yellow fruit about the size of a small apricot. Chill the can and serve in small dessert bowls with the syrup.

Lychee Nuts Chill the can and serve the lychees alone or with a ginger syrup (page 336) garnished with fresh berries. A twenty-ounce can contains about twenty-four lychees.

Fresh Fruit

Almost any fresh fruit can be served at the end of a Chinese meal. The fruit should be perfectly ripe and as unblemished as possible. Ripe fruit that is less than perfect can be cut up and marinated in a fruit liqueur like Chambord, Grand Marnier, or ginger liqueur. Top-quality fruit is best served unadorned. I chill the fruit and place it on pretty dessert plates of a contrasting color, garnished with a sprig of mint or lined with a pretty leaf from our grapevine.

The following are some of my favorite fruits. You can add favorites of your own. Remember, you don't have to serve a lot as long as what you do serve is ripe and sweet. Let the bounty of mother nature be your guide.

Berries It doesn't sound very Chinese, but fresh berries are such a satisfying way to end a meal and since their season is so short, I take advantage of every opportunity to serve them. Since we grow blueberries, raspberries, and blackberries in our garden, a favorite dessert of ours is a bowl of just-picked berries with a dollop of sweetened whipped cream. Local strawberries are always welcome, too.

Mangoes My father loved ripe mangoes more than any other fruit. When I was a child, we would buy mangoes by the case and keep them in the basement to ripen slowly. Each day my father would inspect them, gently pressing the flesh and smelling for that sweet, almost heady fragrance that told him they were ready. Not all the mangoes in the box ripened at the same time, so when there was only one fruit ready, my father would bring it upstairs and we would all lean over the dining table as he almost ceremoniously peeled the skin to expose that deep yellow flesh. He then divided the fruit among us — except for my brother Stephen, who was allergic to mangoes. As a special treat, one of us would be allowed to scrape the remaining mango off the skin.

Mangoes are most flavorful and affordable during the months of June and July. They are hardly ever ripe enough to eat when purchased, so you have to get your mangoes about a week before you plan to serve them. Let them ripen at room temperature. A mango is ripe and ready to eat when the skin is rosy red and the flesh is tender and gives to a gentle squeeze. The stem end should smell sweetly fragrant.

Ripe mangoes are very juicy and difficult to eat gracefully. It would be cruel and unusual punishment to serve a whole mango to a guest. See page 337 for directions on cutting and serving mangoes.

Melons Nothing is so refreshing at the end of a meal as a slice or wedge of chilled ripe melon.

Cantaloupe melons. This sometimes ordinary fruit can be out of this world when properly ripened. I serve a small wedge already sliced away from its rind. If you have both cantaloupe and honeydew, a dish of melon cubes makes a very attractive dessert.

Honeydew melons. Asians love the honeydew melon. When it's ripe and sweet with a lot of juice, there's nothing that can compare to it. In Japan there is a melon much like our honeydew. You see the melons beautifully packaged in wooden presentation boxes with a part of the stem still attached. These melons can cost up to $100 each!

Watermelon. The Chinese are partial to watermelon. For many years cold drinks were not easily available in China, and the summer beverage came from a slice of watermelon. In China, my mother and her friends would take a whole watermelon on a picnic. The watermelon was placed in a net and lowered into a cool well. On more formal occasions, serve a small wedge or triangle of watermelon to each person or cut the watermelon into small pieces and serve them in dessert dishes. I like to serve seedless watermelon for easier eating and yellow watermelon for a change when it's available.

Oranges Oranges are believed to be lucky and are given as tokens of good fortune during the lunar New Year. Mandarin oranges appear in the market around February — just in time for the lunar New Year. Many kinds of easy-to-peel oranges are called tangerines or mandarins.

One of my favorite varieties is the Honey tangerine, also known as the Murcott. It is a little tighter skinned than some of the others, but the flesh is as sweet as its name implies. Other kinds of mandarins are the tiny clementines and bright orange mineolas. Serve a whole mandarin to each guest. I also use canned mandarin oranges in several of my desserts.

Peaches and Nectarines The peach is a symbol of long life; it is always held by the god of longevity. Cut them into cubes (toss peaches with lemon juice to prevent discoloring) and serve in little dessert bowls, garnished perhaps with a strawberry or a dash of Grand Marnier or Chambord liqueur.

Persimmons Persimmons were another of my father's passions. They grow abundantly in northern China; in the winter months they are lined up on the rooftops to sweeten and dry. Persimmons have a short season, from

Desserts

October to January. Except for the Fuji persimmon, the ripe fruit is soft and the thin tomatolike skin a bit shriveled. Underripe persimmons are very astringent and impossible to eat. Fuji persimmons are hard and crisp. I was afraid to buy them because I always thought they were not yet ripe. Then one day one was served to me. To my surprise and delight, it was sweet and crisp, just like an apple. To serve soft persimmons, place a fruit, with stem side down, on a plate. Cut an X at the tip so the persimmon may be peeled easily. Each person peels the skin halfway down, then eats the soft flesh with a small dessert spoon.

Lychees with Sweet Ginger Sauce

Serves 4

*T*he lychee is not a nut but a juicy soft, white fruit. It's not easy to obtain fresh lychees even during their short season in the summer, but the canned ones, although not quite as tasty as the fresh, are perfectly acceptable and refreshing. They are available in Asian markets and some larger supermarkets.

健康

1 (20-ounce) can lychees in syrup
1 tablespoon coarsely chopped peeled gingerroot
2 tablespoons light brown sugar
Sprigs of fresh mint, for garnish (optional)

1. Drain the lychees, reserving the syrup. You should have about 1 cup of syrup. Set aside. Place the lychees in a bowl. Set aside.

2. Combine the gingerroot, sugar, ¼ cup of water, and the lychee syrup in a small saucepan. Bring to a boil, reduce the heat to low, and simmer for 5 minutes. Remove from the heat and allow it to cool for 15 minutes. Strain and discard the gingerroot.

3. Let the liquid cool to room temperature and add it to the drained lychee nuts. Cover and refrigerate for 1 hour or overnight. Serve the lychees in small dessert bowls with the ginger sauce. Decorate with a sprig of fresh mint, if desired.

Porcupine Mangoes

Serves 2

*I*n *Asia mangoes are enjoyed by nearly everyone. Ripe mangoes are indescribably deli-cious but messy to eat. Here's a neat way to serve mangoes even at dinner parties. The first time I saw this done, I thought the mangoes looked a bit like the back of a porcupine, with the bright yellow cubes of fruit sticking up.*

福

1 ripe mango
2 mint sprigs, for garnish

1.   With a sharp knife, slice the flesh off either side of the pit. Cut as close to the pit as you can. The pit is flat at the widest part of the mango.

2.   Holding a piece that was just sliced off, make evenly spaced diagonal cuts in a diamond design through the flesh but not into the skin. Do the same for the other piece.

3.   Holding a mango piece in your hands, push the center up so that the skin flips up and the mango pieces separate and stand out. Serve with a sprig of mint. Or slice off the cubes and serve them in a dessert bowl with a fork or toothpicks.

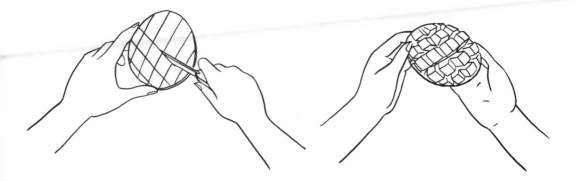

Note   There is always some flesh left on the mango pit. I consider it the cook's reward.

Poached Pears in
Spiced Ginger Sauce

Serves 6

*T*his light fruit dessert was inspired by Western poached fruit recipes. You might drizzle a teaspoon or two of ginger liqueur or brandy over each serving of pears or garnish with toasted sliced almonds, shaved chocolate, slivers of crystallized ginger, or a sprig of fresh mint. Serve with Almond Ginger Cookies (page 348).

祿

1 lemon
6 firm pears, Bosc, Anjou, or Bartlett
½ cup plus 2 tablespoons sugar
3 tablespoons candied ginger, minced (about 1 ounce)
6 whole cloves
1 cinnamon stick (about 2 inches)
3 cups water

1. Cut 1 heaping tablespoon of julienne strips from the lemon peel. Avoid taking any of the bitter white pith. Set aside. Cut the lemon in half. Halve the pears, core with a melon baller, and peel. Squeeze the juice of the lemon over the pears. Set aside.

2. Combine the sugar, ginger, cloves, cinnamon, lemon peel, and 3 cups of water in a saucepan large enough to hold the pears. Bring to a boil, stir to dissolve the sugar. Add the pears and reduce the heat to a simmer. Cook, covered for 15 to 25 minutes, or until the pears are tender. Insert a toothpick or cake tester into a pear; if it goes in easily, the pears are ready. Be careful not to overcook or they will become too soft and mushy.

3. Uncover the pan and cool in the cooking liquid. Transfer the pears to a bowl, strain the liquid, and return to the pears. Serve warm or cold with the cooking liquid in individual dessert dishes.

Almond Tea

Serves 4

My mother recalls how vendors in Peking (Beijing) used to sell almond tea from door to door in the morning, afternoon, and evening. It was made by hand grinding soaked raw rice and almonds together. My mother took out the elbow grease by using pure almond paste and fresh rice flour. Using pureed nuts to make thick sweet soups is quite common in China. Almonds, walnuts, peanuts, and black and white sesame seeds are all popular.

Asian markets often carry powdered instant sweet soups that just need to have water added. Some from Japan come in thick pouches that can be heated in boiling water. All of these are easy, but none taste as good as soups made from scratch.

⅓ cup rice flour

2 tablespoons almond paste

4 cups cold water

⅓ cup sugar

1 teaspoon almond extract

Light brown sugar, for garnish (optional)

1.   Combine the rice flour, almond paste, and ½ cup of the water in a blender. Blend on high until you have a very smooth thin paste. Add the remaining water, 1 cup at a time, and continue blending until smooth.

2.   Transfer the liquid to a heavy-bottomed saucepan and heat over medium heat, stirring constantly, until it boils. You must keep stirring to keep the liquid from burning on the bottom or becoming lumpy. When it comes to a boil, add the sugar and almond extract and stir to dissolve thoroughly. Remove from the heat and serve hot in cups, mugs, or bowls. Sprinkle with ½ to 1 teaspoon brown sugar, if desired. If not serving immediately, press a piece of plastic film directly on the surface of the tea to prevent a skin from forming. Remove plastic wrap when reheating.

Note   I sometimes use sweet rice flour, also called glutinous rice flour or powder, for a thicker consistency. I prefer a brand called Mochiko (the Japanese name for sweet rice flour) made by Koda Farms in California and sold under their Blue Star label. If you like the tea thinner, simply add more water and adjust the sugar to taste.

Desserts

The Emperor's Nectar

Serves 6 to 8

T he name for this soup dessert, with its tiny glutinous rice balls and orange segments, was coined by our friend Barry Lockard as we were sitting at the table one winter evening enjoying this dessert. He insisted that I include it in my book. It's a good dessert to follow a spicy meal of Szechuan food.

1 (13-ounce) jar or 1½ cups sweet rice wine, both liquid and rice

½ cup sugar

½ cup glutinous rice flour

1 (11-ounce) can mandarin orange segments in syrup

1. Combine the rice wine, 6 cups of water, and the sugar in a 3-quart or larger saucepan.

2. Mix the rice powder with 3 to 3½ tablespoons water to make a dry dough. Working with ¼ teaspoon at a time, roll the dough between your palms into tiny pearl-shaped balls. You should have about 50 balls. Line the rice balls on a plate and set aside.

3. Bring the rice wine mixture to a boil over medium heat. Drop in the rice balls a few at a time until all the balls are in the hot liquid and stir. When the balls float to the surface, they are cooked. The mixture will remain very liquid. Add the mandarin oranges with their syrup. Taste and add more sugar, if desired. Serve hot in bowls.

福

Note   This dessert is best served fresh, but it does reheat very well. Store it in the refrigerator; the rice balls will soften, but that does not affect the taste. Reheat gently in a saucepan over medium heat, stirring so the rice balls don't burn.

Sweet rice wine (jiu niang), sometimes called fermented rice wine, is steamed glutinous rice that has been mixed with a yeast starter and allowed to ferment, producing a fragrant sweet alcoholic liquid. Both the liquid and fermented rice are used in cooking and desserts. Like many Chinese, my mother made her own, but today it is possible to purchase it in jars at Chinese grocery stores.

Orange and Pearl Tapioca Sweet Soup

Serves 6

*I*n China, this slightly thick soup is often served at formal banquets. When my cousin May Chen first came to America from Shanghai, I made it for her as a midnight snack. It really hit the spot and reminded her of home.

禄

¼ pound large pearl tapioca (about ¾ cup)

½ cup sugar, or to taste

1 teaspoon almond extract

1 (11-ounce) can mandarin oranges in syrup

1. Soak the tapioca in 2 cups of cold water for at least 2 hours or overnight.

2. Pour the soaked tapioca with the soaking water into a saucepan and add another 3 cups of water. Bring to a boil over medium heat. Cover and simmer over very low heat for 30 minutes. Stir occasionally to avoid burning.

3. Remove the saucepan from the heat and let stand, covered, for 20 minutes. The tapioca pearls will become completely transparent.

4. Add the sugar, almond extract, and mandarin oranges with their syrup. Stir until the sugar is dissolved. Bring to a boil over medium heat, stirring occasionally. Stir gently to avoid breaking the orange segments. Serve hot in Chinese rice bowls or dessert bowls.

Note The tapioca thickens as it cools. If the soup gets too thick (it should have the consistency of heavy syrup), thin it with water and add more sugar to taste.

Sweet Red Bean Soup

Serves 6 to 8

*R*ed bean soups are especially popular in the southern part of China. For special occasions, this soup is sometimes enriched with lily root segments and lotus seeds. In summer it is often made thicker and sweeter and served cold over shaved ice (a favorite with the Japanese) or thinned with water and light cream into an iced drink.

Red azuki beans may be purchased in Asian markets or health food stores.

禧

1 cup azuki beans (8 ounces)
2-inch square dried tangerine peel (optional)
1 cup granulated or (firmly packed) light brown sugar, or to taste

1. Rinse the beans and discard any black or damaged ones. Cover the beans with cold water and soak overnight or for at least 4 hours. Drain.

2. Place the beans and tangerine peel, if using, in a large saucepan with 8 cups of water. Bring to a boil, reduce the heat, and simmer, partly covered, stirring occasionally, until tender, about 1½ to 2 hours.

3. When the beans are tender and beginning to break apart, add the sugar. Stir to dissolve and remove from the heat. Serve hot or at room temperature in hot weather.

Note The soup can be made in advance, and refrigerated, covered. Reheat just before serving. Place in saucepan over medium heat and be sure to stir frequently as the beans fall to the bottom of the saucepan.

Variation A thicker version of this soup can be made by adding 5 tablespoons of glutinous rice with the beans in step 2. You may want to add more than 1 cup of sugar in step 3. The soup thickens as it cools. When reheating, add more water and sugar to taste, if desired.

Desserts

Almond Float

Serves 6

M y mother adapted this dessert from a classic Chinese recipe and it quickly became a favorite at our first restaurant on Concord Avenue in Cambridge. She substituted gelatin for the agar agar called for in the original recipe. She used almond extract instead of grinding almonds by hand and added mandarin oranges.

I've made Almond Float into a festive dessert for the Fourth of July by combining the white almond jelly with red strawberries and blueberries for a patriotic red, white, and blue dessert. If you do that, be sure to make a double portion of the syrup so everything will float.

禄

1 tablespoon unflavored gelatin
⅓ cup cold water
¾ cup boiling water
⅔ cup sugar, divided
1 cup milk
1½ teaspoons almond extract
2 (11-ounce) cans mandarin orange segments in syrup, chilled

1. Sprinkle the gelatin into a 10-inch square baking dish. Add the cold water and let stand until the gelatin softens, about 3 minutes. Add the boiling water and ⅓ cup of the sugar and stir until the sugar and gelatin have dissolved. Pour in the milk and 1 teaspoon of the almond extract. Cover the dish with plastic wrap and chill in the refrigerator for at least 3 hours or overnight. It will be softly firm.

2. To make the syrup, mix the remaining ⅓ cup of sugar, 2 cups of water, and the remaining ½ teaspoon of almond extract together in a small bowl and stir until the sugar is dissolved. Chill the syrup in the refrigerator.

3. To serve, cut the almond gelatin into ½-inch squares. With a rubber spatula, carefully scrape the cubes out of the dish and place in a serving bowl. Add the 2 cans of mandarin orange segments with their syrup to the bowl. Pour on the chilled almond syrup. Stir gently to mix. Serve in small dessert bowls with enough liquid so that the almond gelatin floats.

Variation Add raspberries, blueberries, or quartered strawberries along with the mandarin oranges.

Eight Treasure Pudding

Eight Treasure Pudding is not difficult to make, but it is usually reserved for special occasions and banquets. The Chinese like to refer to dishes so as to express wealth, prosperity, longevity, happiness, and so on. The candied fruit that crowns the pudding represents the treasures, precious gems like rubies, jade, and onyx.

2 cups glutinous rice

3 tablespoons vegetable shortening

¼ cup assorted dried fruit, such as Maraschino cherries, cut in half; dark or golden raisins; candied citron; candied kumquats, cut into thin shreds; candied ginger, cut into thin shreds; Chinese black or red dates, pits removed and cut into slivers

⅔ cup plus 2 tablespoons sugar, divided

1 cup canned sweetened red bean paste

2 tablespoons cornstarch, dissolved in 3 tablespoons water

½ teaspoon almond extract

1. Soak the rice in at least 4 cups of cold water for 2 hours; it will almost double in volume. Drain in a strainer and put in a 1½-quart heatproof bowl. Add 1¾ cups of water and steam over boiling water for 30 minutes. (For this recipe, the steamer is the best way to cook the rice because it prevents any burning or hard crust from forming.) Allow the rice to cool enough to be handled. It should remain warm.

2. Coat a heatproof 1½-quart bowl generously with 1 tablespoon of the shortening. Arrange the dried fruit in a design on the bottom and up the sides of the bowl. The design will be on the top of the pudding when it is unmolded. Set aside.

3. When the rice is cool enough to handle, transfer to a large mixing bowl and mix in the remaining 2 tablespoons of shortening and ⅓ cup of the sugar. Mix with your hands to keep the rice grains from breaking.

4. Press half the rice around the sides and bottom of the prepared bowl, being careful not to disturb the fruit design. The rice should be thicker at the bottom than around the sides.

5.   Spoon the bean paste into the center of the bowl on top of the rice. Press lightly with a rubber spatula to flatten. Add the remaining rice around and on top of the bean paste. Press gently as you work to eliminate any air pockets. Smooth the surface with a rubber spatula.

6.   Heat water in a steamer large enough to hold the bowl with enough room above it for the steam to circulate freely. Seal the top of the bowl with plastic wrap, cover the pan with a lid, and steam for 1 hour over simmering water. (Covering the bowl with plastic prevents any condensation from dripping onto the rice. The old Chinese way to do this was to wrap the steamer lid with a cloth. Be sure to remove the plastic carefully so that the accumulated water doesn't fall into the rice.) The pudding can stay in the steamer with the water at a simmer until ready to unmold and serve. The extra steaming will not affect its quality.

7.   To make the sauce, combine 1½ cups of water and the remaining sugar in a small saucepan. Bring to a boil and stir until the sugar dissolves. Slowly pour in the cornstarch slurry and stir until the sauce thickens and becomes translucent. Stir in the almond extract and keep warm.

8.   Remove the pudding from the steamer and carefully remove the plastic wrap. Run the tip of a knife around the edge of the pudding to loosen. Be careful not to disturb the fruit design. Place a rimmed platter — it needs some depth to capture the sauce that will be poured over the pudding — over the bowl and invert so the pudding unmolds onto the platter. Pour the sauce over. Serve immediately.

禧

Note   The pudding is meant to be served hot. You can prepare it ahead of time and steam it while having dinner, or prepare it and seal it with aluminum foil or plastic wrap and refrigerate or freeze until ready to steam. Freezing and reheating does not alter the taste or texture of this dessert. The sauce, however, should be freshly made. The cooked pudding can also be reheated by steaming.

Almond Rice Pudding

Serves 6 to 8

lthough rice pudding made with dairy products is not Chinese, I like a well-made rice pudding — and, of course, I always have rice on hand. This recipe is adapted from The Periyali Cookbook. *The Periyali Restaurant in New York City has the best rice pudding I've ever tasted. Instead of cooking the rice on the stove, where it has to be monitored and stirred almost constantly for about an hour, I cook it in a steamer. The rice cooks evenly, won't burn, and doesn't need to be stirred while cooking.*

健康

4 cups low-fat milk
2 pieces lemon peel, about ¾ × 4 inches each
¾ cup long-grain rice
¾ cup sugar
1 egg yolk
½ cup heavy cream
1 teaspoon almond extract
Toasted sliced almonds, for garnish
Ground cinnamon, for garnish

1. Combine the milk, lemon peel, and rice in a 1½-quart heatproof bowl. Bring water to a boil in a steamer and steam the rice for 40 to 50 minutes, or until the grains are tender. The mixture will remain very soupy.

2. Transfer the rice and the liquid into a 3-quart or larger saucepan. Separate the rice grains with a wooden spoon or fork. Heat over medium heat just until the liquid comes to a boil. Stir frequently to prevent sticking.

3. In a small bowl, mix the sugar into the egg yolk with a fork until the mixture is crumbly. Stir in a few spoonfuls of the hot liquid from the rice to warm the egg. Remove the rice from the heat and quickly stir in the egg mixture, stirring constantly to prevent the yolk from cooking.

4. Return the pan to the stove and continue cooking over low heat for a few minutes. Stir constantly to prevent burning and a skin from forming on the surface. Add the cream and continue stirring until the mixture is steaming. Remove from the heat and stir in the almond extract. Stir for 1 minute, then pour the pudding into a serving bowl. If not serving immediately, press plastic wrap on top of the pudding to prevent a skin from forming. Serve warm or chilled with a generous sprinkling of toasted almond slivers and cinnamon.

Desserts

Steamed Egg Cake

Serves 6

*W*hen the Chinese make cakes or bread, they steam them. It may seem unusual, but the results are quite delicious — and healthy, too, when you consider that this recipe calls for no butter, oil, or shortening. The steamed cake can be eaten hot, warm, or cold. It's at its best piping hot, right from the steamer. For a festive touch, my mother sometimes dusted the top of the cake lightly with colored sugar crystals.

福

3 eggs, separated
½ teaspoon pure vanilla extract
1 cup all-purpose flour
¼ teaspoon baking powder
1¼ cups sugar

1.   Line the bottom of an 8-inch round cake pan with wax paper or aluminum foil. Bring water to a boil in the bottom of a steamer. The water should not be high enough to touch the bottom of the cake pan.

2.   While the water is coming to a boil, beat the egg yolks with the vanilla and ⅓ cup of water just until blended. Sift the flour with the baking powder. Add the sugar and sift again. Stir the flour mixture into the egg yolks.

3.   Beat the egg whites until stiff but not dry. Fold the whites into the batter and pour the batter into the prepared pan. Rap the pan sharply on the counter several times to remove any large air bubbles.

4.   Place the pan in the steamer and steam over medium-high heat for 20 to 25 minutes, or until a toothpick inserted into the cake comes out clean. Remove the cake from the steamer.

5.   Invert the cake pan onto a plate, pull off and discard the paper, and turn the cake right side up. It is best served hot or warm.

Almond Ginger Cookies

Makes about 4 dozen 2½-inch cookies

*T*hese cookies were inspired by a recipe given to me by Valarie Hart Ross, our Oregon sales representative. The cookies are rich in almond flavor and have the cracked surface of traditional Chinese almond cookies.

Chinese almond cookies are commonly garnished with whole blanched almonds but I use natural almonds. I'm lucky to have a steady supply since my brother-in-law Cliff Ohmart, who is an entomologist, collects them in the almond groves of California. He goes into the groves to check the trees and almonds to determine the optimum time for farmers to spray. He always has more than he needs.

祿

2½ cups unbleached all-purpose flour
1 teaspoon baking powder
3 teaspoons ground ginger
½ teaspoon salt
¾ cup vegetable shortening
1 cup (firmly packed) light brown sugar
¼ cup honey
1 large egg
½ cup almond paste (4 ounces)
About 48 whole almonds

1. Preheat the oven to 350°F.

2. Sift the flour, baking powder, ginger, and salt together into a mixing bowl. Set aside.

3. Blend the vegetable shortening with the brown sugar, honey, and egg in a food processor fitted with a steel blade until smooth. Cut the almond paste into small pieces, add to the mixture, and process until it is smooth and the almond paste well incorporated. Add the flour mixture a third at a time, turning the processor on and off at 5-second intervals, until a firm dough is formed.

4. Roll about 1 rounded tablespoon of dough between the palms of your hands into a ball. Continue with all the dough. Place on an ungreased cookie sheet 2 inches apart. Press an almond into the center of each.

Desserts

5. Bake for 10 to 12 minutes, or until the cookies are lightly browned. Cool for about 1 minute on the sheet, then transfer to a rack. Cool thoroughly. Store in a tightly sealed container.

Ginger Pound Cake

Makes two 9 × 5-inch cakes

G inger is often used at the end of Chinese meals as a digestive. This ginger-flavored cake is a perfect ending to a Chinese meal and goes exceptionally well with Chinese tea.

3 cups unbleached all-purpose flour

1 tablespoon baking powder

½ teaspoon salt

¾ cup light cream

2 teaspoons pure vanilla extract

2¼ cups sugar

1½ cups (3 sticks) butter, at room temperature

6 eggs, at room temperature

1 cup candied ginger (8 ounces)

¼ cup poppy seeds (optional)

1. Preheat the oven to 350°F. Butter two 9 × 5-inch loaf pans and line the bottoms with parchment or wax paper. Butter the paper and dust the pans lightly with flour, tapping out the excess.

2. Sift 2½ cups of the flour with the baking powder and salt. Set aside. Stir the cream and vanilla together. Set aside.

3. With a stand mixer or a handheld beater, cream the sugar and butter together until light and fluffy. Beat in the eggs, one at a time, beating well after each one. With a spoon or the beater on slow speed, add the flour mixture alternately with the cream and stir until smooth. Increase the beater speed to high and beat just until smooth.

(continued)

4. Toss the candied ginger with a few tablespoons of the remaining ½ cup of flour and cut into small diced pieces. Fold the ginger, remaining flour, and poppy seeds, if used, into the batter until well mixed. Divide the batter evenly between the 2 loaf pans and tap them on the counter to remove any air pockets.

5. Bake for about 1 hour, or until the loaves are golden brown and the cakes pull away from the sides of the pan. A cake tester inserted in the center should come out clean. Set the pans on racks and cool for about 30 minutes. Unmold, remove the paper, and turn the loaves right side up to cool completely.

禧

Note   This keeps in the refrigerator up to 2 weeks or in the freezer for 2 months.

Index

Index

Index